THE HERO WITHIN

Corinne,

This book gave me insight as well as inspiration towards life & living it fully! I thought you might enjoy reading it - With a friend or alone!

The excersizes in the back are fun!

love you XXOO

Tricia

THE HERO WITHIN

Six Archetypes We Live By

Expanded Edition

Carol S. Pearson, Ph.D.

HarperSanFrancisco

A Division of HarperCollins*Publishers*

Carol S. Pearson and her colleagues at Meristem offer workshops, seminars, and individual and organizational consultation designed to help people further their heroic journeys in their work and private lives. For more information, call or write: Meristem, 4307 Underwood Street, University Park, Maryland, 20782, or phone: (301) 277-8042.

Revised Edition

Library of Congress Cataloging-in-Publication Data
Pearson, Carol, 1944–
    The hero within: six archetypes we live by / Carol S. Pearson.—

    Expanded ed.
    p.   cm.
    Bibliography: p.
    ISBN 0-06-254862-X
    1. Archetype (Psychology)   2. Self-actualization (Psychology)
3. New Age movement.   I. Title.
BF175.5.A72P43   1989   85-51996
150.19′54—dc 19   CIP

        91   92   93   MUR   10   9

With love and gratitude
For the depth of his faith
And the power of his example,
I dedicate this book to my father,

JOHN A. PEARSON

Here we are opening into the "the religion of psychology" by suggesting that psychology is a variety of religious experience.

Psychology as religion implies imagining all psychological events as effects of Gods in the soul, and all activities to do with soul, such as therapy, to be operations of ritual in relation to these Gods. . . . It is not a question of religion turning to psychology—no, psychology is simply going home.
—JAMES HILLMAN, *Re-Visioning Psychology*

ACKNOWLEDGMENTS

My standard of "truth" in writing this book was not an external measure but my own practical knowledge. What I have said has served me well in my own life. I have applied and tested what I have discovered from my reading, observation, research, and listening to my friends, colleagues, and students and in my interactions with others. I share here the truths that have survived this test.

You also should know about certain people and groups who have had a profound impact on my thinking and my life, without whom I would not have written this book. To Katherine Pope, with whom I wrote two books, I give thanks for sharpening my ideas and for the experience of sisterly collaboration.

To Anne Schaef my heartfelt thanks for being the closest thing I have ever had to a mentor. In the six years I worked on staff in her Intensives for Professional Women, my ideas about life were changed profoundly. Anne Schaef's ideas about the differences between male and female systems, her articulation of the ways in which mental and emotional health comes when we learn to "live in process," and the experience of working with her radically transformed my life and my work. I am equally grateful to others on her staff, especially Liv Estrup, Deborah Carver Marstellar, Rosemary Rocco, and Jill Schumacher, who taught me much about living in process and about personal responsibility and spirituality.

Thanks also to Marni Harmony, who introduced me to the ideas of Patricia Sun and the New Age Movement, and to the "Miracles Group" in Charlotte, North Carolina, for what they taught me about the Magician, especially Carol Rupert, Judy Billman, Fan Watson, and Mary Dawn Liston.

To Josephine Withers, Dorothy Franklin, Carol Robertson, Bud Early, Sharon Seivert, Laurie Lippin, Mary Leonard, and others in my spiritual community for what they have taught me about claiming abundance and prosperity and for their love and support. I can no longer imagine living without such a loving community. To my husband, David Merkowitz, and my children, Jeff, Steve, and Shanna, my deep appreciation for their love, support, and tolerance of my long hours at the word processor and my general abstractedness during the process of writing this book.

I also am deeply indebted for their encouragement and criticism to colleagues and students who read and commented upon the manuscript: Sharon Seivert was particularly supportive and generous with her time, making specific editorial suggestions, spending many long lunches discussing potential ideas and ways to structure the book's chapters and increase its readability. I had the good fortune to take David Oldfield's "Hero's Journey" workshop as I was completing the process of revising the manuscript, and his ideas and suggestions were invaluable for my last-minute reordering and fine tuning of concepts. I also am grateful for David Merkowitz's expert assistance in final editing and proofing of the manuscript.

Other people who read and commented on the manuscript and whose insights were essential included Lee Knefelkamp, Josephine Withers, Deborah Marstellar, Dorothy Franklin, Gary Ferraro, Jessy Leonard, Judy Touchton, and the students of my Fall 1984 course, "Women's Culture and Social Change," at the University of Maryland.

Finally, I wish to thank the Women's Studies Program at the University of Maryland for providing a supportive and challenging working environment, the university for the sabbatical leave that provided me with the time to write this book, and to the students of my course, "Women, Art, and Culture" for motivating me to do so.

CONTENTS

PREFACE TO THE EXPANDED EDITION

I was inspired initially to write *The Hero Within* out of a concern that we would not be able to solve the great political, social, and philosophical problems of our time if so many of us persisted in seeing the hero as "out there" or "up there," beyond ourselves. The book was meant as a call to the quest, to challenge readers to claim their own heroism and to take their own journeys. This call is not about becoming bigger or better or more important than anyone else. We *all* matter. Every one of us has an essential contribution to make, and we can do so only by taking the risk of being uniquely our own selves.

Underneath the frantic absorption in the pursuit of money, status, power, and pleasure and the addictive and obsessive behaviors current today is, we all know, a sense of emptiness and a common human hunger to go deeper. In writing *The Hero Within* it seemed to me that each one of us wants and needs to find, if not the "meaning of life," then the meaning of our own, individual lives, so that we can find ways of living and being that are rich, empowered, and authentic.

Yet, even with knowing this, the massive cultural response to the Bill Moyers interviews with Joseph Campbell on the PBS series "The Power of Myth," along with the enthusiastic reader response to *The Hero Within*, was a pleasant surprise to me. More people than I ever dared imagine seem prepared and even eager to respond to the call to the heroic quest with an enthusiastic "yes."

The first edition of *The Hero Within* sold almost entirely by word of mouth. I was fascinated to learn how many readers bought multiple copies to give to their friends and coworkers as a way of calling them to the quest and, at the same time, creating a sense of community that would support their own journeys. Many readers have complained that copies of the book had a way of disappearing from their offices and living rooms, by way, I gather, of friends, lovers, relatives, clients, and coworkers.

Many readers also have written or called to say how *The Hero Within* either named their own experience, or in some other way empowered them. I was particularly touched by a man from Perth, Australia, who called three times, long-distance, to thank me for writing the book, apparently undeterred by always getting my answering machine. But most of all, I have been moved by stories of personal transformation. One young man from the Pacific Northwest told me that he had been on drugs and had lost everything. By the time a friend gave him *The Hero Within*, he was living in the woods alone. He said he read it, believed it, and changed his life. By the time he brought his tattered copy of the book to a lecture for me to sign, he was an executive in a small company and generally doing well. Such *is* the power of myth.

Of course, I do not mean to suggest that every reader of *The Hero Within* was empowered, or even liked the book. One woman, for instance, railed at me for writing the "Magician" chapter, wondering how the author of such an otherwise useful book could write such garbage! Another woman, explaining why she could not get into the book told me, "It's clear to me that you want spiritual depth. I just want the pain to stop," a response coming from such a deep sense of loss and vulnerability that I could not help sympathizing with her point of view, no matter how committed I might be to moving through the pain to find meaning and thus joy.

This new expanded edition of *The Hero Within* has been prompted by the most frequent question asked by its readers: "Is it possible to do something to encourage the development of an archetype in one's own life?" The answer is "yes," and the exercises that have been added to the expanded edition are designed to do just that. You may choose to do only the exercises for a particular archetype you wish to develop or all the exercises, as a way of encouraging wholeness. You may work on these exercises by yourself, but doing them with others, if it is convenient to do so, is a great way to build friendships and communities that support one another's heroic journeys.

The second most frequently asked question is, "What have you learned since writing *The Hero Within*? While the more expansive answer to that question awaits the completion of two books now in progress, the simple answer is that I would now underscore even more strongly than I did when I first wrote the book the cyclical nature of the journey and the essential equality of the archetypes. Were I to rewrite *The Hero Within* today, I would expand the discussion of the positive contribution of the archetype of the Innocent and of the downsides of the Magician, especially the dangers of raising havoc, as does the Sorcerer's Apprentice, if we take on more than we can handle, or do harm, as does the Evil Sorcerer, if we use the Magician's power for egocentric and inhumane ends.

Finally, readers have asked me about the impact on my own life of publishing this book. The impact on my external life has been considerable, parachuting me out of college teaching and administration into assuming the presidency of an educational and consulting organization. In this role, I am able to write, speak, conduct workshops and training sessions, and consult with organizations full-time, about ways of listening to the heroes within as we take our individual and collective journeys. The impact on my internal life has been no less great. Knowing that so many feel resonance with a mythic perspective on their lives energizes my work and increases my optimism about our society's future. For this and for much, much more, I am deeply thankful.

PREFACE

Writing this book was, in part, an homage to the archetypes that have helped me grow as a person and a scholar. It also was an exercise in synthesis, utilizing insights from a number of traditions besides archetypal psychology that have influenced my work and my life. Among those are feminist theory (including formulations about female systems), process therapy, developmental psychology, and the insights of the New Age movement. This work also is my fourth book-length study of heroic journey patterns and as such grows out of my prior work.

My dissertation focused on heroes and fools in contemporary fiction. In it I defined a cultural paradigm shift from a heroic consciousness to the anti-hero to the fool, or trickster, who provided an alternative, comic, and optimistic vision about possibilities for fullness of life even in the modern world. Later, influenced by the feminist movement, I became interested in images of women in literature. In particular I explored the interaction between the cultural stories that named women as virgins, whores, helpmates, and mothers, and identity formation in women. How is it that we, as women, come to know who we are? How healthy are the stories that have been available to us? The outcome of this research was an anthology, coedited with Katherine Pope, called *Who Am I This Time? Female Portraits in American and British Literature*[1] (McGraw-Hill, 1976). In exploring these portraits, Katherine Pope and I identified three heroic images for women: the sage, the artist, and the warrior.

Writing that book helped me understand not only that many of our socialization patterns are based upon limiting stereotypes, but also that it is not possible simply to decide they are not good for us and then ignore them. The *stereotypes* are laundered, domesticated versions of the *archetypes* from which they derive their power. The shallow stereotype seems controllable and safe, but it brings then less, not more, life. The archetype behind it is full of life and power.

When Katherine Pope and I moved through the limiting stereotypes to the empowering archetypes behind them, we discovered a rich and hitherto unexplored tradition of female heroism. In writing my own dissertation, it had never occurred to me to question whether the patterns I was identifying as characteristic of human heroism in the contemporary world might be different if the hero were female. We determined to explore stories about female protagonists and delineate the pattern of female heroism. We found that, although on the archetypal level the patterns of male and female heroism were quite similar, they differed profoundly in detail, tone, and meaning from analogous stories about men. Moreover, the female hero's journey was more optimistic and more democratic and equalitarian than her male counterpart's.

This research led to the publication of *The Female Hero in American and British Literature*.[2] In the years since, readers' responses to the book have convinced me of the power of making explicit the myths that govern our lives. When we do not name them, we are hostages to them and can do nothing else but live out their plots to the end. When we name them, we have a choice about our response. We can extricate ourselves from undesirable myths (such as the Cinderella myth, recently identified as creating the Cinderella complex), and/or we can respect the archetypal pattern that is exerting control over our lives and learn its lesson.

When I began the study of women's journeys, not much had been done—at least not much that took into account a feminist perspective. The great books on the hero, such as Joseph Campbell's *The Hero with a Thousand Faces*, assumed either that the hero was male or that male heroism and female heroism were essentially the same.[3] Now, with the development of women's studies and widespread interest in feminist scholarship, many theorists have begun studying women's journey patterns and how they differ from men's. Most such works, however, overemphasize differences.

There is a need now to explore female and male journey patterns together, giving serious attention to ways we are the same and ways we differ. We still are members of the same species, yet our biology and our conditioning are different, as are the opportunities afforded us by society. As a result, the texture and tone of our journeys differ, and so do the plots we act out.

For groundbreaking conceptualizations about gender differences I am indebted especially to the theoretical works of Carol Gilligan (*In a Different Voice: Psychological Theory and Women's Development*),[4] Jessie Bernard (*The Female World*),[5] and Anne Wilson Schaef (*Women's Reality: An Emerging Female System in the White Male Society*).[6] I also am grateful to Anne Schaef, with whom I worked for many years, for my understanding of the principles behind process therapy, and in particular a firm belief that we can trust our own processes. Shirley Gehrke Luthman's published works (especially *Collections* and *Energy and Personal Power*)[7] were important to me in refining these understandings, especially with regard to the concept of mirroring discussed in Chapter 6, The Magician. Starhawk's work on feminist spirituality (*The Spiral Dance* and *Dreaming the Dark*) also was influential.[8]

My work differs from that of many theorists of gender difference in that I emphasize the basic similarities between the sexes as well as their differences. I hope that by naming some of the similarities and differences, my work will not only make the journey easier and less painful for men and women, but improve the communication between them.

Shirley Luthman, along with other New Age thinkers such as Gerald G. Jampolsky (*Love Is Letting Go of Fear*)[9] and W. Brugh Joy (*Joy's Way*),[10] helped me understand that in many ways we choose the world we live in. In writing this book, I realized that each of the archetypes carries with it a way of seeing the world. The external world tends to oblige us by reinforcing our beliefs about it. For example, people who see themselves as victims get victimized. Further, even when the world does not mirror us, we see only those aspects of the world that fit our current scripts, unless, that is, we are developmentally ready to move on.

I have reservations, however, about some New Age thinking, such as that found in books like Richard Bach's *Illusions*. The external world exists and is not totally in a single individual's control. It is one thing to believe that we have total responsibility for our lives and at the soul level choose the events of our lives, and quite another to see everything external to us as illusory. It is critical to developing into a responsible human to see that other people exist, as do poverty, sickness, and suffering. Further, I fear that some New Age thinking encourages people to believe they can skip their journeys and live returned to Eden without completing critical developmental tasks.

This book could not have been written without the insights of post-Jungian theorists James Hillman and Joseph Campbell.[11] In addition to these archetypal psychologists, I am indebted to those developmental psychologists who work in the area of cognitive and moral development such as William Perry (*Forms of Intellectual and Ethical Development in the College Years: A Scheme*),[12] Lawrence Kohlberg (*The Philosophy of Moral Development*),[13] and, again, Carol Gilligan, and to my colleagues at the University of Maryland, especially Faith Gabelnick and Lee Knefelkamp, for what I have learned from them.

Concepts from developmental psychology basic to this book are the belief that all human beings go through phases and stages, and that the successful completion of one stage makes possible movement to the next, although men and women are likely to experience them in different orders and to enact the themes differently. Embedded in each stage is a developmental task. Therefore, once you learn how to do it, you continue to have that ability. Thus, the stages are additive and not strictly linear. As you grow and change, you add themes and your life becomes fuller. This theory departs from many stage theories in that it dissociates stage from chronological age, it deemphasizes the importance of addressing each learning task in sequence, and it recognizes, at least as acknowledged in this preface, cultural relativity. It makes no claim to universal truth.

Indeed, although this book is the result of many years of study of literature and myth and of careful observation of the lives of those around me, it is a very personal and subjective offering. A friend suggested I might call this book "Carol Pearson at Forty," for it was written to acknowledge the end of one phase of my life. I wrote it as I was moving out of full-time teaching, as something to hand to my students to summarize what I know about life that I most want to share with them.

I am very conscious of the limitations of my own knowledge and experience. What I have been able to see and the patterns I have been able to identify are biased toward my own experience as a white, middle-class woman with a Christian background, a feminist, a wife and mother, not to mention an academic. I trust that the reader whose life and experience may be very different from mine and who thus will know slightly or very different truths from those I share here will use this as one point of reference in an ongoing dialogue, and will take some time to ponder what he or she knows about the gods and goddesses who inform our lives. I certainly will continue to do so. But if you happen to see me after a lapse of several years, do not ask me to defend ideas in this book. Very likely I will know more and may no longer agree with what I have said. Tell me what you think, and ask me, if you wish to ask me something, what I have learned since writing it.

INTRODUCTION

This is a book about the stories that help us make meaning of our lives. Our experience quite literally is defined by our assumptions about life. We make stories about the world and to a large degree live out their plots. What our lives are like depends to great extent on the script we consciously, or more likely, unconsciously, have adopted.

Any culture's or individual's myths of the hero tell us about what attributes are seen as the good, the beautiful, and the true, and thereby teach us culturally valued aspirations. Many of these stories are archetypal. Archetypes, as Carl Jung postulated, are deep and abiding patterns in the human psyche that remain powerful and present over time. These may exist, to use Jung's terminology, in the "collective unconscious," the "objective psyche," or may even be coded into the make-up of the human brain. We can see these archetypes clearly in dreams, art, literature, and myth that seem to us profound, moving, universal, and sometimes even terrifying. We also can recognize them when we look at our own lives and those of our friends. By observing what we do and how we interpret what we do, we can identify the archetypes that inform our lives. Sometimes we even can recognize the archetypes dominant in someone's life by their body language. A person trudging along in a stoop as if every step were a chore is possessed by the Martyr archetype, while another person, whose life is controlled by the archetype of the Warrior, walks purposefully, chin jutting out aggressively, body leaning forward as if striving to meet a goal.

Archetypes are numerous. How is it then that I write a book about only six of them? Although there may be quite a large number of archetypal plots available to us, most do not have the influence upon our development that these six do. For an archetype to have a major influence upon our lives, there must be some external duplication or reinforcement of the pattern: an event in one's life or stories recounted in the culture that activate the pattern. Therefore, both our personal histories and our culture influence which archetypes will be dominant in our lives. Although the archetypes may, as Jung argues, be timeless and transcend culture, this book about them is more culture-specific, for what I am describing here are some of the archetypal patterns, or stories, that preside over individual development in Western culture. Were I writing about heroism in African or Japanese culture, this book would be quite different (although because of the degree to which Western culture influences these societies, many of its insights might have contemporary relevance for them).

Furthermore, the archetypes discussed in this work are those important to the *hero's* journey, that is, a journey of individuation. These are the archetypes manifested in our daylight worlds that help us define a strong ego, and then expand the boundaries of the ego to allow for the full flowering of the self and its opening up to the experience of oneness with other people and with the natural and spiritual worlds.

Here I am using Carl Jung's terminology, according to which the ego is that part of the psyche that experiences separation. At first, the young child feels little or no separation from the environment, and especially none from the mother. It is only as the adult completes the task of strong ego development that his or her boundaries can expand and make way for the self. This includes (in each of us) not only the full conscious self, but the personal unconscious and access to archetypal images emerging from the collective unconscious. The result is not only a renewed sense of wonder and oneness with the cosmos, but a reclaiming and redefinition of magical thinking.[1]

The journey described here is more circular or spiral than linear. It begins with the complete trust of the Innocent, moves on to the longing for safety of the Orphan, the self-sacrifice of the Martyr, the exploring of the Wanderer, the competition and triumph of the Warrior, and then the authenticity and wholeness of the Magician. In much-simplified, graphic form, the archetypes' approach to life looks like this:

	Innocent	Orphan	Martyr	Wanderer	Warrior	Magician
Goal	None	Safety	Goodness	Autonomy	Strength	Wholeness
Task	Fall	Hope	Ability to give up	Identity	Courage	Joy/faith
Fear	Loss of Paradise	Abandonment	Selfishness	Conformity	Weakness	Superficiality

(A more detailed chart appears on pages 20 and 21.)

The archetypes identified here are not the typical ones usually included by Jungians as critical to the individuation process. Most works of Jungian psychology use dreams and rather exotic mythic texts to get at unconscious psychological formulations. Our purpose here is to explore the archetypes active in our *conscious* lives. Most Jungians focus on dreams because our culture and hence our socialization patterns have defined so much archetypal material as bad or wrong. In fact, diving into the depths of the unconscious too often has been discouraged because it is going, according to cultural mythic geography, into the underworld—the devil's place. So we repress and censor what goes on there to keep it from our conscious minds.

This work can look at the more conscious manifestations of archetypes partly because it addresses those that are congruent with our culture's present point in its evolution, and because the culture we live in now is less repressive. Exploring the unconscious has become culturally acceptable, even desirable. Different approaches are appropriate for different times. Jung was writing at a time and place that greatly encouraged psychological repression. Most people had little or no understanding of their inner motivations. Our time, however, is greatly influenced by psychology, and a large percentage of the population is quite literate about the workings of the psyche. Therefore, we do not always have to move to dreams or other forms of uncensored expression to find out what is true for us. We simply have more access now to unconscious material, more skills for dealing with it, and more cultural permission to experiment with different feelings and ways of being and acting in the world than Jung's patients did. Our psyches need not hide so much from us, and the archetypes need not seem so foreign and threatening. Indeed, that is why I used ordinary, well-known words to describe them, rather than the exotic names of ancient gods and goddesses or psychological terms, such as anima or animus, which may seem intimidating to some.

The point is that we can be safe and at home in our own psyches, and we need not spend years studying psychology to be able to converse with ourselves. We know the language of the archetypes, for they live within us. Ancient folk also knew the language. For them, the archetypes were the gods and goddesses who were concerned with everything in their lives from the most ordinary to the most profound. Archetypal psychology, in a sense, brings back insights from ancient polytheistic theologies, which teach us about the wonderfully multiple nature of the human psyche. When these deities, or archetypes, are denied, they do not go away. Instead they possess us, and what we experience is enslavement, not the liberation they ultimately hold out to us. So beware of scorning the gods, for ironically, it is our very attempts to deny and repress the gods that cause their destructive manifestations.

The archetypes are fundamentally friendly. They are here to help us evolve, collectively and individually. In honoring them we grow.

THE HERO WITHIN

Chapter 1

THE HERO'S JOURNEY

Heroes take journeys, confront dragons, and discover the treasure of their true selves. Although they may feel very alone during the quest, at its end their reward is a sense of community: with themselves, with other people, and with the earth. Every time we confront death-in-life we confront a dragon, and every time we choose life over nonlife and move deeper into the ongoing discovery of who we are, we vanquish the dragon; we bring new life to ourselves and to our culture. We change the world. The need to take the journey is innate in the species. If we do not risk, if we play prescribed social roles instead of taking our journeys, we feel numb; we experience a sense of alienation, a void, an emptiness inside. People who are discouraged from slaying dragons internalize the urge and slay themselves by declaring war on their fat, their selfishness, or some other attribute they think does not please. Or they become ill and have to struggle to get well. In shying away from the quest, we experience nonlife and, accordingly, we call forth less life in the culture.

The primary subject of modern literature is this experience of alienation and despair. The antihero has replaced the hero as the central figure in literature precisely because the myth of the hero that dominates our culture's view of what it means to take our journeys has become anachronistic. What we imagine immediately when we think of the hero really is only one heroic archetype: the Warrior.

The Warrior typically takes a long, usually solitary journey, saves the day, and rescues the damsel-in-distress by slaying a dragon or in some other way defeating the enemy.

Gender and the Redefinition of Heroism

In our culture, the heroic ideal of the Warrior has been reserved for men—usually only white men at that. Women in this plot are cast as damsels-in-distress to be rescued, as witches to be slain, or as princesses who, with half the kingdom, serve as the hero's reward. Minority men, at least in American literature, typically are cast as the loyal sidekick (think of Huck and Jim in Mark Twain's *Huck Finn* or the Lone Ranger and Tonto).

In *The Hero With a Thousand Faces* Joseph Campbell wrote that the hero is "master of the world."[1] And it is the masters of the world—the kings, the princes, and their poets—who have defined for us *what* the heroic ideal is and *whose* it is. Of course, they designed it in their own image and saw heroism as the province of the few. With the rise of democracy and the development of the ideal of an equalitarian society, first working-class white men and then women and minority men began claiming the heroic archetype as their own.

Ironically, just as women, working-class men, and minority men are embracing the Warrior archetype, many white middle- and upper-class men are expressing great alienation from it. In part, I think that is so because, although this archetype is a myth that presides over a healthy capacity for assertion and mastery, it also, in its usual form, is based upon separation—upon cutting oneself off from other people and the earth. Many men have discovered that, however satisfying it is in the short run, the urge to be better than, to dominate and control, brings only emptiness and despair.

The Warrior archetype is also an elitist myth, which at its base embodies the notion that some people take their heroic journeys while others simply serve and sacrifice. Yet we are all really one; as long as we are not all taking our journeys, finding our voices, our talents, and making our unique contributions to the world, we start feeling less and less alive—even the most privileged among us. No one can truly profit for long at another's expense.

When I first began to examine this myth, I thought virtually all of modern malaise was due to the prevalence of the Warrior archetype. Surely, having a "slaying-the-dragon" paradigm for problem solving was not going to bring us world peace or eliminate world hunger. Later I came to realize that the Warrior archetype is not the problem per se, for it is developmentally critical to the evolution of human consciousness. Certainly it is as critical for women and minority men as it is for white men, even though the archetype gets redefined somewhat when everyone gets into the act instead of only a privileged few. The problem is that focusing on *only* this heroic archetype limits everyone's options. Many white men, for example, feel ennui because they need to grow beyond the Warrior modality, yet they find themselves stuck there because it not only is defined as *the* heroic ideal but is also equated with masculinity. Men consciously or unconsciously believe they cannot give up that definition of themselves without also giving up their sense of superiority to others—especially to women.

In doing research for *Who Am I This Time?* and later for *The Female Hero in American and British Literature*,[2] I realized that the belief that there are no true heroines in modern literature simply is not accurate. Women, for example, as Katherine Pope and I showed in *The Female Hero*, often are portrayed heroically. Encouraged by feminism, many women enact the Warrior archetype. But that is not the whole story. They also are exploring patterns of heroism that, at first, seemed to me to be specific to women. This mode, which is different from men's, is based upon integrity rather than on slaying dragons. Female heroes often even flee dragons! While male heroes like Owen Wister's Virginian (in *The Virginian*) would leave even their bride on the wedding day to fight a duel (for honor's sake), women tend to assume that it simply is good sense to run from danger. Further, they do not see slaying dragons as very practical, since the people who often entrap women are husbands, mothers, fathers, children, friends—people who insist that good women forgo their own journeys to serve others. That is why there often are no true villains in stories about female heroes. Or at least it does not occur to the hero to slay them.

I was pleased to discover that women had developed an alternative to the hero-kills-the-villain-and-rescues-the-victim plot, one with no real villains or victims—just heroes. This mode of heroism seemed to offer hope that there is a form of heroism that can not only bring new life to us all, but do it in an equalitarian way. However, this mode of heroism could never fully blossom if only one sex seemed to know about it. While I observed all around me women optimistically playing out a hero/hero/hero script, most men I knew were acting out the old hero/villain/victim one. Men who could not be the hero in that old definition found the only other role available to them was the victim, or antihero. But then I noticed some men and some male characters in literature who had also discovered the hero/hero/hero plot and were feeling fully alive, joyous, and heroic in acting it out.

I began to recognize that men and women go through—albeit in somewhat different forms and sometimes in a slightly different order—the same basic stages of growth in claiming their heroism. And ultimately for both, heroism is a matter of integrity, of becoming more and more themselves at each stage in their development. Paradoxically, there are archetypal patterns that govern the process each of us goes through to discover our uniqueness, so we are always both very particularly ourselves and very much like one another in the stages of our journeys. In fact, there is a rather predictable sequence of human development presided over respectively by the archetypes of the Innocent, the Orphan, the Wanderer, the Warrior, the Martyr, and the Magician, even though our culture has encouraged men and women to identify with them differently.

The Archetypes and Human Development

The Innocent and the Orphan set the stage: The Innocent lives in the prefallen state of grace; the Orphan confronts the reality of the Fall. The next few stages are strategies for living in a fallen world: The Wanderer begins the task of finding oneself apart from others; the Warrior learns to fight to defend oneself and to change the world in one's own image; and the Martyr learns to give, to commit, and to sacrifice for others. The progression, then, is from suffering, to self-definition, to struggle, to love.

It was clear to me that the heroism of the Wanderer is not defined by fighting. It is the very act of leaving an oppressive situation and going out alone to face the unknown that is the Wanderer's heroic act—for men or women.

But at first I missed the heroism of the Martyr, since more modern literature celebrates liberation from the older ideal of sacrifice. The antimartyr feeling is particularly strong in literature about women, because female socialization and cultural norms have reinforced martyrdom and sacrifice for women well into the twentieth century. Women have been cramped by the Martyr role even more than white men have been by the Warrior-only role. Looking again at the archetype of the Martyr, I began to respect its power and to see why, for example, Christianity, with the centrality of the image of Christ martyred on the cross, so appealed to women and minorities, and also why suffering and martyrdom have been so important in Judaism, especially in the many times and places marked by anti-Semitism.

I discovered the emergence of an ancient archetype heretofore reserved for even fewer people than the Warrior and that now is being redefined as a mode of heroism available to everyone. In this mode, the hero is a Magician or Shaman. After learning to change one's environment by great discipline, will, and struggle, the Magician learns to move with the energy of the universe and to attract what is needed by laws of synchronicity, so that the ease of the Magician's interaction with the universe seems like magic. Having learned to trust the self, the Magician comes full circle and, like the Innocent, finds that it is safe to trust.

Each of the archetypes carries with it a worldview, and with that different life goals and theories about what gives life meaning. Orphans seek safety and fear exploitation and abandonment. Martyrs want to be good, and see the world as a conflict between good (care and responsibility) and bad (selfishness and exploitation). Wanderers want independence and fear conformity. Warriors strive to be strong, to have an impact upon the world, and to avoid ineffectiveness and passivity. Magicians aim to be true to their inner wisdom and to be in balance with the energies of the universe. Conversely, they try to avoid the inauthentic and the superficial.

Each archetype projects its own learning task onto the world. People governed by an archetype will see its goal as ennobling and its worst fear as the root of all the world's problems. They complain about other people's ruthlessness, conformism, weakness, selfishness, or shallowness. Many misunderstandings arise from this. The Wanderer's independence often looks to the Martyr like the selfishness Martyrs abhor. The Warrior's assertiveness may appear to the Orphan like ruthlessness. And when the Magician proclaims that if the response is genuine, it is perfectly fine to act in any way, including all the ways you formerly feared and rejected (selfish, lazy, etc.), it sounds to almost everyone else like the worst kind of license!

At the Magician's level, however, dualities begin to break down. The Orphan's fear of pain and suffering is seen as the inevitable underside of a definition of safety that assumes that life should be only pleasurable and easy. Magicians believe that in fact we are safe even though we often experience pain and suffering. They are part of life, and ultimately we all are held in God's hand. Similarly, Magicians see that it is an unbalanced focus on giving that creates selfishness. The task is not to be caring of others *instead* of thinking about oneself, but to learn how to love and care for ourselves *as well as* our neighbor.

Magicians see beyond the notion of individualism versus conformity to the knowledge that we each are unique *and* we all are one. Beyond strength versus weakness, they come to understand that assertion and receptivity are yang and yin—a life rhythm, not a dualism. Finally, they know that it is not even possible to be inauthentic, for we can be only who we are. Inevitably, we do take our rightful place in the universe.

Each archetype moves us through duality into paradox. Within each is a continuum from a primitive to a more sophisticated and complex expression of its essential energy. The chapters that follow describe the archetypes and the stages of awareness the hero encounters in exploring each one. The pattern described is schematic, however, so it is important to recognize while reading it that people do not go through these stages lockstep. Individuals chart their own unique courses through these "stages," and there are predictable differences in the ways people encounter them. This holds true in general for many cultural groups—different ethnic or racial groups, people from different countries or regions—but in this work, because of my own background and experience, I will focus on differences between men and women.

For example, male and female modes of heroism seem different because men linger longer in some stages and women in others. Because women are socialized to nurture and serve, and perhaps also because women give birth, their lives tend to be overly dominated by the Martyr archetype even before they have had the opportunity to explore the possibilities embodied by the Wanderer and the Warrior. Men, on the other hand, are pushed into having control over their lives and power over others, into being Warriors, before they know who they are. They get to the Warrior stage quickly but then get stuck there—and not only *there*, but often at its more primitive levels. They often have little or no encouragement and few male role models for developing their capacities for sensitivity, care, and commitment.

Women often do not like the Warrior stage and, hence, either refuse that journey or, if they embark upon it, whiz right on through it to become Magicians. That's why, I think, the changes I describe as the Wandering and Warrioring stages appear in Carol Gilligan's pioneering work, *In a Different Voice: Psychological Theory and Women's Development*, as a mere "transition" stage between a morality based on care of others (sacrifice) and, at a higher level, one in which the self is filtered back into the picture (interdependence).[3]

Women seem to linger in the stages that emphasize affiliation (Martyr and Magician) and men in those that emphasize separateness and opposition (Wanderer and Warrior). As Gilligan has shown, women are more likely to see the world in terms of nets and webs of connectedness; men see it in terms of ladders and hierarchies, where people compete for power. When we look at where most women or men are, without seeing the overall developmental pattern, it may look as if there are distinct and different male and female paths. Or, if one looks just at the paths and not at the different time and intensity of commitment to each archetype, it appears that men and women are developmentally the same. Neither is true. Men and women are developmentally the same; *and* they are different.

The typical male pattern of development in this culture is to go directly from the Orphan to the Warrior stage and stay there. Movement occurs, if at all, during the mid-life crisis, when a man is forced into confronting identity issues. Often the result is a more compelling concern with issues of intimacy, care, and commitment than he has known before. His typical progression looks something like this:

Orphan   Warrior   Wanderer   Martyr   Magician

The traditional female, on the other hand, moves from the Orphan into the Martyr stage, where she may stay the rest of her life, unless something propels her to grow. Sometimes when the children leave, the husband strays, her self-esteem sinks, or she encounters liberated ideas, the resulting identity crisis forces her to ask herself who she is, after which she learns to be more assertive. Here is her pattern:

Orphan   Martyr   Wanderer   Warrior   Magician

A career woman who strives to be independent early in life may work on warrioring and martyring simultaneously, being tough at the office and all-giving at home. Many men also organize their lives this way as well. Whether male or female, the pattern reduces to this:

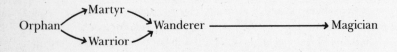

In this case, identity issues are forced when the split seems untenable and the conflicting values of the Martyr and the Warrior find enough integration that we feel whole again.

It is important to recognize that men and women, however, do not always and inevitably experience these stages in different orders. Individual differences are great. Moreover, there is a variation on the pattern described here by personality type. In Jung's type theory, some people are governed by their analytical, thinking process, and others by their empathic, feeling modes. Feeling types have a greater affinity with the Martyr archetype and thinking types with the Warrior mode. What we like we often develop first, waiting to explore our less preferred attributes at a later time. Therefore, both women with a preference for thinking and men with a preference for feeling are likely to work on martyring and warrioring simultaneously because one urge is reinforced by sex role conditioning and the other by their personality type.[4]

But some generalizations about gender seem to hold up. At this particular time, most men's values are very much defined by the Warrior ethic. The way of contemporary women, however, is split. Most women either are Martyrs or they have moved quickly through the Wanderer and Warrior stages and are beginning to experiment with being Magicians. Depending on which group of women you notice, you can argue that the Martyr archetype is distinctly female in contrast to the Warrior mode, which is distinctly male, *or* that the Magician mode is the new emerging female system in contrast to the old patriarchal Warrior way of being in the world. The first position has been adopted by conservatives and the second by many feminists. Neither is wrong, but neither gives us the whole story, either.

In the cultural mind, feminists generally are associated with the archetype of the Amazon, but truly liberated women seem to have a particular affinity for the Magician's way of operating and are leading the way into exploring the archetype that presides over the current transformation of human consciousness—a transformation as important as when men led the way in exploring the possibilities for positive (yang) action and aggressiveness as a means to improve the world. The discovery that the Magician's wand and staff are appropriate tools for today's world is a profoundly hopeful one for both men and women, promising a restoration of peace and loving energy between them and between humankind and the earth.

A New Heroic Paradigm

The Warrior's life, with its focus on power over other people and the earth, is lonely and ultimately tragic. We may complete our journeys, be rewarded by being made king or queen, but we all know that the story goes on. We will, we know, lose power, be replaced by the new hero, and die. And our last moments on this earth will be marked by the least control over ourselves, other people, the future, and even our bodily functions of any time in life—except perhaps birth. And it is the end of the story that traditionally determines whether the plot is comic or tragic. No wonder modern literature and philosophy are so despairing!

But what if we simply shift our expectations a bit? What if the goal of life is not to prevail, but simply to learn? Then the end of the story can seem very different; and so can what happens in between birth and death. Heroism is redefined as not only *moving* mountains but *knowing* mountains: being fully oneself and seeing, without denial, what is, and being open to learning the lessons life offers us.

Box-Car Bertha's autobiography, *Sister of the Road*, ends with Bertha looking back over a life that has included abandonment by her mother at a very young age; a dehumanizing stint as a prostitute (culminating in a case of syphilis); and the experience of looking on helplessly when one lover was hanged and another run over by a train. She declares: "Everything I had ever struggled to learn I found I had already survived. . . . I had achieved my purpose—everything I had set out in life to do, I had accomplished. I had wanted to know how it felt to be a hobo, a radical, a prostitute, a thief, a reformer, a social worker and a revolutionist. Now I knew. I shuddered. Yes, it was all worthwhile to me. There were no tragedies in my life. Yes, my prayers had been answered."[5] Bertha sees herself as neither a suffering Martyr nor a Warrior, but as a Magician who received everything she asked for. She both takes responsibility for her choices and is thankful for the gift of her life.

Similarly, Annie Dillard in *Pilgrim at Tinker Creek* surmises that life "is often cruel, but always beautiful . . . the least we can do is try to be there," to be fully in life. She imagines that "the dying pray at the last not 'please,' but 'thank you' as a guest thanks his host at the door. . . . The universe," she explains, "was not made in jest but in solemn, incomprehensible earnest. By a power that is unfathomably secret, and holy, and fleet. There is nothing to be done about it, but ignore it, or see."[6]

Magicians view life as a gift. Our job here is to give our own gift and to engage fully with life and other people, letting in and receiving some gifts and, of course, taking responsibility to decline others. Tragedy, in this view, is a loss of the knowledge of who you are, with the result that you do not contribute what you are here to do.

For example, Gertie, in Harriette Arnow's *The Dollmaker*,[7] is a six-foot-tall hillbilly who is extremely wise, but she habitually discounts her wisdom. Becuase she does so, she slowly loses almost everything she loves: She loses the Tipton Place (a farm she had planned to buy) because she listens to her mother, who says a woman's duty is to be with her husband, and forgoes the farm to join her husband in Detroit; she loses her favorite daughter because she listens to a neighbor who tells her she must not let Cassie play with the doll that is her imaginary friend (Cassie sneaks off to play with the doll and is run over by a train); she does not take her vocation as a sculptor seriously, calling it "whittlin' foolishness," and her ultimate act of self-disrespect is chopping up a block of fine cherry wood, out of which she has been carving a "laughing Christ," to make cheap figurines and crucifixes. The "laughing Christ" is a visual image of her life-affirming philosophy in contrast to the deathly Puritanism she had been taught by her mother. To chop up that block of wood is equivalent to killing or maiming herself. Lest we miss this, earlier in the novel Cassie enjoins her to finish the statue and "let *her* out." "Her," of course, is Gertie.

The moment in which she chops up the cherry block is genuinely tragic, because in doing so she has denied herself and her own vision, yet even then it is not without hope. We all have moments of cowardice, when we deny our wisdom, our integrity, and our divinity. Although the novel ends here, we do find that Gertie's self-destructive act has forced her into a new level of understanding. Her excuse to chop up the cherry block when her family needed money was that she could not find the right face for Christ. At the novel's close, she says, "They's millions an millions a faces plenty fine enough . . . some a my neighbors down there in th alley—they would ha done."

From the vantage point of the Martyr, Gertie may have been seen as admirable, because she does almost nothing except sacrifice for her husband and children or to please her mother. What makes this novel different from conventional stories about women is that Arnow portrays her sacrifices as unnecessary and destructive. However, even though Gertie often does not claim either her own wisdom or the power to change her life, Arnow does not cast her as an antihero, either. Gertie is still a hero. While it is clear in the novel how many forces—external and internal—acted on her to reinforce her inability to trust herself, she is not portrayed as a helpless victim but as someone with responsibility for the choices she has made. Her life is tragic because she cannot act more fully on her heroism. This is, of course, similar to Shakespeare's portrayal of Hamlet or Lear. A major difference is that Gertie does not die in the end, so we have a sense of life as a process that continues.

From the Warrior's perspective, Gertie's story is tragic. But what of the Magician? What if we assumed, as Shirley Luthman does in *Energy and Personal Power*, that our beings attract to us the things we need, that we all are working out exactly what we need to learn in this life for our growth and development?[8] From this point of view, we would posit that Gertie propelled herself into situations from which she could learn to trust herself. In doing so, she had first to learn—with all the attendant pain—what happens when she does not do so.

The point is not for her to prove her heroism, as it is for the Warrior, but to claim it. The idea of proving heroism is tied up in the notion that it is a scarce commodity and that there is a hierarchy of people. When we come to understand that the real task is not to work hard to prove ourselves but to allow ourselves to be who we are, things seem very different. Throughout the novel, Gertie always is trying hard to *do* the right thing or sometimes just to learn what the right thing is. She comes to understand at the end that had she simply allowed herself to be herself and to go for what she honestly wanted, her dreams could have come true. Most likely she would have been the owner of the Tipton Place, surrounded by her family, completing her sculpture. She realizes in retrospect that she even had plenty of support for staying on that farm, but in her self-distrust she listened to those voices that undercut her. Even her husband explains that he would have supported her had she only trusted him enough to tell him what she was doing.

In the initial stages the Martyr assumes that suffering is simply what is. It must be endured by someone, so the Martyr suffers either so that others might be happier or to purchase happiness for another time. The Warrior discovers that with courage and hard work people can take a stand and can make changes—for themselves and for others. The Magician learns that neither suffering nor struggle is the ground of life. Joy is also our birthright. We can attract joy as easily as we attract pain, and we need neither martyr ourselves nor struggle unduly to make abundant life for ourselves or those we love.

It is this new mode—embodied in the journey of the Magician—that is the cutting edge of consciousness in contemporary culture, and it is the awareness that the Magician's archetype is now an appropriate, available, and powerful model for ordinary human life that motivates me to write this book. I also write it out of a need to honor the Martyr, the Wanderer, and the Warrior. We learn key lessons from each—lessons we never outgrow.

Growth as Spiral Toward Wholeness

These heroic modes are developmental, but they actually are not experienced in linear, ever-advancing steps. I would illustrate the typical hero's progression as a cone or three-dimensional spiral, in which it is possible to move forward while frequently circling back. Each stage has its own lesson to teach us, and we reencounter situations that throw us back into prior stages so that we may learn and relearn the lessons at new levels of intellectual and emotional complexity and subtlety. In our first tries at warrioring, for example, we may come on like Attila the Hun, but later we may learn to assert our own wishes so appropriately and gently that we are able to negotiate for what we want without any noticeable conflict. And it is not so much that the spiral gets higher, but that it gets wider as we are capable of a larger range of responses to life and, hence, able to have more life. We take in more and have more choices.

The chart on page 14 summarizes the stages within each archetype. The first time around the wheel, many people move through the center circle twice until they can move out by mastering the second and third levels of learning. While this schematic is helpful conceptually, human development is rarely that neat and tidy. The point is, however, that the archetypes are interrelated, and often one cannot resolve the psychological or cognitive dilemma embedded in one without working through another. Warrior and Martyr are two sides of a dualistic formulation about life in which you either take or you give. *Until you can do both, you can do neither freely.* Therefore, we go to school with each archetype many times in our lives. Further, events in our lives influence the order and intensity of our learning. Any massive change or crisis requires a reconsideration of identity issues. Any new commitment raises questions about sacrifice. Each time we encounter the same archetype, we have the opportunity to do so at a deeper level of understanding.

The virtues that the hero learns in each guise are never lost or outgrown. They just become more subtle. As Innocent, the hero

Three Turns Around the Hero's Wheel

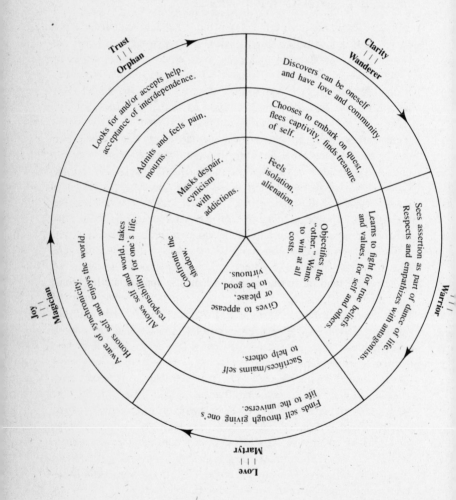

learns to trust; as Orphan, to mourn. As Wanderer, the hero learns to find and name one's own truth; as Warrior, to assert that truth so that it affects and changes the world; and as Martyr, to love, to commit, and to let go.

These virtues all involve some degree of pain or struggle. The virtue the Magician adds to these is the ability to recognize and receive the abundance of the universe. As the circle widens, the Magician gains what the Orphan longed for, the return to the lost Eden, first on the microcosmic, personal level, and later on the most cosmic level; but instead of experiencing plenty from a childlike, dependent position, the Magician enters the garden on the basis of interdependence—with other people, with nature, and with God. The last lesson the hero learns, then, is happiness.

We carry with us the lesson of each stage into the next, and when we do so, its meaning is transformed, but the lesson itself is not lost or outgrown. For example, at the first level of martyrdom, heroes sacrifice to propitiate the gods or some authority figure. Later, they do so simply to help other people. In becoming a Warrior, the hero transforms sacrifice into discipline: Some things are sacrificed so that other things can be achieved. As Magicians, heroes understand that nothing essential ever is lost: Sacrifice becomes the organic and gentle letting go of the old to make way for new growth, new life.

To people who move into a stage when it is appropriate for them, the myth brings life. When those who are at an earlier stage of development jump prematurely into a role, the same archetype makes for deadness, for it is not where their true growth lies. Men or women who are developmentally ready to move out of the Warrior stage, for example, may not be able to do so because they do not know there is anything else. They will feel deadened, claustrophobic, trapped, just as women who have been trapped in the Martyr role may get stuck because they have been told that the archetypes of the Wanderer and the Warrior are roles reserved only for men. Many women have expressed their excitement about *The Female Hero in American and British Literature* because the book reclaimed heroism—especially the Wanderer's and the Warrior's journeys—as an appropriate aspiration for women, and thus helped them move along on their journeys. I now hope that by reclaiming what is valuable in the Martyr archetype and by describing the archetype of the Magician

I can help make the journey easier and less painful for both women and men.

I also believe that we all have access to every mode all the time. What "stage" we are in has to do with where we "hang out" the most, where we spend the greatest percentage of our time. The most oppressed victim will have moments of transcendence. And none of us gets so advanced that we stop feeling, every once in awhile, like a motherless child. In fact, each stage has a gift for us, something critical to teach us about being human.

Suggestions to the Reader

Because I have indicated that there is a kind of predictable order in which people address certain developmental tasks, I hasten to emphasize again that *we do not leave one behind in a linear fashion and go on to another*. The deeper levels of understanding and performance associated with any of the archetypes are dependent upon also deepening our investment in the others. We continually are sharpening and refining skills in each category, for this journey is truly a matter of high-level skill development. Ultimately, we gain a repertoire of possible responses to life, so we have incrementally more choices about how we will respond in any given situation.

Actually, encountering these archetypes is a bit like redecorating a house. We begin by moving into a house furnished in part by attitudes, beliefs, and habits passed on to us by our families and by our culture. Some people never make the house their own and so do not develop a distinct identity or style. Those who do take their journeys and (to continue the metaphor) furnish their own houses do so at different paces and in different orders.

Some people do one room at a time, finish that, and go on to the next. Others may do a bit in each room, paint the whole house, then put up all the drapes, etc. Some people hurry and finish quickly and others are more leisurely in their work. Of course, this psychological house is a bit different from most homes because there are some rooms that cannot quite be finished until you have worked a bit on the adjacent one(s). While people do explore their learning tasks in many different orders, the archetypes are related and interdependent. Ultimately, we do not finish any of them completely until we finish them all. Like a house, moreover, the task is never quite done. Inevitably, whenever you think you have completed decorating it, you notice that the couch you bought first is worn or the wallpaper is torn, and there you go again!

Most people, then, work on all the learning tasks all their lives. But, like interior decorating, it is easier to work on, say, the Martyr room when you already have put some sustained effort into it over time and have made it yours. You begin to get the hang of it. So, too, when you learn the lessons offered by each archetype, you can "do" that archetype elegantly. Whether you are in Martyr, Wanderer, Warrior, etc., your reactions will be graceful and appropriate to the situation. If you have learned discretion, the responses you choose will fit who you are in the moment and the situation at hand. You will know you are on target because you feel centered and clear. When you feel awful and off-center, it is appropriate to take some time to focus on what response would have been more authentic or might have acknowledged more fully the other's realities as well as your own.

You might find that the theories in this book can help you get moving when you are feeling stuck. For instance, it sometimes is useful to remember that when you feel powerless and Orphan-like, it is time to look for help. When you feel alienated and cut off from people, you probably are dealing with wandering issues. Instead of worrying about how to be more intimate, attend to your identity issues. When you work them out so that you can be more fully authentic, relationships often fall into place. Similarly, if you feel martyred and can see that you are giving and giving, hoping to make a situation turn out right, then *let go* of your image of what "right" means and pay attention to taking your journey.

If you feel compulsive about remaking the world or getting another person to agree with you, the issue is always fear that if your environment does not change, you cannot be or have what you want. Your survival feels threatened, but the issue is not getting others to change, it is your own courage. This is the time to take a leap of faith, act authentically *now*, and contribute your own truth to the world without insisting that others agree with you. When you do that, change almost always happens (although you cannot control the outcome of that change).

Trusting yourself and your own process means believing that your task is to be fully yourself and that if you are, you will have everything you genuinely need for your soul's growth. If you find you are too attached to a particular outcome, that you are trying to force it to happen the way you want it to, and that you are suffering with lack of success in doing so, this is the time to cultivate the Magician's faith in the universe, in mystery, in the capacity of the unknown to provide you with what you need. Recognize that what you want and what you need often are not the same and that it is quite rational to trust the universe, God, or your higher self and let go.

Using these theories requires an awareness that we are multidimensional creatures. Most people work with different archetypes in different arenas of their life. For example, some are highly influenced by the Magician's consciousness when they think about spiritual issues but not when they think about their health. Exploring possibilities inherent in each archetype in different parts of your life may be a way of broadening your skills, or it may be stultifying. You may find that you are just stuck in roles that are defined by the context, and your responses do not, or no longer, reflect your true feelings.

You may fear that people will be thrown off if, say, you experiment with some of your Warrior skills at home or your Martyr ways of proceeding at work. Or you might fear a loss of power as you put aside highly developed skills to try out ones you may be awkward and unsure with at first. Yet you might find it interesting, challenging, and even fun to vary your repertoire and experiment with new approaches to old situations. Being assertive in your private life is different in style and in substance from what it is in public life, for instance. You learn new aspects of each archetype according to the context you are in.

Also note that the more primitive versions of any of the stages are jarring to people, simply because they are blunt, not yet refined. Remember that in their more refined and subtle forms none of the approaches are difficult for most other people to deal with. If people do have difficulty, it may be that they are just disoriented by change of any kind. Or, as you change and grow, a few people may always drift away, but your compensation is that gradually you will attract to you people who have mastered more of the skills you have and hence there can be more appreciation and reciprocity between you.

The chart that follows summarizes the various ways of approaching life characteristic of the most typical worldview associated with each archetype. Notice how in any month—or week—you may have all the responses listed. It is useful in thinking about these archetypes to recognize that we all really know about all of them. When I am feeling like an Orphan, I want the world to be handed to me on a silver platter, and I am annoyed that it is not. When I feel like a Wanderer, I really distrust association and need to do things alone.

After reading the book, use the following chart and take the test in the Appendix to refresh your memory. You will see which approach you take most often and therefore get some indication about what your primary lessons are at this point in your life. Being conscious of where you are can help you move on, if you wish to. For instance, if you feel rather practiced in a certain approach to life, try moving on to another level and try out some new responses to see how they feel. Note that the chart gives the more typical characteristics of each archetype rather than its most highly developed aspect. However, the most advanced stages of all the modalities, taken together, give a prescription for good mental health.

We are all so practiced in thinking linearly (and this chart is so linear) that I hasten to remind you that it is not necessarily better to be a Magician than an Orphan. Both the Magician and the Warrior run the risk of pride when, as a result of their real increase in power and self-confidence, they forget how dependent we all ultimately are on each other and the earth for our very survival. Not too long ago, I was feeling particularly proud of my (Warrior) achievements and competence; but I found myself waking up one morning, asking, "Why me?" when a series of challenges, inconveniences, and catastrophes hit me all at once. I experienced all the classic Orphan responses: victimization, the wish to be rescued, self-blame, and the urge to scapegoat others. Ultimately, however, the gift was the reminder of my real vulnerability and interdependence, as I was forced to ask my friends, family, and colleagues for help. Having a tendency toward too much self-reliance, I needed the reminder through their loving help that I was not alone.

Summary of Approaches of Each Archetype*

	Orphan	Martyr	Wanderer	Warrior	Magician
Goal	Safety	Goodness, care, responsibility	Independence, autonomy	Strength, effectiveness	Authenticity, wholeness, balance
Worst Fear	Abandonment, exploitation	Selfishness, callousness	Conformity	Weakness, ineffectuality	Uncentered superficiality, alienation from self, others
Response to Dragon	Denies it exists or waits for rescue	Appeases or sacrifices self to save others	Flees	Slays	Incorporates and affirms
Spirituality	Wants deity that will rescue and religious counselor for permission	Pleases God by suffering, suffers to help others	Searches for God alone	Evangelizes, converts others, spiritual regimes, disciplines	Celebrates experience of God in everyone, respects different ways of experiencing the sacred
Intellect/ Education	Wants authority to give answers	Learns or forgoes learning to help others	Explores new ideas in own way	Learns through competition, achievement, motivation	Allows curiosity, learns in group or alone because it is fun
Relationships	Wants caretaker(s)	Takes care of others, sacrifices	Goes it alone, becomes own person	Changes or molds others to please self, takes on pygmalion projects	Appreciates difference, wants peer relationships
Emotions	Out of control or numbed	Negative ones repressed so as not to hurt others	Dealt with alone, stoic	Controlled, repressed to achieve or prevail	Allowed and learned from in self and others

Physical Health	Wants quick fix, immediate gratification	Deprives self, diets, suffers to be beautiful	Distrusts experts, does it alone, alternative healthcare, enjoys isolated sports	Adopts regimes, discipline, enjoys team sports	Allows health, treats body to exercise, good food
Work	Wants an easy life, would rather not work	Sees as hard and unpleasant but necessary, works for others' sake	"I'll do it myself," searches for vocation	Works hard for goal, expects reward	Works at true vocations, sees work as its own reward
Material World	Feels poor, wants to win lottery, inherit money	Believes it is more blessed to give than to receive, more virtuous to be poor than rich	Becomes self-made man or woman, may sacrifice money for independence	Works hard to succeed, makes system work for self, prefers to be rich	Feels prosperous with a little or a lot, has faith will always have necessities, does not hoard
Task/Achievement	Overcoming denial, hope, innocence	Ability to care, to give up and give away	Autonomy, identity, vocation	Assertiveness, confidence, courage, respect	Joy, abundance, acceptance, faith

*The Innocent is not included on the chart because it is not an heroic archetype. When we live in paradise, there is no need for goals, fears, tasks, work, etc. The Innocent is both pre- and post-heroic.

The point is to be more complete, whole, and to have a wider repertoire of choices—not to be higher up a developmental ladder. (Imagine tearing out the chart and pasting the top and bottom together to make a circle.) Indeed, the Innocent is simply a Magician who has not yet encountered the other archetypes and learned their lessons. If you decide that being a Magician is better than being a Warrior or a Martyr and you try to limit your ways of responding to the world to those of this one archetype, you will be as one-sided and incomplete as the Orphan who has not yet gained skill in any other modality.

We do not outgrow any lessons. A nice example of this is in politics. Each archetype has its own contribution to make. Orphans want to follow a great leader who will rescue them. Wanderers identify as outsiders and see little or no hope, especially in conventional politics. (That is why people seem so apolitical these days.) Many of the kinds of people who used to be engaged in politics are now responding to major cultural change by removing themselves and addressing identity and values issues that help make a new politics possible. Warriors get involved in conventional politics and causes and try to make change happen. Magicians are more likely to emphasize the creation of new alternative communities, institutions, and ways of relating to one another without trying to get people to change who are not ready to do so.

The point is that none of these responses by themselves are adequate and none are bad. There are times for recognizing that someone else knows more or is a better leader and following them. There are times for removing yourself from the action to be sure of your values. There are times for political engagement, and there are times to focus on what you can create right where you are.

However, we do not always feel so tolerant and appreciative. Sometimes when we first move into a stage, we are a bit dogmatic about it and see it as the only way to be. When we leave that position, we usually flip-flop and reject where we have been.

For people just moving out of the early-stage Martyr mode, any positive statement about the value of sacrifice is likely to seem masochistic. And, of course, the point is that they are right—for them. If we are just moving from Martyr into being a Wanderer, the temptation to stop the journey and give to others is an ever-present and real threat. It is like leaving a love affair. Few of us can just say to our partner that we are ready to move on and leave with a simple thank you for what has been. Instead, we spend a great deal of time chronicling the faults of our former lover and how bad the relationship was. Often we create high drama this way to divert ourselves from our fear of the unknown, or because we do not believe we have a right to leave anything unless it is positively awful.

We also may reject stages we are not ready to move into yet, the ones we have had little or no experience with. Instead, we may redefine them in terms we know, and thus completely misunderstand the point. That is all right, too, because at that point the truth that we do not understand is not yet relevant to us developmentally. For instance, to a person just confronting the fall from Eden, just learning some rudimentary sense of realism, the Magician's claim that the universe is safe will sound like the worst possible example of denial![9]

I recently shared these ideas with a class, and it became clear to me that many students wanted to skip to Magician without paying their dues to the other archetypes. I do not believe that can be done— or if it can be done, it cannot be sustained over time. We do have to pay our dues by spending some time in each stage. What I hope, in such cases, is that knowing where we likely are going will free us up somewhat from the fear that often paralyzes us as we confront our dragons.

There is a paradigm shift that occurs when people move from being Warriors to being Magicians: their perception of reality actually changes. They come to realize that seeing the world as a place full of danger, pain, and isolation is not how the world is, but only their perception of it during the formative parts of their journey. This new knowledge can be very freeing.

While most people are concentrating on the news reported in the media—news that focuses primarily on disasters, wars, and contests—something transformative is happening in the culture that you do not see until you begin to change. Learning about this change is like learning a new word that you never knew before; suddenly, to your surprise, you hear it everywhere you go. Probably it was always there somewhere in your environment, but you did not notice it. When you learn a new way of being and relating in the world, all of a sudden you start meeting people like yourself, and pretty soon you are living in a new society, a new world, that operates on principles different from the old. The fact that you are reading this book suggests that it is time for you at least to know that world exists— if you are not living in it already.

People who must have power over others in order to feel safe themselves sometimes are threatened by others' moves into the Magician's domain, because Magicians cannot be controlled and manipulated very easily. "Power over" is dependent upon fear and a belief in scarcity—that there is not enough, so we all must compete for it. This fear keeps people docile, dependent, conformist, hoping to stay in the good graces of those in power, and/or jostling for power themselves. In the most affluent country in the world, people are motivated to work by their fear of poverty. Surrounded by others, people are motivated to buy this and that product in order to be loved. As Philip Slater explains in *The Pursuit of Loneliness*, in our society advertising augments the cultural belief in scarcity by creating artificial needs.[10] Instead of fearing poverty per se, people may fear that they will not be able to buy a fancy car or designer jeans.

People in power reinforce artificial scarcity because it sells products and keeps the work force compliant. The rest of us do not reject or dismiss the belief that resources and talent are scarce because we need to believe they are. We all need to go on our perilous journeys, and we must believe our fears are real. Unless we fear hunger, want, isolation, and despair, how will we ever learn to confront our fears? We are not ready for abundance, for a safe universe, until we have proven ourselves—to ourselves—by taking our journeys. It does not matter how many people love us, how much wealth we have at our disposal; we will attract problems and we will feel alone and poor as long as we need to. Have you ever known someone rich who, like Dickens's Scrooge, lived in terror of losing money, and as a result became a veritable slave to making and hoarding it? Similarly, no matter how much we are loved, until we are ready to let it in, we will feel lonely.

Ultimately, there is no way to avoid the hero's quest. It comes and finds us if we do not move out bravely to meet it. And while we may strive to avoid the pain, hardship, and struggle it inevitably brings, life takes us eventually to the promised land, where we can be genuinely prosperous, loving, and happy. The only way out is through.

Chapter 2

FROM INNOCENT TO ORPHAN

Heaven lies about us in our infancy!
Shades of the prison-house begin to close
  Upon the growing Boy. . . .
At length the man perceives it die away,
And fade into the light of common day.
                    —WILLIAM WORDSWORTH, *"Ode: Intimations of Immortality*
                              from Recollections of Early Childhood"

The Innocent lives in an unfallen world, a green Eden where life is sweet and all one's needs are met in an atmosphere of care and love. The closest ordinary equivalents to this experience occur in early childhood—for people with happy childhoods—or in the first stages of romance or in mystic experiments of Oneness with the cosmos. For many people this myth serves as an ideal of the way things should be.

Shel Silverstein's award-winning children's story *The Giving Tree* speaks to us of this yearning to be cared for totally. In it a young boy plays in a tree's branches and eats her apples. When he grows up, she gives him her branches to build a house. Many years later, when he yearns to sail the seven seas, she gives him her trunk to make a boat. Finally, when he returns to her in old age, she is sad because she has nothing left to give him, but he explains he only needs a place to sit down. So he sits upon her stump, and, like every other time she has given to him, "He's happy and she's happy."[1]

This story is seen as beautiful and ideal only if one identifies with the boy rather than with the tree! To Innocents, other people, the natural world, everything exists to serve and satisfy them. God's whole reason for being is to answer prayers. Any pain, any suffering, is an indication that something is wrong—with them (God is punishing them) or with God (maybe God is dead). To Innocents, the earth is there for their pleasure. They have every right to ravage it,

despoil it, pollute it, for it is here solely for them. For male Innocents, a woman's whole role is to care for men, to support them and
please them. For female Innocents, men's role is to protect them and
provide for them. For neither one is the other fully human.

Innocence is a natural state for children, but when carried into
adulthood it requires an astonishing amount of denial and narcissism;
and yet it is not uncommon for adults to believe that others should
be making their life Edenic. That God, their mother and father,
spouses, lovers, friends, employers, employees do not do so is a
constant source of annoyance, anger, or even cynicism.

The promise of a return of the mythic Edenic state is one of the
most powerful forces in human life. Much of what we do—and what
we fail to do—is defined by it. We objectify the earth and each other
in a frantic attempt to remain, or become, safe and secure, cared
for, in Eden. The irony here is that *we can and do return to safety,
love, and abundance but only as a result of taking our journeys.*
Understandably, most people seem to want to skip theirs and go
straight to the reward!

Eden, after all, is not a matter of getting all one's narcissistic
whims satisfied; it is a state of walking in grace that requires a deep
acknowledgment of and reverence for oneself and for others. No
amount of taking, by itself, will get us there, and no amount of
giving, either. Innocents, who are confronted with the necessity to
make their own way in life, feel abandoned, betrayed, even outraged,
and do not know that it is, indeed, a fortunate fall. At the deepest
level of their being, they want to go.

The Fall

Many cultures have myths that recount a golden age from which
humankind fell. In our culture, the primary story that gives this
meaning to us is the myth of Adam and Eve, according to which
(1) the Fall results from human sin, (2) that sin is more woman's
fault than man's, and (3) the penalty for sin is suffering. (For Adam
it is making a living by the sweat of his brow; for Eve it is childbirth;
and ultimately for both it is death.) Out of this myth comes a belief
that it is possible for humankind to reenter paradise, but only through
the expiation of suffering and sacrifice.

It is clear that the myth of the Fall has archetypal elements, for not only do versions of it exist in most cultures and religions, but in our own culture even people who are not practicing Jews or Christians experience something like the Fall. For many people it comes in the form of disillusionment with their parents. Parents are supposed to be like the "giving tree." If their parents were not, then they feel cheated, as if the world is not what it is supposed to be. Or perhaps their parents were terrific when they were little, but then they come to discover that their parents are not perfect. Suddenly those who are supposed to care for them cannot be trusted.

The Fall also takes the form of political, religious, or personal disappointment and disillusionment. Innocents become Orphans when they discover that God is dead or uncaring, the government is not always good, the laws are not always fair, or the courts may not protect them. Traditional men may experience extreme disillusionment upon discovering that women are not always "giving trees" but have sexual desires and career ambitions of their own. Women may be equally disappointed and angered to discover that men not only are unlikely to protect women but also have promoted and benefited from the oppression of women. Disillusionment comes to us all as we learn that the world is not always—or perhaps never is—how we have been taught it should be. For some, it is disappointing to discover that real life is not like life portrayed on television.

The Orphan is a disappointed idealist, and the greater the ideals about the world, the worse reality appears. Feeling like the Orphan after the Fall is an exceptionally difficult mode. The world is seen as dangerous; villains and pitfalls are everywhere. People feel like damsels-in-distress, forced to cope with a hostile environment without appropriate strength or skills. It seems a dog-eat-dog world, where people are either victims or victimizers. Even villainous behavior may be justified by the Orphan as simply realistic because you must "do unto others before they do unto you." The dominant emotion of this worldview is fear, and its basic motivation is survival.

The stage is so painful that people often escape from it using various opiates: drugs, alcohol, work, consumerism, mindless pleasure. Or they may addictively misuse relationships, work, and/or religion as means to dull the pain and provide a spurious sense of safety. Ironically, such addictions have the side effect of increasing our sense of powerlessness, our negativity, and they even, in the cases of drugs and alcohol, foster distrust and paranoia.

Such escapes are defended by those who resort to them as only reasonable strategies for coping with the human condition: "Of course I take a few drinks/pills/etc. every day. It's a tough life. How else would I get through it?" And they believe it is not realistic to expect much of life. One might complain that work is drudgery. "I hate my job, but I have to feed my kids. It's just the way things are." In relationships, a woman might simply assume that men "are just no good," and stay in a relationship in which she is emotionally or even physically battered because "he is better than most men." A man might complain that his wife nags but then shrug it off with "that's just how it is with women."

The archetype of the Orphan is a tricky place to be. His or her accomplishment is to move out of innocence and denial to learn that suffering, pain, scarcity, and death are an inevitable part of life. The anger and pain this engenders will be proportional to one's initial illusions.

The Orphans' story is about a felt powerlessness, about a yearning for a return to a primal kind of innocence, an innocence that is fully childlike, where their every need is cared for by an all-loving mother or father figure. This yearning is juxtaposed against a sense of abandonment, a sense that somehow we are supposed to live in a garden, safe and cared for, and instead are dumped out, orphans, into the wilderness, prey to villains and monsters. It's about looking for people to care for them, about forgoing autonomy and independence to secure that care; it's even about trying to be the all-loving parent—to their lovers, or children, or clients, or constituencies, anything to prove that that protection can be or is there. After the Fall comes the long and sometimes slow climb back to learning to trust and hope. The Orphan's task eventually is to learn self-reliance, but usually that cannot be done until he or she begins to search for the "giving tree": "Maybe there is no one, now, who will watch over me, but maybe I can find someone." Some women look for a Big Daddy; some men look for the "angel in the house," the woman who will provide a sanctuary from that cruel world; many look for the great political leader, the movement, the cause, or the million-dollar deal that will make everything all right.

At base is Orphans' fear of powerlessness and abandonment, a fear so profound that it usually is not experienced directly. The more apparent emotion is anger—either turned inward in a belief that somehow the Fall is our own fault, or else turned outward toward God, the universe, parents, institutions—anything or anyone that can be identified as not properly taking care of them. In a patriarchy, this rage habitually is projected onto women, as, for example, in the stories of Eve and Pandora. Perhaps this happens, as Dorothy Dinnerstein has argued in *The Mermaid and the Minotaur*, because we are cared for in infancy by our mothers, who then seem to be omnipotent. Not only are we disillusioned that they could not or would not make it "all better," but this disappointment also is coupled with that early infantile terror that Mother might leave and then one surely would die.[2] There is a great rage in our culture against women to the degree that they are separate people with needs of their own and not just "giving trees." The rage may explode at the liberated woman for her ambition and independence, or at the traditional woman for her dependence. Both are blamed for wanting and needing something for themselves.

One of the defenses of Orphans is to try to cling to innocence and therefore to be narcissistic and oblivious to other people's pain in addition to denying their own. A self-satisfied man sits reading the paper while his wife is overwhelmed, making dinner while taking care of three demanding, tired, and hungry children. A light-hearted young woman spends the day shopping, oblivious to the fact that her husband hates his job but stays in it to provide for her. The kind of rage often leveled at women seeking independence is evidenced any time narcissistic people are forced to confront assertions of independent humanity from people they previously had assumed were there only for their convenience. We saw this rage in Southern whites during the early days of the civil rights movement; in businessmen confronted by demands from labor; in men at the onset of the women's liberation movement; and perhaps, even before then, in women, when men began to leave their wives to find themselves. We find that rage today among conservatives, when the poor assert their right to a decent life—without even having earned it!

The essence of innocence is a belief in a benevolent hierarchy, in which not only do those with power—God, whites, capitalists, politicians, parents—provide for those in their care, but those they care for (humanity, people of color, workers, the populace, children) show gratitude by serving and nurturing them. It is this hierarchical order that ensures that we all will be cared for. The experience of the Fall is feeling, "I want, I hurt, I need," and discovering that no one either will or can do anything about it.

It is, of course, embarrassing for most adults to feel this way. After all, we are supposed to be mature, independent, self-sufficient, so most people who are in this place cannot acknowledge it, even to themselves. They are usually "just fine," but in fact they feel very lost and empty, even desperate. The roles they play often are varieties of the archetypes that inform the next stages of the journey; however, they get the form right, but not the substance.

If they are attracted by the role of the Martyr, they will be unable—no matter how hard they work at it—to truly sacrifice out of love and care for others, and their sacrifice will not be transformative. If they sacrifice for their children, the children then must pay, and pay, and pay—by being appropriately grateful, by living the life the parents wish *they* had lived; in short, by sacrificing their own lives in return. It is this pseudo-sacrifice, which really is a form of manipulation (think of Mrs. Portnoy in *Portnoy's Complaint*, for example), that has given sacrifice a bad name in the culture.

Virtually everyone these days seems to understand how manipulative the sacrificing mother can be, but another, equally pernicious version is the man who works at a job he hates, says he does it for his wife and children, and then makes them pay by deferring to him, protecting him from criticism or anger, and making him feel safe and secure in his castle. Such a man nearly always requires his wife to sacrifice her own journey to his drama of martyrdom. In these two cases and in others, the underlying message is, "I've sacrificed for you, so don't leave me, stay with me, feed my illusions, help me feel safe and secure."

Instead of the pseudo-Martyr role, the Orphan may choose to play the role of the Warrior. Instead of truly confronting his fear to try to make a better world for himself and for others, he behaves as if in a tantrum. These are the looters, the rapists, the batterers, the businessmen exploiting and polluting for profit. It is the classic macho "I take whatever I want, and baby, I want you" role, played by people who are self-absorbed, oblivious to the pain and destruction they cause. Of course it is not only men who act this way, but I have used the male pronoun because the behavior is so socially unacceptable in women that it is more rare. One of the problems of being male in our culture is that because this kind of behavior is justified as masculine, many men get stuck there.

One female version of the pseudo-Warrior role is conquest by seduction. In one scene in Ntozake Shange's *for colored girls who have considered suicide/when the rainbow is enuf*, a woman picks up a man, treats him to absolutely unbridled and sensuous lovemaking, then wakes him up early in the morning to kick him out. It is a revenge plot. She anticipates his rejection and rejects him first. Like the hardnosed busiessman, "she does unto him before he can do unto her." The game is "hurt first."[3]

However much Orphans might want to sacrifice unselfishly for their children, the movement, the church, etc., or however much they want to fight battles that actually might make a difference in the world, they cannot do so. Their pain will mandate that they be almost totally self-absorbed. Their entire drama will center around themselves. Not truly believing they can either have love and gentleness or make a real difference, they will settle for controlling the terms of their own unhappiness.

In many cases, however, Orphans are simply and honestly Orphans, distrusting their capabilities and sending out the message, "I do not know how to care for myself." During our youths, in new, unexplored situations, and in undeveloped parts of ourselves, we are all Orphans and hence dependent upon others. In normal, healthy human development, the Orphan phase is mild. Disillusionment with parents, institutions, and authority simply motivates us to leave the safety of dependence to take our own journeys in search of new answers. This may be as undramatic in late adolescence as enrolling in college, or leaving home to take a job to support oneself. Later it may be leaving a job, a relationship, or becoming disillusioned with a political party, a religious group, or a philosophy of life and seeking new answers. At any age if we have been dependent upon doctors as health authorities or teachers or other authority figures to provide us with "the Truth," disillusionment spurs us on either to search for more adequate authorities or to learn enough that we can become our own authorities.[4]

When people are brought up in homes where they are safe and loved and where they are taught that they can trust themselves and the world, they do not need to linger in pseudo-heroic stages but can develop organically through them. Having had the experience of being safe and cared for, they know it is safe to trust. (The Orphan is a powerful archetype; no one is completely free of it no matter how fortunate.) For many, however, either their childhood homes were not safe, or some trauma occurred (such as being molested or otherwise mistreated), or they were taught by their families, schools, churches, or synagogues that they could not trust themselves or they could not trust the world.

Many Christian groups, for instance, encourage children to see themselves as sinful and to distrust their impulses as coming from the devil. Similarly, they see "the world" as a sinful and dangerous place, set in contrast to "the church." Jews, traumatized by the Holocaust, may teach their children always to beware of anti-Semitism and to believe that they are always at risk in an oppressive, gentile society. Indeed, any oppressed group, in trying to warn children about very real societal oppression, may, if not very careful about how they express it, inadvertently teach their children an attitude of distrust that fosters paranoia and arrests them in an Orphan mentality.

In trying to protect children from the real threat of abduction and abuse, many parents overstress the danger of talking with strangers. Dominant groups may pass on to their children the belief that they may be able to trust members of that group, but not members of other, "inferior groups": women are hysterical and undependable; blacks are shiftless and lazy; Jews are greedy; Asians are sinister, etc. Some people even believe, and teach their children, that it is not safe to trust anyone.

People who feel powerless and do not know where to turn need to learn to ask for help and, of course, they need to learn discretion about where they safely can turn for answers. They will become arrested at the more primitive manifestations of the Orphan archetype if they are unable to acknowledge to themselves and to others when they feel powerless, or lack skills, and need help, or when they are so distrustful that they believe others would take advantage of their plight to oppress them further. At this primitive level, Orphans almost always either distrust themselves and fundamentally believe they do not deserve to have the safety they long for, or believe the world outside them is hostile to them—or both.

Rescue

The Orphan's problem is despair, so the key to movement is hope. There is no use telling Orphans to grow up and take responsibility for their lives if they do not feel capable of it! They must be provided, first, with some hope that they *will* be cared for. The stories, then, that the culture has evolved for the Orphan are rags-to-riches plots and very conventional love stories. The subtheme of these plots is that suffering will be redemptive and will bring back the absent parent. In Charles Dickens's novels, for instance, an orphan suffers poverty and mistreatment until finally it is discovered that he is the long lost heir to a huge fortune. Reunited with his father, he will be cared for forever. In the classic version of the romantic love story (for instance, Samuel Richardson's *Pamela, or Virtue Rewarded*), the heroine suffers greatly—sometimes from poverty, but almost always from assaults on her virtue. If she manages to suffer without losing her virginity, she is rewarded with marriage to a rich man, a Sugar Daddy who very clearly is a father substitute. The happy ending promises that she will be cared for the rest of her life.

The romantic love myth and the rags-to-riches plot are often intertwined. In the traditional romantic love plot, the heroine finds not only true love but also someone to support her. In novels like F. Scott Fitzgerald's *The Great Gatsby*, the hero is motivated to make a fortune so that he may win the affections of Daisy, the golden girl. In both cases, Eden is the attainment of riches *and* love.

It is their hope that love or riches (or both) might be possible that sometimes gets Orphans to embark upon a quest. The "savior" then can be a lover *or* it can be a business venture, a job, or professional training that might allow them to make enough money to buy a sense of total security and control over their lives. The promise is that never again will they have to experience that terrible sense of powerlessness of having needs—deep-seated survival needs—and being unable to meet them.

As students, Orphans want teachers who know all the answers; as patients, they want doctors or therapists to be all-wise and all-knowing and "make it all better"; as lovers they want perfect, cosmic mates rather than fellow mortals. The only theology that seems relevant to Orphans is one that promises that if only they are good, God will take care of them. The only politics Orphans want is the great leader, the great movement, the party that will fix it all so that they will be safe and cared for forever. As consumers, Orphans buy products that promise the quick fix: Use this detergent and you will be a good mother. Drive this car and gorgeous women will climb all over you. Try this diet candy, and men will find you irresistible.

Whether the rescuer is a therapist, a case worker, a religion, or a political movement, any criticism of it seems deeply threatening because all hope—the hedge against despair—is invested there. Women who seek salvation through romantic love may be actively hostile to feminism. People seeking salvation in a religion or a political movement may try to avoid hearing anything that might shake their faith, to silence those who feel differently from them. Of course, those seeking salvation through money are enraged at any criticism of capitalism, while those who seek perfect safety and security through socialism are equally incensed and even more insistent on silencing those who find fault with Marxism.

It also is helpful to remember that no matter how sophisticated their thinking may be in other parts of their lives, in the part that promises rescue, people will be at a fairly rudimentary level of cognitive development, marked by absolutism and dualistic thinking. They believe there are authorities who know what the truth is. The trick is to find them and follow their advice, for they will save them from powerlessness, ignorance, and error.

To the true believer, whatever is not their liberating truth is falsehood and perhaps even evil. At this stage, then, in Christianity, anything other than this truth will be seen as the work of the devil. In business and politics it may be attacked as communist. For women and men who believe that women should find salvation through their attachment to a man, women who do not seek to do so are seen as manhaters or whores.

Further, any indication that the therapist, the teacher, the rabbi or minister, or the lover is not perfect is profoundly threatening. Perhaps that is why therapists and educators often find it best not to let their clients or students know very much about them. Perhaps that is why men like to be seen as the strong silent type, and women opt to be mysterious. Yet when someone is feeling entirely out of control, the simple decision to put faith and trust in another's hands can be liberating. Furthermore, the discipline to be faithful to that decision daily reinforces a sense of being able to choose correctly what is life affirming at this stage.

Whether rescuers are lovers, husbands, therapists, case workers, feminists, preachers, etc., the difficulty arises from the Orphans' belief that they owe their lives to their saviors. In theological terms, this is evidenced in an image of a "jealous God," who shows concern by punishing wrongdoing, especially idolatry. In the theology of romantic love, it evidences itself in the notion that if your boyfriend or husband really loves you, he will be jealous; moreover, he will punish any failure of complete fidelity in thought and action— whether that punishment is in the form of physical or emotional battering, or mere aloofness. Not trusting their own goodness, Orphans also see it as a sign of care when rescuers call their wrongdoings to their attention.

Realize here that at this stage Orphans feel extremely undeserving and dependent. It seems not only logical but comforting that, in exchange for love and care, they give their life and service to their saviors—a small price to pay. The sad thing is that this trust can be, and often is, misused because the rescuers' need to feel safe, needed, valuable requires that the victims continue to be dependent, passive, clinging, and grateful. If this need is strong, the supposed rescuers depend, in a very deep-seated way, upon the continued allegiance of the persons being saved.

We see this frequently in spiritual gurus and evangelists, in political "great leaders," in battering or possessive husbands, in nagging wives. And it is an occupational hazard in the helping professions. In each case, the rescuer plays on the dependent's fears: without this religion, this form of therapy, this political movement, our lives will be lost in sin, we will be hopelessly sick, or we will be overrun by communists (or capitalist imperialists). Men convince wives and girlfriends that no one else ever will love them and that they never will be able to support themselves, repair the car or washer, or take care of themselves out in the world. Women convince husbands and boyfriends that no one else ever will love them and that they never will be able to fix their own dinner, arrange their own social life, or meet their own emotional needs.

This problem is natural because many rescuers are not that far ahead of the people they help; for one possible next step after placing one's trust in a person, a movement, or a spiritual force is to trust oneself to help others (in the guise of either a Martyr or a Warrior). The hard part is to help people find themselves without entrapping them. It is this phenomenon that explains the relative failures of both Marxism and the liberal welfare state. Neither has evolved strategies to move people into responsibility for their own lives—the strategies that would get people off welfare or make possible the eventual withering away of the state. The people in charge have a vested interest in maintaining control because they too are afraid to face the unknown, the truly new.

The rescuer needs to find or be given ways to help the Orphan move through this manipulative stage into a more healthy and productive mode of caring that includes the development of a positive sense of an autonomous self. To move on, however, one first must fully *be* in the Orphan stage, and that means confronting one's own pain, despair, and cynicism; and it means mourning the loss of Eden, letting oneself know that there is no safety, that God (at least that childish notion of a "Daddy God") is dead. Of course, Orphans cannot do this all at once. Denial is a much underrated survival mechanism. They can face their pain only in proportion to their hope. The first time they find someone who promises rescue, they can let go and feel some of their pain, but they must hold on to much of it because of their inevitable sense that there will be a cost for the rescue. Inevitably, too, they will be disillusioned with their rescuers because, of course, they are not perfect, do not have all the answers, and cannot make Orphans safe.

The first time Orphans meet someone who is willing to love and help them, they think he or she is the only one, and they would die rather than leave that person—even if the relationship becomes very destructive. If they never leave, they get stuck. Most people, however, circle back to this stage in a series of relationships that they come to look at more and more realistically, in terms of what the relationship can bring them. As they gain more experience, slowly but surely their trust is based not upon the rescuer, but rather on the universe; they begin to trust that there always will be someone for them.

Because most of what they believe about the world is actually projection, however, they cannot truly believe that there are other people who would give to them without manipulation until they are able to do so themselves. They feel less and less like Orphans as they are able to stop clutching for safety and give without any thought of return. As we will see in the chapter on the Martyr, Orphans learn that there can be some safety and love in the world after they learn to give and to care for others.

Orphans' denial mechanisms protect them from full awareness of how powerless and needy they really are. Often they will feel it only in retrospect as they begin to experience more success. As they learn to love, they begin to be able to discriminate between genuine love and the daily failures of love: the times we just cannot give; the times we give manipulatively; the times we cannot see one another for our projections. They then can mourn these lapses without giving up on a belief in the power of human caring. So, too, when Orphans learn to fight for themselves and begin to feel the power to change their worlds to some extent, they are able to differentiate between situations in which power can be exercised and those genuine instances—like mortality—in which acceptance of powerlessness is a more appropriate and realistic response than struggle. They then can not only allow their sense of powerlessness in these instances but go back and permit themselves in retrospect to feel the full impact of earlier despair, yearning, pain, and rage.

The Orphan and the Innocent actually are preheroic archetypes. Life inevitably will liberate Innocents from their illusions, but Orphans, more than any other type, need help crossing the threshold and embarking upon their heroic journey. Those who do not linger in this stage are those who have had help all along. People who have not, or who do not recognize or accept help when it is there, tend to get stuck in their helplessness. To get unstuck, Orphans must confront the assumption that the Fall somehow is their fault and, in so doing, go through and then beyond their notions about blame, fault, and sin. Our culture has used guilt and shame as the primary means to motivate people to be good by its standards, so it is no surprise that people feel guilty, and that they need to atone—or sometimes to have someone else atone for them. In Christianity, it is Christ. Men often have tried to make it women.

However, something else is at work here. During the experience of the Fall, Orphans make meaning of their experience and try to feel in control by believing that the Fall happened because they sinned. The logic is simple: If it is our fault, then maybe we can do something about it. Otherwise, our suffering just seems capricious, and then where are we? Without hope!

The psychological strategy that at first offers Orphans some respite ultimately entraps. People do not want to be at fault and will do almost anything not to admit they are. Thus a kind of massive denial sets in on the conscious level, while on the unconscious level they keep choosing suffering as a way to atone.

A major impediment to embarking on their heroic journeys is this denial, which results from a deep-seated belief in their own unworthiness and that suffering is somehow their fault. At some level, for example, white women and racial minorities tend to see sexism and racism as resulting from their own inferiority. White men feel personally inadequate for not living up to their superior image. All people brought up in the dominant Western religions tend to feel inadequate because they do not live up to the image of a good (i.e., selfless) person.

Although heroism is about learning responsibility for one's own life, it is counterproductive to tell Orphans that they can take charge of their lives because it sounds to them as if you are saying that their suffering is their fault.

Recently I taught an advanced class that did not meet well the needs of one of the students in it. About halfway through the class the student became hostile, so we had a long talk. Because the course was designed to foster responsibility in students, the format changed significantly during the semester to address their stated concerns. My hope in talking to this student was to have her realize that at any time the course could have been different had she simply asked for what she wanted.

During our conversation, I learned an immense amount. For one thing, I learned that some people ask for what they want by complaining. They know no other way. I had not understood her form of communication. I also learned about "fault." She explained her anger by saying that at first she thought it was her "fault" that she was not learning, but then she realized that it was my "fault"—that I was not teaching the class well. We talked for some time, and I felt more and more frustrated. Finally, I realized that for her the situation had to be someone's fault, and better mine than hers. It could not be just a bad fit between a teaching method and one student.

I had wanted to teach her responsibility for her life—a responsibility that could lead her to drop such a class or to ask for what she needed. What I did not yet understand—and the reason I had not been able to help her—is that when responsibility is equated with fault and blame, saying "you are responsible for your learning" can be heard only as an accusation that she was to blame for not understanding. She was not yet capable of taking such responsibility. She quite simply needed more help from me.

What *can* make movement happen for people immobilized by insecurity or self-recrimination? Love, hope, and the message that their suffering indeed is not their fault, and that someone else who is not so powerless and lost and needy will help them. After exploring this process for a while, I have come to believe that a variety of contents for this message is useful for different people, or for the same people in different situations. It is the *process* here that is important. For example, people in the Orphan mode will be attracted to the forms of Christianity that emphasize sin and redemption. What is empowering for them is the notion that their suffering is caused by the devil and can be alleviated by Christ; that no matter how unworthy they are, Christ loves them, and although they themselves are powerless, Christ's sacrifice can save them and bring them back to a state of grace.

For women, the message that feminism can bring at this stage is that women are powerless victims of patriarchy (or of men). Individually they are powerless but together, working as a movement, sacrificing together, they can make a difference and change the world. For men, the message is the same. It is not their fault that they have repressed their feelings. They too are victims of the pa-triarchal system. For people with addictions to chemicals, the Al-coholics Anonymous program, in which people recognize their powerlessness, teaches that fundamentally it is not their fault but the result of an illness, and although as individuals they are not strong enough to do anything about it, they can be saved by putting their faith in a higher power and in that group.

In therapy or analysis, the effective message is to encourage clients to tell their story in a way that helps them see that their pain comes from somewhere outside the self, that it is a result of early childhood trauma, of social conditions, of their parents, etc.—in short, that it is not their fault. Further, it establishes that the therapist will help them deal with and move beyond their pain.

Self-blame is not only crippling because it makes it impossible for Orphans to trust themselves; it also is counterproductive because it fosters free-floating projection. In order to feel less bad about them-selves, Orphans often will project blame onto others: the people close to them (lovers, friends, mates, parents, employers, or teachers), God, or the culture as a whole. The result is to increase their sense of living in an unsafe world. Further, to the extent that they blame those around them for all the suffering in their lives, they alienate others and make their lives more isolated and hopeless. By not only locating the blame outside themselves but also fixing it firmly in one location, they free themselves from the general process of blaming the world. Further, as they identify ways to deal with that root cause, to establish that we do not have to be at the mercy of evil, of our illness, of patriarchy, capitalism, etc., they can begin to believe it is possible to take responsibility for their own lives.

Temporarily relying on someone outside themselves—a higher power, the therapist, the analyst, the group, the movement, the church—begins to move people at this stage beyond the dualism of dependence/independence, for unless they have the misfortune to hook up with someone who wants to use their dependency, they will be encouraged to take charge of their lives—gradually and with sup-port. They do not have to do it all themselves, nor do they have to wait passively for rescue or just take orders. They learn the skills of taking charge of their lives and also of getting appropriate help—

from experts, from friends, from God. They can open up to receiving love and grace.

Orphans may believe that they have put their lives in the therapist's, priest's, or guru's hands, and that belief provides the security to start moving and putting their lives in order, but it is critical that they make decisions themselves and carry them out. Later they can look back and see that they did it themselves. Remember Glinda the Good Witch in *The Wizard of Oz*, who tells Dorothy at the end of her journey that she could have gone home anytime she wanted to? Dorothy asks why she did not tell her that before, and Glinda explains that Dorothy would not have believed her. First she had to convince her that there was a Great and Powerful Wizard who could fix things for her. In journeying to find him, Dorothy developed and experienced her competence, so that ultimately she was able to understand that it was she who killed the Wicked Witch, and it was her own power that would get her home. Until she had experienced these things, however, she would have felt too powerless to proceed except under the illusion that she was about to be rescued.

By linking the examples of Christianity, Alcoholics Anonymous, feminism, and analysis or therapy, in no way do I mean to suggest a lack of respect for the integrity and worth of each, nor do I suggest that they are merely interchangeable. What I do mean to suggest is that each uses a process that works in aiding someone in the transition from despair to hope, to claiming some sense of self-worth and agency. The essential tools for helping Orphans are (1) love—an individual or a group who shows care and concern; (2) an opportunity for the Orphans to tell and retell their story in a way that overcomes denial (retelling how painful it was before they were saved, stopped drinking, became a feminist, etc.); (3) an analysis that moves the locus of the blame outside the individual, that says the fault lies elsewhere; and (4) once it is established that they are not guilty, encouragement to begin to talk about taking responsibility for their own lives.

In many religions, in Alcoholics Anonymous, in therapy or analysis, and in feminist consciousness-raising groups, people may allow themselves to begin to feel their pain. Although their lives may have been exceedingly difficult, they often are so scared of their pain that they block it. In the safety of the group, they may feel their pain more consciously in the telling of their story than they did in the living of it. They also may borrow courage from the therapist, the analyst, the minister, or the group to allow themselves to feel the full horror of their lives. Or, if their life has been simply ordinary, they may need permission to understand that they have a right to their own pain, even though it has not been as great as that of others they know.

Years ago, for example, my own pain was rough and glaring, but I denied it because it was not as great as that of other people I knew. It was quite a breakthrough for me to acknowledge that I had pain even though I came from a relatively happy, middle-class family. As I came to recognize and legitimize my own pain, I could overcome my denial and act to change my life. I could not make my life better until I acknowledged where things were not working for me.

Some people in the Orphan stage, however, have learned to use their pain manipulatively—to get others to feel sorry for them, or to feel guilty, and hence to do what they want. Those who are members of a group that is oppressed in some way can play on other people's liberal guilt and thus gain control. Using their pain as a vehicle for manipulation, they can avoid fully confronting their justifiable rage and feelings of powerlessness. Ultimately, it keeps them stuck.

It is critical for both more privileged and relatively more oppressed groups to listen to each other's pain without playing the who-is-more-oppressed game. We see the same thing done in families or between couples who argue about who has suffered more. Presumably, the person who has suffered less is supposed to give in to the greater sufferer's demands. If this is allowed, suffering is encouraged because it brings with it power. The point, of course, is not to get people further hooked on suffering but to free them to learn about joy, effectiveness, productivity, abundance, and liberation. They need to listen to their own and to others' stories and to acknowledge where their pain is so they can open up the door to growth and change—not to bludgeon each other with it.

It is a major step for Orphans to move out of denial and self-involvement and learn to help others. In many religions, Alcoholics Anonymous, feminist consciousness-raising groups, group therapy, and analysis, individuals are actively encouraged to do so. Sometimes the context for this is evangelism—go out and seek new converts—but what matters in terms of development is that such pressure helps people begin to learn the lessons represented by the archetypes of the Martyr and the Warrior. They assert their own truth in order to improve the world, *and* they give to others.

These same strategies can be used in the classroom. Orphans, of course, see teachers as experts or authorities who know "the Truth" with a capital T. If they do not, they are phony, fake, incompetent. Or, worse, they are abandoning the students unfairly to their own resources. Teachers, then, can tell Orphans what to do, and if Orphans see them as the authority, they will do what they say. Teachers may explain that they really do not know everything, but they may not be heard the way they want to be by some students.

In one of my introductory Women's Studies classes, I assign a project in which people tell their stories and then share them with their small group. They meet with a small group every week all semester to share their own experiences and to make connections between the course content and their lives. The course reading does two things: It provides models for hope and it overcomes denial about the oppression of women. Such an approach can be tailored for many subjects in the arts, humanities, and social sciences so that the classroom can actively support growth.

By providing a structure that requires students to go through the steps of overcoming denial, sharing their story, and developing trust in a group of peers, the teacher can use the authority invested by the institution and projected by students seeking "the Truth" to help students claim their own authority. Initially, some students go through the process because they are told to or for the grade, and only later see what they have gained from the experience. More cognitively complex and autonomous students go through a process of choosing whether or not to invest in this activity. The act of choosing either to do it or not encourages their development at yet another level.

Self-Help and Cultural Transformation

Some people who do not have the benefit of any of these support systems unconsciously set up situations on their own in which their denial systems are assaulted. Usually they place themselves in circumstances that are so life-threatening that they no longer can see that they are in trouble and need help. This may take the form of serious chemical addiction, illness, loss of jobs, increasingly destructive personal relationships, but in every case the individual bottoms out and is forced past denial to recognize the pain that motivates the irrational addiction to self-defeating behavior.

For people who experience less extreme forms of pain and denial, less painful forms of self-help work well. Some people tell their stories in journals. More visually oriented people may paint; some write music. Some may feel a compelling need to work, sculpt, paint, or compose because they are finding their true vocation. And/or, they may feel an equal compulsion because it is their means of working through denial by telling their story in a way that they themselves can hear. For people who express their wisdom with their hands, the story may never be told in a way more verbal people can understand, but it may be encoded in the pattern of a quilt, in weaving, in the shape of a piece of pottery. What matters most is that the individuals involved can see or hear their own truth, and as a result can act to change their lives.

It also is important to recognize that, although far too many people right now are stuck in the Orphan modality, there is massive activity in the culture helping people confront their problems and get on with their journeys. Support groups exist based on either the feminist consciousness-raising or the AA models for all sorts of problems, from overeating to child abuse, to getting clear about one's sexuality, to understanding the impact on one's socialization of one's sexual, racial, or ethnic identities. There has been a rebirth of interest in Eastern as well as Western religion, and a proliferation of forms of therapy and analysis as well as the many groups in the Human Potential and New Age movements. Even contemporary political movements—the civil rights movement, feminism, the ecology and antinuclear movements—emphasize the personal growth and liberation of their proponents. All this energy is focused at this time in history on helping people take responsibility for their own lives so that we might not only save the planet but make the world a more genuinely humane and free place to be.

Cumulatively, this means we are moving from a cultural milieu in which there are a few heroes into one in which we *all* are expected to take our journeys and embark upon the heroic, responsible life. Much of modern philosophy and literature is designed to help us overcome our cultural denial and our clinging to childlike innocence. The legacy of sin, the belief that suffering is somehow "our fault," has been so debilitating, and so interferes with our cultural need to take responsibility for our lives and our future, that much of our art and philosophy have focused on dispelling this idea. Nineteenth- and early twentieth-century naturalism and modern existentialism brought these themes home to us powerfully. Central to these traditions is the declaration that God is dead; nature is inert, or at the least uncaring, and there is no inherent meaning to life. Suffering does not happen to us for a reason or because God is displeased with us. It happens simply by chance—inhuman, uncaring chance. Nothing that happens means anything beyond itself. These philosophically nihilistic beliefs and the art and literature they inspire operate as a kind of collective therapy that help us overcome our denial. They tell the human story in a way that focuses on our pain—on meaninglessness, loss, alienation, the difficulty of human connection; on a sense that the economic world has become a machine and we mere cogs in it, that life has lost grace and meaning, and that basically there is no one who will take care of us. They counter the denial that keeps us in innocence and tell us we are not to blame for our pain, and finally, in the best cases, force us to confront the urgency of action. Modern literature and philosophy push us to stop looking for rescuers and to grow up and take responsibility for our lives and our future. It may be that we as humans have created the current threat to the planet—in the form of nuclear holocaust or environmental accident—to force ourselves into maturity. We no longer can deny the need to take responsibility for our lives—individually or collectively.

Doing so requires increased cognitive complexity and the capacity to differentiate between what suffering is harmful and should be alleviated and what is an inevitable part of growth and change. The intensity of the pain the Orphan experiences after the Fall is partially the result of simple-minded either/or thinking. It is only the belief that there should be a Daddy God caring for us and protecting us that makes the contemporary confrontation with the notion that "God is dead" so painful. Who said life was going to be Edenic anyway?

Where did we get the notion someone was supposed to take care of us? When we begin accepting adult responsibility for our lives, we can accept some degree of suffering and sacrifice as essential to life without defining suffering as what life *is*. It is not so much that God is dead, but God *the Father* is dead. If humankind is to grow up, we must envision and act upon a less childlike and more peer relationship with divinity.

Instead of seeing life dualistically (i.e., either getting everything you want *or* living in a fallen world), we can see suffering as only part of a process—the process of letting go: of Eden, of childhood, of parents, of lovers, of children, of our lives as we know them, and ultimately, in death, of life itself. Our lives will be transformed as we let go and trust our new directions, however fearful we may be about the unknown and however much grieving we may need to do about what we leave behind.

Beyond the dualism that sees "life as suffering" or "life as Eden" is an awareness of pain and suffering as part of the flow of life. Indeed, pain and loss are personally transformative not as a constant mode of life, but as part of an ongoing process whereby we give up what no longer serves us or those we love and move into the unknown. Our pain, our suffering, would be too great were we to do all our growing at once. We give things up little by little. That's the psychological reason for denial—it keeps us from having to confront all our problems at once!

Our denial structures work to protect us from the knowledge of the extent of our suffering, precisely because we are not equipped to deal with all of it at once. Each time we become aware that we are suffering, it is a signal that we are ready to move on and make changes in our lives. Our task, then, is to explore the suffering, to be aware of it, to claim fully that we indeed are hurting. But we can do that only if we have at least a glimmer of hope that our suffering is not necessary, that it can be alleviated, that it is not simply the human condition—or not simply our lot as a man or a woman. In this way, suffering is a gift. It captures our attention and signals that it is time for us to move, to learn new behaviors, to try new challenges.

Suffering also may be a gift in other ways. Particularly later on in the quest, our problem may not be so much a sense of powerlessness as an inflated sense of power, a belief that we have it all together, that we are better, more competent, more worthy than other people. Suffering is the leveler that reminds us of our common mortality, that none of us is exempt from the difficulties of human life. When suffering and despair come together, they provide us with the opportunity to affirm hope, love ourselves, and to say, against all odds, "And yet I will love, and yet I will hope." It is then that we learn transcendence; it is then that we know the beauty of oneness, of being part of the network of mortal connectedness, of being fundamentally—for all our accomplishments—like other people.

Most important of all, it is suffering that helps us face our worst fears and thus frees us from the paralysis of the Orphan hopelessly seeking ways to stay safe. There is often in people to whom "the worst" has happened an almost transcendent freedom, for they have faced "the worst" and survived it. They know they can face anything. Life does not have to be just so, it does not have to be Eden, for them to love it. As Christ taught us, even death by crucifixion is followed by resurrection. Similarly, Elisabeth Kübler-Ross in *Death: The Final Stage of Growth* tells about the peace and freedom experienced by people who have been declared clinically dead and come back to life—how their experiences of love and light freed them from the fear of death that so interferes with most people's lives.[5]

How we deal with death, of course, is tied in with how we respond to all the little deaths in our lives—the loss of friends, family, lovers, of particularly special times and places, of jobs or opportunities, hopes and dreams, or belief systems. What is interesting to me is that it does not seem necessary for many people to suffer in large ways if they learn the small, daily ways of giving to others and of letting go of the present to meet the unknown. Some people need to face "the worst" to learn this lesson. Other people do not. The dailyness of giving and letting go gives them the skills they need to cope when a loved one dies or they find themselves critically ill.

Some people block out these little deaths. They leave without saying good-bye. They graduate from high school or college and neither celebrate nor mourn the life that will be no more. They pretend that birthdays are just like any other day. It is as if there will not be a loss if they do not acknowledge it. Such people always must pick a fight to get out of a relationship or pretend it never meant anything to them. People who block all their endings become so constipated emotionally that there is no room to let anything else in. They start feeling uncomfortable and numb.

Other people who have gained more wisdom know they sometimes must leave someone, someplace, or a job because it is time to grow, to move on. They know that growing older holds new opportunities, but it also means the end of youth. Such people can celebrate the future and their new area of growth while fully acknowledging what it has meant to them to be with that person, in that job or school, or in that place. They can take time also to be thankful for what has been and to mourn their loss. This thanksgiving and mourning empties them out and makes way for the new. Having felt those feelings, they now are ready to feel the excitement of new growth.

This is the meaning of the concept of the "fortunate fall," which propels us out of dependency into our journeys. On the road, we learn through experience that pain need not be meaningless affliction, but that it can fuel continued growth and change. From the initial scared and needy ways in which we experience the Orphan archetype, we may experience any of the other archetypes in their initial stages. If we allow the Wanderer archetype to emerge in our consciousness, it may take the form (as we have seen) of the quest for rescue, during which we begin to gain confidence in ourselves and our abilities. As such, our sense of guilt and inadequacy will be balanced by pride in the demonstration of a capacity to survive on our own, without someone to care for us.

If we encounter our inner Martyr first, we undoubtedly will sacrifice more than is necessary in the service of others. However, in doing so, we become the "giving tree" parent figure we had hoped for, and, in acting out the archetype, develop faith that, since we are good and nurturing to others, it is more believable that *we* will be cared for. If we move initially into the consciousness of the Warrior, we will learn to defend ourselves against threats from without and to control our terrors so that they do not immobilize us. Indeed, we become the powerful rescue figure we had hoped might save us. In doing so, we begin the process of rescuing ourselves.

Finally, if we allow for the emergence of the Magician's consciousness as we begin to expand our options, we will experience increased trust in the universe through giving over our fears into the hands of a benevolent deity, saying "Thy will be done," or through the belief propounded in New Age books like *A Course in Miracles*[6] that suffering and pain are illusory and not reality.

We may cycle through these archetypes and the stages they represent many times until the alchemical miracle has been achieved: Somehow both our own baseness and the world's has become transmuted into gold. At that point, we return to Eden and to Innocence, understanding that it is safe to trust ourselves, each other, and the universe. As we learn we can be counted on, we come to understand that it is realistic to trust others.

It seems important here to stop and reconsider the archetype of the Innocent. Like Don Quixote and other "wise fools," the Innocent can be in touch with a world beyond that of consensus reality. New Age literature puts modern dress upon ancient mystic traditions (in Buddhism, Judaism, and Christianity) that view the world of ordinary consciousness as illusory, beyond which, it is believed, lies a perfect world where each of us is always safe, secure, and happy. In such traditions the task is to avoid seduction by the illusions and to live entirely in this "real," other, good world.

Yet one need not try to escape the everyday. Embracing the illusion eventually does return us to a condition of innocence. However, for many, the existence of another, spiritual realm persists through the journey and lightens their load. To others, they may appear misguided or hopelessly naive, if not actually crazy. Yet, whether or not we are aware of this alternative reality as we go along, at the close of the hero's journey we experience it again.

As we journey, the archetype of the Innocent reminds us at critical junctures to hope and trust, while the Orphan archetype continues to teach us that no matter how developed we get, we still are dependent. We depend on the earth for our very survival, for the air we breathe and the food we eat. We depend on each other. None of us has all the gifts necessary to create the full and rich lives that our combined talents make possible.

Returning to Eden, we are not powerless, childlike dependents, but people who also take responsibility for caring for others and the planet. This return requires interdependency, which necessitates not only the claiming of personal responsibility for the maintenance of our earthly paradise and a trust that some pain and suffering are rightly a part of even Edenic life, but also ultimately a childlike attitude of trust and gratitude for all that is given us. This requires a dawning awareness that, however painful our lives might have seemed, we always have been held in the palm of God's hand. As T. S. Eliot wrote in the "Four Quartets,"

> We shall not cease from exploration
> And the end of all our exploring
> Will be to arrive where we started
> And know the place for the first time . . .
> A condition of complete simplicity
> (Costing no less than everything)
> And all shall be well and
> All manner of things shall be well
> When the tongues of flame are in-folded
> Into the crowned knot of fire
> And the fire and the rose are one.[7]

Chapter 3

THE WANDERER

I fear me this—is Loneliness—
The Maker of the soul
Its Caverns and its Corridors
Illuminate—or seal—

—EMILY DICKINSON, *318*

The archetype of the Wanderer is exemplified by stories of the knight, the cowboy, and the explorer who set off alone to see the world. During their travels they find a treasure that symbolically represents the gift of their true selves. Consciously taking one's journey, setting out to confront the unknown, marks the beginning of life lived at a new level. For one thing, the Wanderer makes the radical assertion that life is not primarily suffering; it is an *adventure*.

Whether Wanderers journey only inward or also outward, they make a leap of faith to discard the old social roles, which they have worn to please and to ensure safety, and try instead to discover who they are and what they want. We often are aware of the Wanderers who externalize their journeys and either literally travel or experiment widely with new behaviors; but there are also heroes whose external behavior seems conventional enough, yet whose explorations of their inner world and whose independence of mind in exploring their relationships in the universe are profound. Such a one was Emily Dickinson. In the latter years of her life, she hardly ever ventured even downstairs, yet no one who reads her poetry can miss the uniqueness, importance, or intense vitality of her quest.

Wanderers may be self-made men or women of business, or hippies living on the edge of society, but they definitely will define themselves in direct opposition to a conformist norm. In philosophy, politics, health, and education they are likely to distrust orthodox solutions, choosing instead to be very conservative, very radical, or just idiosyncratic. In fitness, they are likely to choose solitary exercise, like long-distance running or swimming. As learners, they distrust the answers given by authorities and search out their own truths. The Wanderers' identity comes from being the outsiders. In their spiritual life, they may experience doubt, especially since they usually have been taught that God rewards a measure of conformity and traditional morality—qualities likely to be at variance with the needs of their developing, experimenting psyches. Yet the dark night of the soul they experience often leads to a more mature and adequate faith.

Captivity

If the Orphan's story starts in paradise, the Wanderer's begins in captivity. In fairy tales, the prospective Wanderer may be entrapped in a tower or cave and is usually the captive of a witch, an ogre tyrant, a dragon, or some other fearsome beast. Often the captor is a symbol for the status quo, for conformity and false identity imposed by prevailing cultural roles. Or the hero—especially if she is female—may be imaged as enchanted by a mirror, which suggests a preoccupation with her appearance and with pleasing, rather than with what she sees and what pleases her. Often the hero is told that the cage is Eden and that leaving inevitably will require a fall from grace: that is, the cage is as good as it gets. The first job of the Wanderer is true sight: to declare or acknowledge that the cage is a cage and the captor is a villain. This is especially hard to do because the hero may not only be frightened of the quest but disapprove of it, and these feelings and judgments are likely to be reinforced by those of others.

To the Martyr, the urge to the quest may seem selfish and therefore wrong because it involves turning one's back on care and duty in the pursuit of self-discovery and self-actualization. For the Warrior, it may seem escapist and weak. If Wanderers choose to go on their journey, they may even feel guilty, for the act of claiming one's identity and developing an ego classically is portrayed as an insult to the gods. Think for example of Eve eating the apple or Prometheus stealing fire. To the Orphan the quest sounds unspeakably dangerous!

Because we often are afraid of major changes in others as well as ourselves, we may discourage budding heroes from embarking on their quests. We want them to stay the way they are. For one thing, we may be afraid of losing our lovers, spouses, friends, even parents, if they seem to be changing too much. We may be particularly threatened if someone who has lived to please or serve us all of a sudden declines to do so!

The pressure to conform, to do one's duty, to do what others want is strong for both men and women, but it is strongest for women because women's role has been defined in terms of nurturance and duty. Often women forbear taking their journey because they fear it will hurt their husbands, fathers, mothers, children, or friends; yet women daily hurt others when they do *not* do so. For example, one of the worst things a woman can do for a man's soul is to allow him to oppress her. If a woman loves a man, she should reverence his soul enough to know that whatever the scared little boy in him wants, his deepest core of being—the part of him that is healthy—wants only good for himself and others. If that is not true, then she needs to leave him. If it *is* true, then she is condescending to him when she indulges his less-developed self; indeed, she is acting with real contempt to assume that he is more meanspirited than she is.

Similarly, many men are trapped in their protector role and do not dare take their journeys because of a sense of responsibility not only to their children but to wives who appear to be fragile and incapable of taking care of themselves. If a man loves his partner, then he should reinforce that part of her that can be independent, competent, risk-taking. Every time he holds back his own journey because of her apparent ineptitude and dependence, he reinforces in her that attitude about herself and hence helps cripple her. Her stronger, wiser self wants to grow and wants him to grow too.

The nice thing about Wanderers taking their journey is that it has a ripple effect, allowing loved ones to take theirs as well. Perhaps at first they will be threatened and angry; but sooner or later, they will either have to leave or come along. If they leave, Wanderers may experience aloneness for a while, but sooner or later, if they so desire, they will develop better relationships, ones that are more genuinely satisfying because they are based on respect for that journey. Of course, when Wanderers step outside consensus reality and begin to see the world and themselves with their own eyes, they always face the fear that the punishment for doing so will be perpetual isolation or, in a more extreme sense, a friendless death in poverty. In spite of that fear—which speaks to the heart of one's infantile terror that one cannot survive if not pleasing others (parents first, teachers, bosses, sometimes even mates)—Wanderers make the decision to leave the world of the known for the unknown.

However much people have learned about giving and letting go, their sacrifices will be for nothing unless they also learn who they are. It is not helpful to tell people to transcend ego until they have developed an ego. It is not useful to tell people to transcend desire until they have allowed themselves fully to go for what they want. For this reason, I am uncomfortable with the Buddhist notion of transcending desire because it may have the effect of keeping some people focused on the lessons of letting go just when their growing edge is to find out what they want!

I maintain that not everyone knows what he or she desires. Certainly, narcissistic Orphans seem to live entirely by desire: I want this! I want that! But their desires are not really true, educated desires at all. Mainly they are forms of addiction, masking a primal emptiness and hunger for the real. Narcissists do not yet have a genuine sense of identity and consequently feel an emptiness. Their wants are programmed by the culture—they say "I want a cigarette," "I want a new convertible." They think getting these things will help them feel good. Even strategies for personal growth may not emerge out of a true self, but out of a compulsion to satisfy addictive cravings: "I want to lose ten pounds so I can attract more men and have a better sex life." "I want to go to college so I can make lots of money and have a great stereo system, be the envy of my friends."

When they have not developed much sense of a separate, autonomous self, people basically are run by what they think to be other people's opinions. I just returned from my husband's twenty-fifth high school reunion, where one woman told me that a number of people who had been invited said they did not want to come because they looked too fat or too old and/or they were not successful enough! Clearly, these people had not developed, even in their forties, a sense of themselves apart from such external considerations.

One of the major addictions in our culture is to traditional sex roles. This works because the culture has made sex and love artificially scarce commodities, so people spend endless hours trying to manipulate the world so they will get enough. We are taught that we need to conform to certain images of feminine and masculine behavior to be loved and to be thought sexually appealing. Yet, as long as we play roles rather than take our journeys, we never feel loved for ourselves, and we never experience the power of truly intimate sexual connection. Thus we may have lots of lovers but still feel empty, needy, and wanting something more.

If that were not enough, our economic system, and before it our educational system, work out of this shortage of love. We are taught to work hard so we can have things that will make us loved, respected, or admired. This includes buying nice clothes and cars, finding attractive places to live, having the money to buy good health and dental care, and perhaps even to join a health club—all this to attract a mate. It certainly is a powerful way to motivate a work force. The strategy however, ultimately does not work in the best interest of people.

For one thing, people who are driven by their addictions in this way do not have the time or the inclination to develop a sense of self. Instead they settle for stylish pseudo-independence, buying monogrammed towels, briefcases, or individualized Cabbage Patch dolls, using products that are pitched to appeal to their urge to be different and fashionably iconoclastic. Pseudo-Wanderers, even in their urge to wander, get channeled into conforming to whatever is considered to be the "in" way to be. Without a self, it really is not possible to either give much love or take it in. In the latter case, when people play a role to get love or respect—and hide who they really are (which may well be a mass of neediness)—they never really feel loved for themselves. It is the role that feels loved.

Further, even their loving ultimately may be harmful to other people, for it is likely to be compulsive, proprietary, controlling, and dependent. Because their sense of identity comes from having (as in possessing) that child, that boyfriend, that girlfriend, they need them to be a certain way. They need them to stay around even if their own journey calls them away. The role players may need others to act in certain ways to make themselves look good. They also may abridge their own growth so as not to threaten a relationship, or out of fear that if they do not sacrifice their good to the other's, some harm will come to that loved one.

The Orphan and the Martyr at their first levels of understanding, and sometimes even at the second, believe that in order to have love they must compromise who they are. At some level, they believe that if they were to be fully themselves, they would end up alone, friendless, and poor.

Many women do not like the Wanderer stage. As Carol Gilligan has pointed out in *In a Different Voice: Psychological Theory and Women's Development*, while men fear intimacy, women fear aloneness.[1] I see here two different responses to the same belief system. In our culture, we tend to believe we can have intimacy *or* we can have autonomy and selfhood. So women tend to choose intimacy and men choose independence. The irony is that in choosing this way, neither really get what they want. For one thing, people really want both. For another, it is not possible to truly get one without the other.

If we choose intimacy instead of independence, we cannot be fully *ourselves* in a relationship, because we have too much invested in keeping it; we play it "safe," play a role, and wonder why we feel so alone. If, on the other hand, we choose independence, our need for intimacy does not go away. Indeed, because it is repressed and therefore unacknowledged and unexamined, it manifests itself in compulsive and uncontrolled urges and activities. Most men or women who believe in "I-don't-need-anyone" stoicism are dreadfully lonely. Many—while maintaining the illusion of self-sufficiency—are absolutely terrified of abandonment.

Men like this infantilize women, so women (they believe) will not have the confidence to leave them. They want to keep their wives, if not barefoot and pregnant, at least without the skills and confidence needed to have a career that could support them well. Similarly, at work, they define their secretary's role as part mother, part wife, so they always will be taken care of. Finally, they are so dependent upon the regard of their male colleagues, bosses, and oftentimes even their subordinates, that they will violate their own sense of ethics rather than face the possibility of not being one of "the boys."

Such men are particularly vulnerable to charges of being soft, so they would never, for instance, say that they do not want to dispose of chemical waste in the cheapest way—for they would not want to be accused of some idealistic caring for the environment. They can be controlled—even to acting immorally—by the fear that they will seem to care—about the earth, about women, about other people. Women who have adopted this macho ethic act the same way, with the complicating factor that they also seek to gain male approval by acting like one of "the boys."

Accurate generalizations about sex differences are enormously important in helping us understand one another, but often they make men and women seem more distinct and different than we are. Although the fear of aloneness is primary for many women, next to that is a corresponding fear of intimacy. So, too, men who are most conscious and obvious about their fear of intimacy also fear aloneness. As long as the problem is defined (as it is by our culture) as an either/or situation where one can be autonomous and independent or one can have love and can belong, we all will fear both.

We do not move out of this dualistic formulation of the dilemma until we resolve it on its own terms. Wanderers confront the fear that they will be unable to survive alone and decide that whatever the cost in loneliness, isolation, even social ostracism, they will be themselves. It is critical to do both at some time in one's life. Women tend to be so afraid of aloneness that they stay overlong in Martyr; and of course this fear is accentuated by the cultural notion that to be alone and female is to be a failure (clearly you could not get a man). To wish to be alone is either unthinkable or not nurturing, and hence unfeminine.

Men, on the other hand, are so enamored of independence that they get stuck there, since independence in our culture is practically a synonym for masculinity. Furthermore, their independence has a ring of martyrdom to it. It is as if they have sacrificed their need for love to their desire to be separate and whole. This explains Daniel Levinson finding in his famous study of male development, *The Seasons of a Man's Life*, that many high-achieving males could not describe their wives![2]

Male stoicism denies the need for connection and wipes out not only the full awareness of one's need for connection, but also inevitably the awareness of other people as people. It is this blocking out of other people that explains why so many men treat other people as objects.

I do not suggest, however, that doing so is only a male phenomenon. Women do it, too. Whenever we deny our need for other people, we block them out, at least partially. Thus, when we deny our need for other people we stay (at least in the area in which we are doing the blocking) narcissistic. The result of blocking our yearning for connection, then, is loneliness.

Alienation and Escape

We have many ways of being alone. One is actually to live alone, travel alone, spend our time alone. Relatively few people adopt this course for any extended period of time. There are other ways—some of which have the advantage of masking our aloneness, sometimes even to ourselves. One way is to discount what we feel, what we want, and give others what we think they want: to be what *we* think they want us to be. Another way is to treat people as objects for the gratification of our own desires. It is critical here to allow ourselves no real awareness of their separate human identity. Actually, any time a person acts in one up/one down roles with another person, that will be a solitary interaction.

Still another way to be alone, as we have seen with traditional sex roles, is always to act a part—the perfect woman or man, mother or father, boss or employee—to *be* our roles. Or we can continue living with our family if we don't get along with them; we can stay in a bad marriage; we can live with roommates with whom we have little in common. A woman can decide that all men are chauvinists, and a man can decide that all women are scheming bitches. If we are really serious about being alone, we can decide that everyone is out to get us or to get something from us.

Lest I sound unduly negative here, let me hasten to add that in fact, all these strategies demonstrate how imaginative we are in making sure that we take our journeys: The very emptiness and vulnerability that results from such addictive approaches to life motivates many of us to take our journeys and to discover or create a self. Certainly, many people manage to be alienated and lonely all their lives without ever growing or changing, but others use these times to be "secret heroes," thinking new thoughts and imagining new alternatives while on the surface they go about their normal lives as usual. A woman I know looks back on an eleven-year, extremely conventional and superficial marriage as a safe haven, a cocoon in which she hid while she prepared to soar. But when she was in the marriage, she did not know this. In fact, it was the intensification of her sense of emptiness in the traditional role and loneliness in that relationship that was, by its very unpleasantness, her call to the quest. For many people *alienation within captivity is the initial stage of wandering*, followed by a conscious choice to take one's journey.

The archetypal American hero leaves the small town and embraces his journey; the beat hero and later the hippie hit the open road; the Western hero rides off into the sunset. The new feminist hero leaves her parents, husband, or lover and takes off too. For women, leaving the husband, lover, or family is such a recurrent form of the Wanderer archetype in contemporary times that Erica Jong writes in *How to Save Your Own Life*, "Leaving one's husband is the only, the cosmic theme."[3] Yet the individual who does not leave the small town or the spouse who does not leave the limiting marriage is no less alone than the Wanderer. Paradoxically, all the delaying strategies we employ to avoid our journeys may end up being part of them—if we are lucky!

When it is time to take the journey, Wanderers will feel alone whether or not they are married, have children and friends, or hold a prestigious job. There is no way to avoid this experience. All their attempts to do so simply repress their awareness of where they are, so that they are slower at learning lessons and thus stay lonely longer. And, although some people take off on the quest with a high sense of adventure, many experience it as thrust upon them by their feeling of alienation or claustrophobia, by the death of a loved one, by abandonment or betrayal.

Furthermore, it is unlikely that any of our attempts to break through to persons at this stage and to be truly intimate with them will work. They will continue to set up barriers to intimacy because their developmental task is to confront being alone. Very few people, moreover, are conscious enough of their own patterns of growth to tell you that honestly. Most will say, "Sure I want to be close," but then they sabotage intimacy. The only thing that really speeds them up is for them to become conscious that they are, in fact, alone.

Abandonment actually is quite facilitative at this stage. When Wanderers do not let another in, whether it is parent, lover, therapist, analyst, or teacher, it is important for that helper to pull away so that child, lover, client, or student can experience fully the aloneness they have created for their own growth. Otherwise, they will be diverted from recognizing their loneliness by fighting off the assaults of others on their walls. Some people simply will not grow until they are abandoned. Charlotte Brontë's Lucy Snow (in *Villette*) is such a one. She willingly gives her life over to serving almost anyone. Every time Lucy settles in to do so, however, Brontë kills them off.

Some people take their journeys because they cannot find the "right" person to sacrifice for. Because society has taught us that "good" women live to serve, many women explain their independent state by bemoaning the scarcity of available men. Sometimes this is real, and sometimes it is rationalization. A mother of a friend of mine once defended her newly divorced daughter by explaining: "She wanted a man to take care of her (and to take care of) but no one would." Sometimes a woman does find a man but comes to realize that while she has been sacrificing for him, not only has he not been sacrificing in return, he is contemptuous and unappreciative of her. Perhaps he makes comments about how uninteresting she has become. Or maybe he gets interested in just the kind of "selfish" career woman or party girl he has always claimed was not a real woman.

One of the legacies of the feminist movement is that it has propelled many men on their journeys, just as men's embarking on their quests, leaving women alone, has pushed women into claiming their own autonomy. Many men define their whole lives in terms of their role as provider. I remember one man who kept calling me to talk about his wife, who was going back to work. For him, that was a crisis. He explained that he did not know what the meaning of his life was any more. He hated his job, but did it, he said, for her and for the children. If she worked, he did not know why he was doing it. I naively assumed that he should be thrilled—that he was now free to explore other options, other careers he might find more satisfying—but I was underestimating the degree to which his sense of identity (indeed the meaning of his life) hinged on sacrificing in that way for his family. Without that, he did not know who he was. Her action thrust him—albeit kicking and screaming—on his journey.

We all need a period of solitude to find out who we are. Most of us need some solitude every day just to stay clear. Furthermore, all the strategies we use to avoid this task—searches for Mr. or Ms.

Right, the perfect job that will give us our identity, etc.—do help us, in the end, to learn what we need to learn. They give us practice in desire and assertion.

A woman initially may go to college to get an MRS degree and end up taking herself seriously. A man may become increasingly sophisticated in strategies to score and then learn that women like men who are expressive with their feelings. Pretty soon he is so enamored with being open and honest, he forgets all about the score-card and opens up to loving.

Even when our desires are programmed by the culture, they ultimately can help us grow, especially if we are attentive to feedback. For example, if one of my desires is a cigarette every five minutes, I need to begin to be attentive to the warnings on the package and that developing cough. We get educated partly by throwing ourselves into things and finding out what really pays off in a sense of fulfillment and what does not. Then sometimes we can save ourselves some long detours by thinking and feeling a course through before we actually throw ourselves into it: "Well, I could go after that guy, but if I succeed it likely would break up my marriage. Actually, I want my marriage more than I want that fling." Or, "I'm really nuts about this guy and want to become involved with him whatever the consequences. Besides, this might be the crisis that will get my husband to go into marriage counseling with me." Or, "I see that I am attracted to other men. Perhaps that means that something is wrong with my marriage. Maybe I should explore that first." Or, "I really am not monogamous. Jim and I will have to confront that someday. Why not now?" Or, "I don't approve of adultery. Can I face myself if I do this?"

Of course, life does not always follow our scripts. We get feedback from what really happens; this sharpens our reality principle so we can think things through more intelligently next time. The point is, we live out some options, and we imagine our way through others. In either case, we learn what we want and do not want, what we believe in, what our values are. Sometimes we learn we did not really want what we thought we did, but there is no other way to learn what we want than by trusting our knowledge as we go along. Unless we allow ourselves to admit that we do not really know who we are and what we want, we never will know, nor will we know who we are and what we want if we just sit there without trying anything. This is why sometimes in our journeys we actually must wander a bit to grow.

This process of listening to our own desires and acting to fulfill them is fundamental to building an identity. We come into this world with a self, but it is more a potential than a fully developed identity. We learn about who we are by what we want, what we do, and what we think and feel. The happiest people always are the ones who risk enough to be fully themselves. They are the ones who play the prescribed roles the least, but they also have no particular need to be rebels either. They not only have the strongest sense of who they are, they also can receive and give more love than other people because they have confidence that the love that comes their way is real, and not just a response to the roles they play.

I also hasten to say there probably is no way to build a self *without* playing roles. Our first sense of pride comes from playing roles well, and our choices of which roles to play is a rudimentary stab at choosing an identity. For example, a woman may choose to play dumb blonde, the competent, reliable type, the fearless, devil-may-care adventurer, or the motherly, nurturing type. She also decides whether or not to try to be a good student, whether to try to please her parents or be a rebel. She chooses whether to be a career woman or a housewife, and she chooses whether to study art, science, or whatever. Even not choosing still is choosing by default. As she chooses among all these roles and tries them on for size, she begins to get some notion of who she is.

If she plays the roles well, she may begin to gain enough confidence to ask more fundamental questions about who she is apart from such roles. Or she may have such high standards that she feels inadequate in everything she does, in which case she may sink into a serious depression. Even then, if a therapist or friend is sensitive to the basic nature of the situation, the crisis can be used to help her find a sense of herself outside the parts she plays. At some point, if we are to continue to grow we begin to differentiate ourselves from the roles we play. Often we do this when roles that felt good initially now feel empty. In practice this usually means that we have stopped making choices and asserting what we want. For example, a woman sees that everything she now does was preordained by the roles she chose last year, ten years ago, even thirty years ago. More, she may come to understand that even those choices were so influenced by expectations of the culture or by her family or friends that they were not free at all. Maybe she got married, had kids, quit her job just because everyone else did.

Actually, when she made those choices, she was not very experienced and not very clear about what she really wanted. Making them helped her become someone capable of better ones. However, expectations that she choose who she is at twenty-one and act that out for the rest of her life militate against her freedom to make new life choices. Ultimately, of course, that is easy enough to redress. She can decide that the culture, other people, or voices in her own head are wrong to give her "life sentences" for prior bad decisions, and she can start making new ones. But even then her situation remains complicated. Perhaps she decides she does not want to be a wife because she married before she ever experimented with life and gained a sense of competence in the world. She still is unlikely to be able to leave the marriage and save the relationship. And, if she is a mother, the odds are great that she will continue that responsibility whether or not she now feels ready for parenthood. (I have known people to be really innovative here, finding someone to care for their children for a year or two, for example; but mainly people feel pretty trapped by the choices they have made.)

Society is more forgiving of men in such circumstances who forgo caretaking and parental responsibilities to take their journey than it is of women. However, men who continue to support their children both financially and emotionally while they also are "finding themselves" experience wandering as do many women—as a tenuous balance between caretaking and taking one's journey. Paradoxically, often it is in resolving what sometimes seems an intolerable opposition that people find out more fully who they are. They come to know themselves moment by moment by the decisions they make, trying to reconcile their care for others with their responsibility to themselves. Maturity comes with that curious mixture of taking responsibility for their prior choices while being as imaginative as possible in finding ways to continue their journey.

Wanderers do not learn their lesson all at once. Like all the archetypes they learn an initial lesson and then circle back. The first time they take independent action may be as a child, expressing an opinion unpopular with friends or teachers. They may be very influenced by the archetype as they pull away from parents and explore what it means to be an adult and not a child. They may experience it many more times as adults when they follow their heart or convictions and risk the loss of marriages, jobs, friendships, or popularity with friends. This is a lifelong process that sometimes requires more than mere risking.

Like those of Martyrs and Warriors, Wanderers' first choices for themselves are crude and clumsy. Usually they have gone along with someone else, over their own wishes, too long, so that their resentment is deep by the time they act in their own interest. The result is that they choose themselves in the midst of a veritable explosion of rage. Or they may put off making a hard decision in their conscious mind so that their unconscious mind takes over and makes them break some rule that gets them thrown out, as Eve was thrown out of the garden, instead of actively choosing to explore the new world.

When people have grown up in an environment that glorifies martyrdom, being good, and making others happy, their desire for autonomy and independence will be interpreted, even by themselves, as wrong. Their first forays into wandering, accordingly, will consist of seemingly uncontrollable acting out. They will be noticeably bad! Maybe they hang out in bars, take drugs, become promiscuous, even steal, and seem always to be hurting and letting down those they love. They do so, of course, because the price of that love is being good, and being good tends to mean, in such circles, forgoing one's quest to please others. Unfortunately, this pattern can be catastrophic, because those caught in it become increasingly convinced of their worthlessness. They can be helped if they are encouraged to see that, even though their loved ones might immediately be threatened and disapproving, they do, nevertheless, have a responsibility to take their journeys and find out who they are.

Another similar pattern may emerge when we do not wander when we need to—illness. We may become sick as an unconscious way to stop the cycle we are in. As we become more practiced at staying with ourselves, we find that we no longer have bumpy crises in which we have to leave situations dramatically to save ourselves or in which we have to almost kill ourselves to recognize we need to change. Indeed, the Wanderer ultimately teaches us to be ourselves—to be fully true to ourselves in every moment. This takes enormous discipline and means staying in touch with our body, heart, mind, and soul at every moment and in every interaction. As long as we do this, big explosions need not occur.

Fleeing the Captor

At the first level of Wandering, subtlety is not the issue. The big question is whether one will act at all. While the pivotal person for the Orphan is the rescuer, the transformative person or concept for the Wanderer is the villain or captor. In fact, it is the identification of the villain as a real threat that motivates the journey. At the very least, Wanderers identify a person, an institution, a belief system as the cause of their misery, and then they can avoid or flee the cause.

This is the stage of separation. Feminists who identify men as oppressors, people of color who see whites as the enemy, working class and poor people who conclude that capitalists never can be trusted strive to live as separately from the oppressing groups as possible. To the extent that the identities of the oppressed groups are, or seem to be, defined by internalized values of the oppressing groups, this self-imposed isolation provides time and space for the definition of group identity. Women, for instance, ask themselves the question, "What does it mean to be female apart from the definition of femininity imposed by patriarchal culture?"

In the Wanderer stage, men or women who feel trapped in their marriages initially might be able to justify divorce only if it can be established that their spouse is villainous. This was, of course, the basis of all divorce laws until modern no-fault divorce was introduced. The alternative to divorce, as we will see in the next chapter, was to fix the spouse, to make him or her better, by religious conversion, instilling guilt, or perhaps therapy or counseling.

In the old hero myths, the young hero is motivated to go on his solitary journey because the kingdom has become a wasteland. In these stories, it was thought that the cause for this desolation and alienation was in the old king; maybe he was impotent or had committed a crime. In more realistic stories, it is because he has become a tyrant. The aspiring hero goes off into the unknown and confronts a dragon, finds a treasure (the grail, a sacred fish), and comes back, bringing with him what is needed to provide new life for the kingdom. He is then made king.[4]

Now, the interesting thing about this story is that its cyclical nature is built in; not everyone goes on a quest. When someone does and gains some wisdom and power, he is made king and everyone does what he says. Of course, eventually something will be wrong with that new king too. The world keeps changing, and he is not encouraged to keep on with his journey but instead to forgo it so that he might rule the kingdom. So he goes a bit dead. All the other people follow him rather than find their own wisdom and power. They are, then, *all* in captivity. When the young challenger comes along, he sees the deadness, but instead of interpreting the problem as one inherent in the system, he declares that the old king is the villain.

The Orphan wants to be taken care of, and the Martyr will deal with the situation by giving more and more to shore up the king and/ or to help make the kingdom work better. But the part of each of us that is a Wanderer sooner or later will experience our "kings" and "queens"—the people we serve or who we thought would save us— as villains and tyrants. Our job, then, is to leave them, actually or simply by distancing enough to claim ourselves. What is critical in either case is to stop postponing our journey for them.

A friend of mine was complaining to me recently about a woman who comes to her for marital counseling. In spite of the fact that her husband is a very sweet fellow who was willing to do just about anything to keep her and make her happy, this woman persisted in seeing him as a villain. The counselor was most irritated at her because the woman had a perfect opportunity for an extremely happy marriage. What my friend did not see was that her client could not have a happy marriage because she as yet was incapable of taking her own journey while staying with him. As long as she was with him, she would compromise, try to please him, and in any number of ways do things that aborted her own quest. No matter how wonderful her husband was, he was a captor to her and she needed to leave him—at least until she had developed sufficient boundaries so that she could be with him and with herself at the same time.

This is, of course, the same reason teenagers decide their parents are uptight, or oppressive, or that they just do not understand. Very few people feel justified in leaving anyone—a parent, a child, a lover, a mentor, a job, a way of life—without coming to the conclusion that *what they are leaving is bad.* It is not conceivable just to want to leave because one needs to grow. The awareness that one's rescuer always becomes an oppressor if one does not move on when it is time to do so comes later, if at all.

As a rule of thumb, if someone else suddenly becomes hostile to you or if ways of behaving that used to please them do not anymore, it is useful to recognize that unless you have changed radically, the other person probably is changing, and your relationship no longer fits. Your old friend or lover probably will need some distance from you. If you do not allow the distance, the other person will pick fights and make you the villain to enforce it.

However, if you do allow separateness and decide to let go of the other person fully, it is very likely that eventually you will be rewarded with a new, deeper, and more honest relationship with that person, or at worst with the knowledge that in letting go you did a good thing—for both of you. If you are terrified of being left and want to control those you love and hence try to make them abort their journeys, you are truly a dragon in your willingness to devour them to feed your own fears and insecurities. In this case it is time to pause, go back, face your fears and loneliness, process them, *and let go.*

For most of us, opposition is critical to the formation of identity. It is the pressure in the culture in general and in our families, schools, etc., to conform to a particular mode of behavior that forces us to confront our differences and thus sharpen our sense of identity. When fitting in does not work for us—and sooner or later we will find ourselves somewhere in which it does not—we are in the crisis of having to choose either to become chameleons or take the risk of dissociating ourselves from other people.

If we take the latter course, doing so forces us onto our "road of trials," which is the initiation into heroism and always is taken alone. Most of us experience this initiation many times in our lives—every time we are pulled between our desire to stay within the known, safe world and our seemingly conflicting need to grow and risk, confronting the unknown. It is this tension that accounts for the pain attendant upon growing up and leaving home experienced by teenagers or young adults; the difficulty of the midlife crisis that challenges us to leave behind a sense of identity based on a role, achievement, or relationship to others in favor of facing deep psychological and spiritual questions about who we are; and even for the most spiritual and trusting, the psychological struggle surrounding death.

The Road of Trials

Jean Auel's bestselling novel, *Clan of the Cave Bear*,[5] portrays the Wanderer's dilemma. Ayla, one of the first homo sapiens, is swimming one day when an earthquake kills her whole tribe. She is only five. Wandering alone for days, she finally is picked up by Iza, the Medicine Woman of the Clan. The Clan, we learn, are humans, but of a different species. They have phenomenal memories but are not very good at abstract thinking or problem solving. They also have absolutely rigid, patriarchal sex role patterns. Deviation on critical points is punishable by death, but the patterns by now are so genetically encoded that no one in the Clan even thinks of deviation anymore.

The tension between the desire for growth, for mastery, for pushing the limits of one's capacity to achieve versus one's desire to please and fit in is a quintessential Wanderer's dilemma. Ayla's story is illustrative of it. She is strikingly different from the people around her and they fear her difference. So does she, because it threatens her survival, which is dependent—when she is a child—upon pleasing the Clan. To find herself, she must leave the people she most loves so that she can stop compromising to please them.

The most important difference Ayla feels is her capacity for androgyny. She is capable of performing both male and female tasks, and she is curious enough to want to learn everything she can. She resolves her dilemma by conforming when with the Clan, but when she is alone she secretly teaches herself to hunt.

When Ayla's ability to hunt inevitably is discovered, her punishment is to be declared dead. Usually, Clan who are pronounced dead actually die, so strong is their belief in the declaration. But there is a provision in Clan mythology that, if a person comes back from the dead after a certain number of "moons," he or she can be accepted into the tribe. That means Ayla has to survive on her own for a long time—and in winter. On her own means dealing with not only physical survival but also the emotional crisis of learning to trust her own sense of the Clan's reality: They said she would be dead; she thinks (but is not sure) she is alive.

When she comes back, she *is* accepted. She very much wants to be part of the Clan again, for she has been dreadfully lonely, yet the experience of making it on her own has made her even more confident and therefore less malleable and more independent of Clan mores. When Ayla has a child, she runs off so that it will not be put to death as a mutant. Ayla figures out that the child is not deformed. It is only half-Clan, half-Other (their term for homo sapiens) and so it looks very different from other Clan babies. Even though this situation is resolved through a combination of her cleverness and the leader's compassion, the clash between the more and more independent and adventurous Ayla and the increasingly disoriented Clan is growing. No resolution seems possible, however, because she so loves them, and they her. Almost no one wants to sever this relationship—except one person.

Enter the villain: Broud, the one Clan who has truly hated Ayla (because he has been envious of the attention she has received), is put in charge. His first action is to declare Ayla dead once again. She goes off to find the Others, people like herself, not knowing whether she ever will. In Auel's sequel, *The Valley of the Horses*,[6] we learn that Ayla ends up spending three years—including three hard winters—away from human society, kept company only by a cave lion and a horse.

Having left the clan, she nevertheless takes with her the belief that the price of being alone is giving up critical pieces of who she is. She can have love at the price of conformity or be alone for the rest of her life. Clan, for instance, do not laugh or cry. Alone in her valley, she debates what of herself she is willing to give up in order to be less lonely. She decides she would be willing to give up hunting but not laughing. It never occurs to her that she could find a community in which she could be *fully* herself. Even when a man of her own kind finds her and falls in love with her—a man who simply assumes that everyone laughs and cries and who prefers and admires women who hunt well—she cannot believe it and keeps acting as if he were a sexist Clan male.

The point here is that originally the threat was real. She was totally dependent for her physical and emotional survival on the Clan. She did need to compromise to please them. She gained major lessons both by disciplining herself to please them—especially in doing it for the love of her parent figures, Creb and Iza—and by choosing herself as much as she could in defiance of custom. One can see here the passage of childhood and adolescence—the dual lessons of obedience and rebellion. Yet Ayla, like most of us, transfers these lessons to situations in which they no longer are relevant.

The belief that we have to compromise critical parts of ourselves to fit in makes visible and real to us both our need for love and our equally strong need to explore who we are. The tension between these incredibly strong and apparently conflicting impulses leads us first to give up important pieces of ourselves in order to fit in, and in that way to learn how much love and belonging means to us, and finally, radically, to choose ourselves and our journeys as even more important to us than care of others or perhaps even our own survival.

Because the culture has overglorified the harsh solitary journey of the classic hero, and because the culture so needs people who can work collaboratively, there has been a good bit of disenchantment with the traditional heroic ideal of the Wanderer. Like that of martyrdom, the problem of the Wanderer is not with the archetype itself, but rather with a confusion about what the archetype means for people. Just as martyrdom is destructive when suffering is justified for its own sake, solitude can be an escape from community—and hence destructive—if it, too, seems like a value in itself. For instance, if maturity is equated with independence—an independence defined as not needing anyone else—it can stop an individual's growth.

However, making an absolute choice for ourselves and our own integrity even if it means being alone and unloved is the prerequisite for heroism and ultimately for being able to love other people while remaining autonomous. It is essential for creating the proper boundaries so that we can see the difference between ourselves and another person—so that we will not have to objectify them to know ourselves and what we want. Only then is it possible to both empathize with and honor another, and yet still do what we need to do for ourselves.

Boundaries also are essential for finding our own vocations. Part of being human is to be a creator, to bring into being things that were not here before. That's what it means to say we were created in God's image. Ayla, in her solitary valley, made and invented tools; she tamed a horse and a cave lion; she experimented with new medicinal recipes, new ways to dress and wear her hair. Only the discovery that she could survive alone freed her to be as creative and competent as she was able to be. By exploring her potential in this way, she not only created things and experiences outside herself, but she discovered herself as someone to be proud of.

Work helps us find our identity, first because it is the way people survive—by toil. When we learn we can support ourselves, we do not have to be dependent on other people. Beyond that, when we find work—in this case paid or avocational—that expresses our souls, we find ourselves by what we bring into being. The Wanderer's quest, then, also is about agency, productivity, creativity.

No matter how much people want to feel loved, appreciated, and a part of things, there will be a loneliness deep in their souls until they make a commitment to themselves, a commitment that is so total that they will give up community and love, if necessary, to be fully who they are. Perhaps this is why some of the most secure people I know—and the people with the clearest sense of who they are—have taken great risks. In this list I would put several friends: a woman who knew in her soul she must be an artist and left a marriage to a wealthy man to tend bar and pursue her art; a man in midlife who left a secure job to start his own business developing a product he had invented; and a number of men and women who risked losing their jobs and/or social ostracism by making public their love of someone of the same sex. I also would include a woman who left a high status job as a scientist to go into the ministry, not even sure that any church in her denomination would accept a woman minister.

Not every Wanderer makes decisions so dramatic, but every one of us—if we are to grow past a certain point—needs to make an absolute commitment to ourselves. Like the Martyr, we do so in stages. We begin angry that we have to make such hard choices. At first we act like Orphans, kicking and screaming that someone else is supposed to be caring for us! Or we may complain that no one loves us for who we really are, that we would like to do such and so, but there are no jobs in that field. In short, we complain that life is hard and we take that secure job that is not what we want to do or stay in relationships that seem safe, even if they are not very satisfying to us.

Then one day, loneliness and a sense of an existential void, sometimes felt in the solar plexus, are accepted as just the way things are: "We all walk alone, each and every one of us." Fully accepting and feeling anything always sends us into another place. It is only struggling against our growth that locks us in. In this case, accepting loneliness leads to rebellion: those quiet or public experiments in acting on what you really want, loving who you really love, doing the work you love, finding out who you are. Then the sense of enjoyment that Ayla discovers in her own company, in which solitude becomes something quite different from loneliness, creeps in. The more we are ourselves, the less alone we feel. For we are never really alone when we have ourselves.

Community

Paradoxically, the movement into isolation and loneliness ultimately leads back to community: Ayla finally can have love and be who she is, and she can live with people like herself—her true family. The archetypal Wanderer, then, moves from dependence to independence to an autonomy defined in the context of interdependence. Many who have learned to embrace their independence and even solitariness find later that they miss human connection. They have become capable of experiencing intimacy at a new level because they have developed a strong enough sense of self that they are not afraid of being swallowed up in the other. To their surprise they often find, just when they are ready, that people, communities, exist who will love them for exactly who they are.

As they resolve the conflict between love and autonomy by choosing themselves without denying their yearning for connection, the seemingly impossible conflict dissolves. In this new way of seeing the world, the *reward* for being fully and wholly ourselves is love, respect, and community. But for most of us, the full enjoyment of this reward does not come until we gain the Warrior's ability to assert our own wishes in the relationship, the Martyr's capacity to give and commit to others, and the Magician's knowledge that there is no scarcity, that we can have all the love we need as our birthright. We do not have to *pay* for it by forfeiting our lives.

Chapter 4

THE WARRIOR

Lives of great men all remind us
    We can make our lives sublime,
And, departing, leave behind us
    Footprints on the sands of time. . . .

Let us, then, be up and doing,
    With a heart for any fate;
Still achieving, still pursuing,
    Learn to labour and to wait

—HENRY WADSWORTH LONGFELLOW
"A Psalm of Life"

The Wanderer identifies the dragon and flees; the Warrior stays and fights. And it is the archetype of the Warrior that *is* our culture's definition of heroism. I have asked many classes and audiences to tell me the central characters in the hero's story. They always give the same answer: the hero, the villain (or the dragon to be slain), and the victim (or damsel-in-distress to be rescued). We all know this plot and these characters. The underlying moral of this story is that good can and will triumph over evil, but even more fundamental than that, the story tells us that when people have the courage to fight for themselves they can affect their worlds.

Any ending in which good does not triumph, therefore, seems fundamentally disempowering because we take it to mean that we are powerless and because, in undermining the major belief system of the culture, it reinforces cynicism, alienation, and despair. When the hero does triumph over the villain, however, it reinforces our faith that it is possible not only to identify the dragon but to slay it: We can take charge of our lives, eliminate our problems, and make a better world. In doing so, we rescue the damsel-in-distress who is the Orphan in all of us. The Warrior says to the Orphan within: "You do not always have to look for someone outside yourself to save you; I can take care of you."

This archetype helps teach us to claim our power and to assert our identity in the world. This power can be physical, psychological, intellectual, and spiritual. On the physical level, the Warrior archetype presides over the assertion that we have a right to be alive. The Warrior consciousness includes self-defense, a willingness and an ability to fight to defend oneself. On the psychological level, it has to do with the creation of healthy boundaries, so we know where we end and other people begin, and an ability to assert ourselves.

Intellectually, the Warrior helps us learn discrimination, to see what path, what ideas, what values are more useful and life-enhancing than others. On the spiritual level, it means learning to differentiate among spiritual energies and theologies: to know which bring more life and which kill or maim the life force within us. The Warrior also helps us to speak out and to fight for what nourishes our minds, our hearts, and our souls, and to vanquish those things that sap and deplete the human spirit by speaking the truth about them and by refusing to countenance them or to allow them into our lives.

The development of warrioring capabilities is essential to a full life, and it is a necessary complement to the virtues associated with the Martyr. Initially, Martyrs see themselves as sacrificing for others, while at the relatively primitive level Warriors assume the necessity of slaying others to protect themselves. And the willingness to do so is an important assertion of commitment to themselves and their own self-worth; it is the fundamental assertion that they have a right to be here and a right to be treated with dignity and respect. That means that they have a right to be honored by loved ones, to be respected by teachers and employers, and to refuse work that is demeaning or to learn ideas that insult them. Unless they value themselves enough to say no to what is hurtful or harmful to them, their choices for sacrifice and for giving for love's sake may be more cowardly than transformative.

Women, minority men, and the working class all have been culturally defined as inferior and, as such, their role is to serve. To the degree that these groups have internalized such ideas, much of their giving and serving is linked unconsciously to their belief that they do not have a right to be here unless they do serve—that they do not have a right to exist for their own sake. Many women, for instance, can conceive of doing things just because they want to only after they have satisfied the needs and wishes of their children, their husbands, their bosses, their friends, and on and on. Because those demands are never wholly met, anything they do for themselves is accompanied by guilt—even if what they are doing is attending to their basic health needs, like going out for a jog. One wonderful friend of mine told me how her new frontier was simply going for a walk because she wanted to just as her husband and stepchildren gathered around expecting her, if not to cook dinner, at least to supervise the process and keep everyone's spirits up. Although she could not yet enjoy her walk—she felt too guilty—at least she was able to take it. This, of course, is a step above the even more rudimentary attempt that many women make at assertion, which is to nag or complain, without having enough confidence to assert their own views on the world, to demand real change.

Men who have not addressed their identity issues in any deep way find their sense of self-worth primarily through the assertion of their superiority. Consequently, their warrioring activities are characterized mainly by a struggle to win—in their work, their recreation, and even their friendships and intimate relationships. One man recognized he was in trouble in this area when he discovered he could not even allow his daughter to beat him at checkers!

Under stress, even women and men who have a pretty good idea who they are will revert, respectively, to appeasing and caring for men and to being competitive, domineering, and opinionated. Whether male or female, the journeyer who has not spent some time under the tutelage of the Wanderer archetype can be only a pseudo-Warrior. And, as I have suggested, the Warrior who has not submitted to the teaching of the Martyr will be stuck at a fairly rudimentary, us/them level of warrioring.

A Warrior Culture

Warriors change their worlds by asserting their will and their image of a better world upon them. Whether in families, schools, workplaces, friendships, communities, or the culture as a whole, this archetype informs Warriors' demands to change their environments to suit their own needs and to conform to their values.

However, people who move into warrioring before dealing with their identities cannot really be Warriors, for they either do not know what they are fighting for or are fighting mainly to prove their superiority—a mechanism for the development of self-confidence that never really substitutes for knowing who you are.

Individuals (and cultures) need to address Wanderer issues every time they go through major transitions to answer the question, "Who am I this time?" Not having resolved this question, they retain the emphasis on the slaying-the-dragon plot, but the form is there without the meaning. Accordingly, many people engage in pseudo-warrioring, in which the myth is acted out for its own sake, but they find the ritual itself cannot transform either the hero or the kingdom. Ironically, those who represent the old cultural values are less conflicted than people who are engaged more fundamentally in grappling with issues of identity raised by changing times. Conservatives, for example, are more comfortable slaying dragons than are progressives, for whom the battle is complicated both by unresolved identity questions and by their desire to reconcile their own values and concerns with the needs of others.

Whether it is an empty ritual, deeply satisfying, or seen as needing redefinition for changing times, the hero/villain/victim myth informs our culture's basic secular belief system. The ritual that underlies the Warrior myth is found, of course, in war, but it also is played out culturally in our sports, our business practices, our religions, and even our economic and educational theories. In the realm of sports, we have seen over the centuries a progression from gladiatorial contests in which the loser actually was killed, to football, baseball, or soccer, in which the antagonist simply loses.

The kind of religion that makes headlines results from the Warrior's method of problem-solving, from the Crusades to modern fundamentalists' waging war on sin, evil, and the devil. The Warrior's approach to spirituality is to identify evil and eliminate it or make it illegal. It is the impetus behind the campaign to get prayer back into the schools, to wipe out pornography, to get rid of sex education, and to deny jobs to homosexuals. The next step up from this is to convert sinners. They do not need to be destroyed if they can be transformed so that they no longer are villains: They can be saved by adopting the same belief system as the hero.

In politics, too, we have an interesting progression. In the most primitive mode, the hero kills the old king (the tyrant) and at least theoretically saves the victimized populace. That is how change occurs. These practices continue into the modern era in many parts of the world where change still is brought about by the bloody coup or by revolution. In our country we have found a way to avoid such bloodshed. The old king is neither ritually dismembered, as in some primitive cultures, nor killed in his sleep, nor tried and executed for his crimes. But as we are reminded each election year, the rhetoric based upon these old practices remains.

The challenger—whether in electoral or intraorganizational politics—explains how he or she will save the country or the organization, and that the incumbent is responsible for all its ills. The incumbent, of course, retaliates by describing how he or she has, in fact, made major improvements in the country/the state/the organization and how the opposition would ruin things were they in power. The language is warlike: We talk about defeating the opposition at the polls. We may even say, "We slaughtered them!" This warlike language, of course, also is basic to business, in which the object is to defeat the competition. The central belief of capitalism is based upon the wisdom of this modality: that competition, a version of the contest, will bring about the good life for all—better products, lower prices. The sports metaphor here is the race. The vitality of our country is seen as depending upon this race, upon competition. Even our legal system is based on the model of the contest.

Although the person defeated in sports, politics, or business no longer is seen as a villain per se, the persistence of this idea is evident in the way losing brings shame on the loser—a response more appropriate to a recognition that one is bad than simply that one has lost a contest. When Richard Nixon won the presidency, George McGovern was pictured by the press as disgraced—even though he ran an incredibly valiant campaign against great odds. The sense that he had been shamed was so great that when he announced his candidacy a second time, it was viewed as an embarrassing thing to do. Presumably, having been defeated by such a landslide at the polls, he was supposed to go hide his face, even though it was an amazing victory for someone so liberal to have been nominated at all. Consequently, when he was able to win back a measure of respect from the other Democratic hopefuls, the press portrayed that as a major "victory."

There is shame attached to being the losing team or the losing candidate, to being poor and hence having lost out in the contest of the free market. Such assumptions may explain why we seem incapable as a culture of designing a welfare system that does not humiliate the recipients. Many educators envision the learning process as a contest (usually a race) with some students marked as early as elementary school as "winners" and others as "losers." Those expectations can become self-fulfilling prophecies. The "losers" internalize a sense of being unworthy, while the "winners" are spurred on to greater efforts by fear of also being failures. Flunking out of school—or, in more advanced cases, college professors being denied tenure—is tantamount to disgrace. People do not want to talk about it. Or if it is talked about at all, it is in one of two ways: Either it is your own fault (i.e., you are the villain) or you have been treated unfairly (you are a victim). But it is clear you are not the hero, unless, of course, you wage a battle to get reinstated.

Our culture so consistently reinforces this basic archetype, at least for those in power, that the slaying-the-dragon pattern appears to them to be the only reality—just as the Orphan sees meaningless suffering to be just the way things are.

Warriors tend to focus on the "facts" in an effort to be tough-minded: A Marxist will insist that material reality *is* reality. Any other focus—on inner, subjective reality, spirituality, etc.—is false. A fundamentalist Christian will, in the same spirit, insist on taking the Bible literally as a blueprint for action. In sports we count plays, keep score; in business we look at the bottom line; in education we increasingly quantify and look for airtight methodologies; in economics we tabulate the Gross National Product. In all cases, too much focus on the impact of these facts on people or people's yearnings for a better world, too much tender-heartedness, too much hope is seen as inappropriate, naive, and unproductive. Good thinking, in this view, is linear, hierarchical, and dualistic.

Thus, Warriors must be tough-minded and realistic in order to change the world by slaying dragons. They need to be able to look their adversary in the eye and say, "You are a dragon and I am going to slay you." Or, "I do not care how you feel, I want to win and that means I have to defeat you." Warriors also have to be on the lookout for inappropriate qualities within themselves to be slain or repressed.

In the Warrior mode, for instance, a critical question for a feminist is to determine who is to blame for sexism. If it is men, then they are the enemy. If it is a patriarchal system, then it must be overthrown. Or (as in the case of some socialist feminists), if it is capitalism, then that system, or even perhaps all capitalists, must be defeated. A feminist's softer feelings of compassion and care, her desires for love with a man or to wear pretty clothes are seen as internalized oppression that must be overcome. For the warrioring Christian, the issue is the devil without and within. For the person in business or for students, it is not only performing at the top of the sales or grading curve, but overcoming tendencies to sloth—that desire just to sit and enjoy the day.

Warriors share with Martyrs a sense that we should suffer for our transgressions. There is a widespread feeling among conservatives that it is only natural that the losers in a contest should suffer; hence, it makes perfect sense to them that the poor, who lost the economic contest, and women, who they see as losing the battle of the sexes, should not have as much as the victors. It also is necessary that the victors should be rewarded for their superiority because the spoils of victory, they believe, inspire excellence. Otherwise, we all might languish around, never accomplishing anything.

Liberals tend to focus more on blaming the oppressors who have, indeed, fixed the contest in their own favor, or on trying to guarantee that the contest will be fair by developing headstart programs, etc. But they rarely question the idea that life is a contest—at least they do not dare suggest publicly that it may not be!

In fact, the belief in the hero/villain/victim plot is dogma in our culture, with power so great that its invocation renders contravening evidence irrelevant.

Academics, for example, will equate increasing competition with quality education, even though most research data supports the view that cooperative approaches to learning actually are more effective.[1]

Many managers continue trying to push employees to greater productivity by promoting an atmosphere of fierce competition when, again, research suggests that the most successful business enterprises build atmospheres of trust in which employees help one another.[2]

It is critical to remember here that in our culture the Warrior hero has been envisioned most often as a white man. Women are cast as damsels-in-distress, as the reward along with half the kingdom, or, if they step outside traditional expectations, perhaps as witches, temptresses, shrews, or other female variations on the villain archetype. Indeed, the initial phase of the Warrior archetype defines a patriarchal way of perceiving and arranging the world, one seen dualistically—as a clash between opposing issues, ideas, or forces—and hierarchically, so that the main concern is always who and what is superior or more worthy. The hero's task is to defeat or subject whatever is inferior, within or without, to his will. This phase typically is not only sexist, but racist and classist.

While the hero/villain/victim plot holds enormous power in our culture, the challenge we face as Warriors depends upon our ability to imagine and assert other truths, other versions of the Warrior myth. The logical consequence of continuing to define life as a contest is world hunger, environmental devastation, racial and gender inequality, nuclear war, and, at the very least, the waste of the talents of all those who see themselves as losers. Fortunately, although the culture is Warrior-possessed, warrioring has other possible stages and forms.

Stages of the Warrior's Journey

Warriors' progress through the archetype is dependent upon how much they have learned from other archetypes. For example, pseudo-Warriors (macho men or women) are really Orphans masquerading as Warriors, covering fear with bravado. If they experiment with wandering before developing their capacity for care or their sense of who they are, they will fight mainly to prove their courage but will not have any good idea what they are fighting for, except perhaps to win. When they have made some inroads in finding out who they are and what they want, they can fight for themselves, and when they have developed some capacity to care for others, they can fight for them.

Furthermore, if Warriors have skipped the lessons of the Wanderer, they will feel very lonely as Warriors. If they have not attended properly to the lessons of the Martyr, they will be possessed by the archetype and martyr themselves to the cause, the business, or the team they, as Warriors, fight for. (So, too, if they do not attend to the lesson of the Warrior, they will become controlling and manipulative.)

Warriors who integrate care with mastery fight for themselves and for others. Soldiers fight for their loved ones, country, and to make the world a better place. Political leaders, social activists, and concerned volunteers struggle to improve the lives of those around them. It is here that one can see how the lessons of sacrifice and the lessons of mastery work together. Gaining a more sophisticated level of skill at one allows the development of a more sophisticated level of skill at the other.

The harmful side effects of warrioring come in its more primitive forms, just as they do in sacrificing. When it is freed from these more dualistic and absolutist forms, warrioring (like sacrificing) becomes a healthy, useful, positive human process. It is the basic process of taking action to protect themselves and those they love from harm. Whether it is killing the predatory animal, heading off the invading band, or identifying acid rain or nuclear proliferation as a threat to humankind, it requires Warriors to take strong action to protect us all.

In each modality explored so far, our hero has learned to deal with a difficult experience: the Orphan has dealt with powerlessness; the Martyr, pain; the Wanderer, loneliness; and now the Warrior confronts fear. The levels Warriors experience, then, also are related to how well they have learned to confront fear. At the early stages— the stages in which the only answer seems to be a literal slaying of the enemy—fear is rampant. The general who cannot imagine enough weapons to counter the communist threat is simply *controlled* by fear. His world is defined by a vision of perpetual threat in which the villain is imagined to be totally irrational and bent on destroying all that he is or holds dear. The only possibility is to kill or be killed. The symbolic contest in politics/business/sports/school is mild in comparison, but its fears are real as well: the fear of losing, of not being the best, of being inadequate, inferior, a loser.

At the next level the villain is seen not as someone to slay or to defeat, but as someone to convert into a hero. The villain is redefined as a victim to be saved. Whether we are talking of crusading Christianity, Marxism, feminism, or pull-yourself-up-by-your-bootstraps capitalism, Warriors take the truth that enabled them to develop some sense of hope and meaning to their life and go out to convert the world. Analogously, in private life, Warriors undertake Pygmalion projects to improve loved ones and friends.

The problem of human difference is hard to confront when you are yearning to make an ideal, humane world. One of the central ways Martyrs try to make the world better is to give up parts of themselves that do not seem to fit what others want. Warriors change other people. In both case, *sameness* is seen as a prerequisite to the creation of a loving community. We either change ourselves, or we get rid of or transform *them*!

I recently talked to a charismatic Christian who told me about a typical process in that movement. The exultation of conversion, a feeling of being reborn and renewed by the church community, often is followed by evangelism. The initial belief is that one will just tell people about Jesus and they will be saved. But then not only do many people show no interest in the "good news," but one's own life may not be going so well. The initial euphoria of salvation has passed and life still has the same struggles, the same ups and downs. The temptation then is to revert to dogmatism and an attempt to impose—by legislation or social pressure—one's views on other people. This urge comes out of a belief that the ideal Christian community cannot come about with so much flagrant sin going on. When conversion does not transform one's life, true military obedience and discipline become required.

I suspect this is also what happened with Marxism in Russia and China. As a liberating truth was put into effect and the Edenic community still looked a long way off, the antidote for cynicism and loss of faith was dogmatism and repression. The same frustration produced McCarthyism in our own country.

Although warrioring, by itself, does not bring a utopian world, it does teach a very important process that contributes to building a better world for each one of us. What do Warriors learn? First, they learn to trust their own truths and act on them with absolute conviction in the face of danger. To do so, moreover, it is necessary for them to take control of, and responsibility for, their own lives. Orphans see themselves as victims, and Wanderers as outsiders. By defining oneself as having no power in the culture, one does not have to take any responsibility for it. To identify oneself as a Warrior is to say, "I am responsible for what happens here," and "I must do what I can to make this a better world for myself and for others." It also requires Warriors to claim authority, that they have a right to assert what they want for themselves and for others. Warriors learn to trust their own judgment about what is harmful and, perhaps most important, they develop the courage to fight for what they want or believe in, even when doing so requires great risk—the loss of a job, a mate, friends, social regard, or even their very lives.

Eventually, if they do not regress to find refuge in dogmatism and become tyrants, they also will develop flexibility and humility. All the liberating truths, by themselves, fail! They fail partly because each is just part of the truth; all of us are like the proverbial blind men, each feeling one part and trying to describe a whole elephant!

The hero ultimately learns not the content per se but a *process*. The process begins with an awareness of suffering, then moves to telling the story and an acknowledgment to oneself and to others that something is painful. Then comes the identification of the cause of that pain and taking appropriate action to stop it. The hero replaces the absolutist belief that in slaying one dragon we solve all problems for all time with a belief that we continue slaying dragons our entire lives. He or she learns that the more we slay, the more confident we become, and therefore the less violent we have to be.

And as we have seen, the content itself changes. Gladiatorial contests are replaced by football. I like to think that war is being replaced by posturing and a build-up of weapons. The woman who a few years ago would have lambasted a man for a sexist remark now says in a fairly bored and disinterested way, "Oh, come off it." Nor is there then the requirement of so much violence to the self. The stronger and more confident Warriors become, the less they must use violence, the more gentle they can be—with themselves and others.

Finally, they need not define the other as villain, opponent, or potential convert, but as another hero like themselves.

Warrioring: Male and Female

Male and female experiences with the Warrior archetype differ significantly. Men are socialized practically from birth to be Warriors, so their issue is whether they can develop other sides of themselves or even deepen and grow in their experience of the archetype insofar as doing so is dependent upon their satisfactory resolution of Orphan, Wanderer, and Martyr dilemmas. For women, the issue is whether they will have the audacity even to enter a contest culturally defined as male, and, if they do, whether they will learn to speak in their own voices, to express their own wisdom. Because women usually enter the Warrior after the Martyr stage, moreover, they often enter at a higher and more complex level.

Books such as Betty Harragan's *Games Mother Never Taught You: Corporate Gamesmanship for Women*[3] explain the rules of male culture to women, for although one can say generally that the Warrior's consciousness informs our culture, that is only because it is a patriarchal culture. Women have been discouraged from doing battle. These kinds of books teach women to enter the contest and to learn men's rules for doing so. Books such as Anne Wilson Schaef's *Women's Reality: The Emerging Female System in a White Male Society* or Carol Gilligan's *In a Different Voice: Psychological Theory and Women's Development* go further to challenge the notion that male culture *is* reality by defining, respectively, an emerging women's culture and the stages of women's moral development. Male culture, as defined in each case, is equivalent to what I call the warrioring modality.

The hero/villain/victim plot is the characteristically macho way of making meaning of the world. Accordingly, there is a certain alienation for women when they first confront it. This follows naturally from male culture's exclusivity. Indeed, both the military and football—the institutions that dramatize the myth in its most primitive and basic forms—have been defined as male-only preserves. Although there are now women in the military (though not in professional football), neither women themselves nor the society as a whole have viewed warrioring as an attribute of womanliness.

But I do not think this alienation means that women do not or should not learn warrioring. Women need to learn to struggle, to fight for themselves and others, and it is this archetypal pattern that teaches them how to do it. Because it has been defined as for men only, the warrioring archetype is the new frontier for women. The real issue for them and for all Warriors is to learn to come from their core and to fight for what they truly believe in and care for. Men are so strongly socialized to be Warriors that it not only prevents them from developing other aspects of themselves but also tends to foster a confusion that sees the battle or contest as justified *for its own sake*.

The contest seems so important to men because it has defined their *identity* as males: Man the hunter lives on through all these pseudo battles. In our culture, mastery and nurturance have been defined in opposition. Women have been charged with nurturance, men with mastery. Women fear achievement, agency, and mastery precisely because the world that has honored these qualities—the male world—is profoundly painful to them, not only because it does not value women, but because it often does not value care.

Women are offended by the male world because they see little love there. Indeed, too often men even have forgotten that the point of the battle or the contest is to make the world a better place. On the other hand, men are horrified by the female world because they see the sacrifice there and fear being swallowed up in it. Because women are more apt to explore care and sacrifice before agency, they are likely to deplore the killing, the defeating of others—all the aspects of the battle that hurt other people. Women, therefore, often are seduced into the fray only to save others. It was women who lent most of the energy to the nineteenth-century reform movements, and today they provide much of it to the environmental and peace movements. Conversely, many men move into warrioring prematurely when they really still are at the narcissistic Orphan stage, and only later begin to see the importance of caring for others.

When agency is separated from care, it becomes will, domination. This is the primary danger of warrioring for men. In Ursula Le Guin's *A Wizard of Earthsea*, Sparrowhawk, as a young student of magic, looses something horrid and evil upon the world when, merely to show off, he summons the dead. His sin, the typical male one, is pride. In his egocentrism, Sparrowhawk does powerful magic just for his own glory, even though he knows that to do so threatens the equilibrium of the world and can have unforeseen effects on everyone. He is so engaged with proving himself, however, that he does not care about the outcome, which is that a Shadow emerges from the underworld that threatens to possess his body and terrorize the world.[4]

Women's socialization to receptivity poses analogous difficulty for them. They may be able to fight for others and not for themselves because they think doing so is selfish. In this case, the fray may be simply another form of martyrdom. So, too, for some men. Those who *have* integrated care and sacrifice into their lives can fight for their country, their company, or their family, but sometimes not truly for themselves. Indeed, that the hero traditionally has been cast as male and the victim as female holds dangers for both men and women. While women may fear the presumption of stepping into the heroic role, men may identify their heroism solely in terms of protecting and rescuing others—especially women and children—while they neglect the captive victim in themselves: men, they believe, are not supposed to need rescue! Neither men nor women can fight intelligently for themselves unless they have taken the time, as Wanderers, to find out who they are and what they want.

In a ground-breaking work on moral development in men and women, *In a Different Voice*, Gilligan argues that men and women solve moral dilemmas differently because they view the world differently. One example she gives is Lawrence Kohlberg's famous Heinz dilemma, in which men and women were given a hypothetical dilemma to solve: Heinz's wife is very ill and will die if she is not given a specific drug. However, the drug is extremely expensive, and Heinz does not have enough money to buy it. He has tried unsuccessfully to borrow the money, and the druggist is not willing to give it to him for less. Should he steal the drug? According to Lawrence Kohlberg, at the highest stage of moral development people resolve this problem by arguing from universal moral principles: Specifically, they will argue the relative merits of property rights versus human life. If life is more important, he should steal the drug. If property rights are more important, he should not, and presumably he then should allow his wife to die. Now, notice that this moral reasoning is not only hierarchical—which value is more important—but dualistic. It is, in fact, the equivalent in moral reasoning to the shoot-out at the O.K. Corral. May the best value win.

Gilligan notes that women rarely scored at Kohlberg's highest levels. Moreover, from a moral development point of view, women seemed to be avoiding the questions, asking for more information (Has he really explained to the druggist that his wife will die, and did anyone try talking with the neighbors or collecting money?) or even, to the annoyance of the interviewers, making pronouncements like, "He shouldn't steal the drug and he shouldn't let his wife die." Gilligan realizes that Kohlberg's formulation of the question—and thus his resulting scale of moral development—was predicated on a male way of thinking. Women think about moral questions differently, and, hence, these women were answering another question: Instead of "*Should* Heinz steal the drug?" they were asking "Should Heinz *steal* the drug?" The women assumed the necessity of action to save the wife's life. Their questions were designed to determine the most effective action.

Beyond the practicality and narrative quality of women's responses (If he stole the drug, he might be sent to jail. If she got sick again, who would steal it for her?) was a different way of envisioning problems. Instead of seeing the world hierarchically as a ladder, the women reenvisioned it as a net or web of human interconnectedness. Accordingly, rather than defining the basis of most problems as an irreconcilable difference between two people/countries/values, women saw the problems as arising from a breakdown in the network of human connection. The solution when that web was broken was communication: Has anybody talked to the neighbors? Has he explained to the druggist? The other approach was to critique the problem: What kind of world is it where a druggist can have a drug, yet let a woman die?[5]

In *Women's Reality*, Anne Wilson Schaef sees an analogous difference between what she calls "white male system" and "female system" modes of negotiation. In the white male system, a sophisticated negotiator recognizes that the situation is one of conflict. The goal is to get as much as you can for yourself, for your side. You do so by asking for or demanding more than you want, playing your cards close to your chest, and then "dealing" until you get something close to what you want. In the female system, the negotiators are seen as essentially on the same side. The goal is to be imaginative enough so that both people can get as much of what they want as they can. So the strategy is to lay your cards on the table and be clear about exactly what you want, what it means to you, and then to put your heads together to find out how both people can get what they want.[6] The former approach is, of course, the basis of our legal system, most labor union negotiations, etc. The latter is the basis for mediation.

Although it probably is true that more women than men negotiate in the "female system" mode, it also is true that many men learn to do so when they move through the more primitive us/them understanding of the Warrior's legacy into more sophisticated (i.e., cognitively and affectively integrated) approaches to problem solving. When Gilligan traced the development of male and female moral reasoning over time and through many levels of understanding reality, she discovered that although men and women still have recognizable differences in the language and metaphors used, they began to sound more and more alike as the thinking of each became more complex and subtle.

I have come to understand that while the emphasis on affiliation and nets of connectedness keeps women overlong in the Martyr mentality, women often are able to maintain an affiliative way of thinking about the world—especially in defining just what they are looking for—even as they choose independence from the net of connectedness to find themselves and to slay dragons. They go through the same stages as men do even though their rhetoric and their basic belief systems may conflict with the us/them mentality of the Wanderer and Warrior. They move quickly, then, pushed by a need to reconcile the discrepancy between their beliefs and the action motivated by the urgency of their own development. Hence they quickly redefine warrioring and learn to have an impact on the world through bridging and communication rather than by slaying dragons or winning contests.

The most important challenge to women's assertiveness today is not entering the male-defined contest but their willingness to speak in their own voices and with their own wisdom. Men appropriately have asserted their own truths in the world, but the suppression of the female voice leaves the culture dangerously lopsided.

Further, the over-reinforcement of the warrioring voice in men retards their development in other areas and leaves them and the culture at a more primitive level of thinking and assertion than is good for many of us. I cannot help noting, however, how many men find this macho level of functioning limiting and inappropriate to their lives. For such men, the issue is analogous to women's: the challenge to become clear enough to speak in a voice that is not yet fully validated and articulated in the culture as a whole, and that may confuse, alienate, or mystify more conventional people around them. As we have seen, men may avoid the lessons of the Martyr and consequently have great difficulty moving on to the more subtle, complex, and affiliative levels of warrioring. For many it takes a crisis to propel them to move on—such as a heart attack, ulcers, or recognition that the cost of their stoic struggle has been the loss of a wife, lover, or children. This crisis usually requires an acknowledgment of the need to care—for oneself and for others. For other men, movement into the hero/hero/hero mode from the hero/villain/victim merely requires that they have so completely experienced the Warrior mentality that their inner need for growth propels them onward.

Beyond Slaying the Dragon

Warrior plots evolve, however, from hero/villain/victim to hero/hero/hero for both male and female heroes. That the Warriors's truth is now simply one among many does not preclude commitment—to ideals, people, causes, beliefs. Warriors embrace their understandings with their whole hearts even in a relativistic world. At this point someone else who asserts a seemingly antithetical truth may be greeted not as an enemy, but as a potential friend: "Here's my truth. I will explain it to you as fully as I can, and you can explain yours to me." The task of the hero, then, is to *bridge*, not to slay or convert.

In the history of justice, we see an evolution from a dictator meting out punishments, to our justice system, in which one person loses and another wins, to a system of mediation that sees neither party as a villain and in which every attempt is made to see that both get satisfied.

The old styles of conflict were jerky, violent, and primitive. Increasingly they have been followed by more gentle and flowing ones. From two people slaughtering each other, we have moved to two people debating and then asking who won; and, finally, we have two people who have grown confident enough to use their differences as a way of finding more adequate and complete truths. They brainstorm with one another, and then both share what they have learned from the exchange.

I have a fantasy of representatives from the Soviet Union sitting down with those of the United States. The U.S.S.R. representatives begin by explaining that they feel they have done a great job at providing economic equity for their people, but they are concerned that it has been at the cost of political repression and a certain dullness to life. The U.S. ambassadors reply by saying that they, too, feel only partly successful. In the U.S. there is much personal freedom and lots of excitement and variety, but there remain great extremes of wealth and humiliating poverty. The two powers proceed to put their heads together, sharing their own piece of the truth, and try to come up with a plan that would combine the best of both systems.

Of course, my fantasy is not realistic today. Such an exchange never happens when people are acting out of fear—not between countries, not between parents and children, and not between men and women.

The developmental gift that comes from confronting one's own most frightening dragons—whether one slays them or merely stands up to them and begins a dialogue—is *courage* and a corresponding freedom from bondage to one's fears. At best the Warrior ultimately learns to make friends with fear by long acquaintance. Instead of being immobilized by it, or coming on like Atilla the Hun, or becoming locked into a paranoid, simplistic mode of addressing problems or even repressing it, the hero comes to see that fear is always an invitation to growth.

One of my favorite examples of a hero who develops such a positive relationship with her fear comes from Susan Griffin's *Women and Nature*. Griffin writes of "an old woman who was wicked in her honesty," who would ask questions of her mirror. When she asks why she is afraid of the dark, her mirror tells her, "Because you have reason to fear. You are small and you might be devoured." The woman determines to become too large to be devoured. But then she discovers that she is afraid to be so big, and the mirror explains, "There is no disputing who you are. And it is not easy for you to hide." The woman then stops hiding. During her next attack of fear, the mirror tells her that she is afraid "because...no one else sees what you see, no one else can tell you if what you see is true." Then she decides to trust herself.

Many years later she realizes she is afraid of birthdays, and her mirror tells her "there is something you have always wanted to do which you have been afraid of doing and you know time is running out." The woman goes immediately away from her mirror to "seize the time."

Over time, she and her mirror become friends and the mirror would weep for her in compassion when her fears were real. Finally, her reflection asked her, "What do you still fear?" And the old woman answered, "I still fear death. I still fear change." And her mirror agreed. "Yes, they are frightening. Death is a closed door," the mirror flourished, "and change is a door hanging open." "Yes, but fear is a key," laughed the wicked old woman, "and we still have our fears." She smiled.[7]

When Warriors become less frightened, their thinking can relax and open to complexity; it then becomes clear how limited the hero/villain/victim formulation of reality is. Tom Robbins' wonderful novel *Even Cowgirls Get the Blues* illustrates this. The Cowgirls of the Rubber Rose Ranch have taken on the shoot-out at the O.K. Corral mentality of the wild-west cowboy. They are preparing to shoot it out with the G-Men. The G-Men have been sent by the U.S. government ostensibly to rescue the Whooping Cranes who are vacationing on the Rubber Rose property, but they really plan to kill these birds. The Cowgirls see themselves as defending the birds (and with them, nature) against the assaults of patriarchal civilization. At the last moment, the leader of the Cowgirls has a vision from the Great Goddess herself, who tells her they should run away. For one thing, there is no way they can defeat the G-Men. The contest is too uneven, but she also calls into question the whole concept of villains and heroes. The enemy of women, she explains, is not men, just as the enemy of blacks is not whites. The enemy is "the tyranny of the dull mind."[8]

The vision interrupts their normal hero/villain/victim way of seeing the world. Note that the battle here is against an abstraction, not people, and that kind of battle requires a different plot. The answer is not to slay anything, but to create something new—in this case, new ways of formulating questions and seeking answers. Furthermore, when thinking becomes reasonably complex, the whole cast of characters is redefined. What does the hero do when the villain is redefined not as a dragon to slay, but as "the tyranny of the dull mind"? Neither violence nor conversion is appropriate. Instead, we need enough imagination to grapple with difference without imposing on it notions of good and bad, better or worse.

The motivation to think more complexly and imaginatively in solving conflict comes from a variety of sources. Sometimes the challenge is forced upon us when we experience the villain as too big to fight. Perhaps this is why women have not taken particularly to combat: Men are physically stronger! Gandhi came up with a more complex and successful approach to liberating India than the typical call to arms because the British had such an incredible military advantage. Combat was not feasible as a way to win the battle.

The outsider almost always comes to understand that those in power consciously or unconsciously rig the contest. Affirmative action, as typically practiced, means that women and minorities, to be seen as worthy, are expected to live up to a pattern designed by white men in their own image. Ultimately, those against whom the contest is rigged lose faith in the contest—even if there are a few visible tokens who do make it. It is not only women and minorities who are losing faith in the shoot-out at the O.K. Corral method, but white men as well. This is happening not only because today's problems seem so overwhelming to white men, too, and so unresponsive to violent solutions, but also because the former damsel-in-distress has redefined herself and is taking her own journey.

One of the major formative experiences for the protagonist of John Irving's *Hotel New Hampshire* is the gang rape of his sister. He is powerless to protect her as a teenager, when it happens, but afterwards he takes up weightlifting. He clearly is determined to be powerful enough to defend her in the future. However, many years later, when he meets the initiator of the gang rape, he does not know what to do, partly because he realizes he does not know what his sister Franny would want him to do. In a moment of anger, he picks up her former attacker, Chipper Dove, and then just puts him down.

He does so because he thinks of Franny not as a classic damsel-in-distress but as a peer, a hero in her own right. So instead of rescuing her, he backs her up as *she* gets revenge on Chipper Dove. It is, he realizes, her story, her tragedy, and ultimately her fight, not his. Because he loves her, however, he helps her.

What he learns is that, even then, revenge is not the answer. It does not take away the pain, and he is left forever with that sense of powerlessness, a sense that he cannot protect the people he loves—one of the hardest lessons for men, trained as they are to find a sense of esteem and identity through the role of protector. He explains, "I would feel, for the rest of my life, as if I were still holding Chipper Dove by his armpits—his feet a few inches above the ground of Seventh Avenue. There was really nothing to do with him except put him down; there never would be anything to do with him, too—with our Chipper Doves we just go on picking them up and putting them down, forever."[9] Irving's hero moves away from warrioring into a more generative mode and devotes his life to caring for his father, supporting his wife's shelter for victims of rape and battering, and finally raising his sister Franny's child. For many men, learning to nurture and care for and, in doing so, gaining an identity that is less confined by the culture's more stereotyped images of masculinity makes it possible to move on to more complex ways of warrioring and provides the prerequisites for becoming Magicians.

The failure of skill and courage for the Warrior also can lead to moments of transcendence and spiritual surrender. Tom Brown, Jr., writes in *The Search* about going into the forest with only the clothes on his back and a knife and not coming out for a year. He was prepared for the year by Stalking Wolf, a Native American teacher, who taught him to be a tracker. He managed not only to survive—even a very hard, cold winter—but to enjoy the time thoroughly.

The most rewarding experience came near the end of his sojourn in the forest when he went on a very long fast. After twelve days, he was about to start eating again when something strange happened. None of his skills served him. For seven more days, every animal he tried to stalk eluded him, and he feared he would starve to death. He was very weak and began to have fainting spells when he had a clear chance of killing a small animal, but his hand stopped and would not move. At that point, he gave up and just surrendered:

Something, some other force, was in charge of my limbs. Or was it? Perhaps there was a deeper level of my consciousness that was now in control of my body, that knew, that realized more than my logical, trained consciousness could ever understand. And that was that I had nothing to fear. That what I must do is wait and surrender myself to the earth around me. To give in to what I was and had always been—and that was not a conquering pioneer. I did not have to give up, only give in. To flow with the spirit of my surroundings. To be different from, and yet a part of the earth. Give *in*. Give *in*. Become…You are it and it is you, and we are all one entity. Like the ant and the bird. Like the leaves and the mulch. Like the earth.[10]

This experience of surrender to himself and to the knowledge of oneness brings him exquisite joy. In the next instant a deer almost walks up to him. He kills it and eats a feast of thanksgiving.

This moment of letting go is not always so transcendent. Sometimes it is motivated by powerlessness, by the heart attack, by loss of a loved one, by a tragic event, and there is nothing to do but accept it. Sometimes it is only maturity and the knowledge that none of the Warrior's skills are effective against death that force the Warrior to "give in" to greater life.

Warriors become burned out because they live life as a struggle against others and against parts of themselves they see as unworthy. I have seen so many men and women finally realize how the struggle to be one up ultimately was killing them—their souls and their heart, and sometimes also their bodies. (Maybe the reason women live longer than men is that they spend less of their lives warrioring.) Warriors who once felt such justifiable pride and exuberance over their attainment of the ability to take charge of their lives and make things happen, years later begin to feel exhausted and drained. The transformation for many occurs when they start looking at all the strategies they are using just to keep going: addictions to caffeine, uppers, alcohol, or simply mobilizing their fear of failure to keep them racing onward and upward. In the latter case, a healthy desire to achieve has become obsessive and addictive. What they need then is to admit their ordinary human vulnerability, their need for love, for other people, for spiritual and physical sustenance and nurturance.

Warriors first develop confidence by proving their superiority to others, because they have taken more control over their own lives than most and can make things happen while others seem to wait passively for things to happen to them. One of the gifts, then, when control fails is the dawning recognition that fundamentally we are not that different from one another. We are all in the same boat, and we are all, ultimately, interdependent: We need other people; we need the earth; we need God.

The Warrior Lover

When Warriors give over control—as Tom Brown does in *The Search*—they move beyond the one up/one down view of life. The only reason to want to be one up is a belief that it is not fine to be just ordinary. Previously, not being special or different was equated with the Orphan's powerlessness, and therefore seemed contemptible to Warriors. In recognizing oneness with the earth and interdependence with other people, they come to honor humanness in people who are in control of their lives and also in those who have given over the control or have had it wrested from them. When heroes give up the need to be better than, they stop having to prove themselves all the time and can, at least occasionally, just *be*.

It is symbolically important that at the end of the old heroic myth, after he has confronted his fear by slaying the dragon, the Warrior comes home and marries. The reward for his battle is that he becomes, finally, a lover. Without the skills of assertion and boundary-setting, there can be no really peer love relationship. Otherwise, one person simply conquers and the other appeases. These skills allow for the creation of a positive relationship with another human being, with institutions, and with the world in general, and ultimately make it possible to love and savor life itself.

Many of the great lovers of literature began by quarreling with one another—for example, William Shakespeare's Beatrice and Benedict (*Much Ado About Nothing*), Jane Austen's Darcy and Elizabeth (*Pride and Prejudice*). They each had the strength, self-respect, and facility for assertion that allowed them to negotiate a mutually satisfactory relationship. Healthy intimacy demands the daily, hourly assertion of who you are and what you want and a willingness to look at how conflicting desires can come together to create a mutually enriching life.

So, too, in business or with friends. You have only part of the equation if you invent a better mousetrap but cannot market it. Being good at your work is only one step toward job satisfaction. The next step is to see that you are appreciated, respected, and rewarded for your work, and that requires an ability to negotiate and to influence your world—to bridge with other people and with institutions.

The first few times Warriors try asserting their own wishes they inevitably will engage in overkill and therefore not get very good results. However, at the next stage, they learn to be more subtle and politic and get what they want more often. Ultimately, however, warriors give over control of the outcome and assert themselves as part of the dance of life. The process of assertion then becomes its own reward because it makes them daily more themselves.

It is then that miracles begin to happen. Often after they have let go of their attachment to a particular outcome, when they have put themselves and their desires out there with no attendant wish to manipulate people or make people satisfy them, Warriors discover that the results are better than they even dared hope for. It is at this point that Buddhist notions of nonattachment and Christian or Jewish mystic beliefs about transcending ego begin to make sense and to be useful to the hero.

Warriors who have proven their ability to defend themselves and fight for what they want tend to be respected and to respect themselves. They can negotiate a way to be true to themselves and to lovers, friends, colleagues, and institutions. Life at this point is not as painful as it once was. Warriors now are ready to lay down their arms and become lovers, and to savor the life they have made, honoring and loving themselves, other people, and the earth.

As we first experience the power of the archetype of the Warrior, we take up arms to defend ourselves and to fight for what we want. As we learn the warrior's lessons more fully, all this seems remote to us, and we are likely to assert, as did a bumper sticker I saw recently, "Arms are for hugging."

Chapter 5

THE MARTYR

Perhaps the dress of flesh
is no more than a familiar garment
that grows looser as one diets
on death, & perhaps we discard it
or give it to the poor in spirit,
who have not learned yet
what blessing it is
to go naked?

—ERICA JONG, *"Is Life the Incurable Disease?"*

The basic plot of the martyr archetype is enacted in ancient rituals of sacrifice in fertility religions. As such, it speaks to us about the cycle of nature, which moves from birth in the spring to summer ripeness, fall harvest, and winter desolation and death. The old Dionysian rites, for instance, included dismembering the god and dispersing his parts until nothing of him seemed left. Basic to every fertility religion is the knowledge that death and sacrifice are prerequisite to rebirth. This is a basic law of the natural and the spiritual worlds.

While the Orphan seeks rescue from suffering, the Martyr embraces it, believing it will bring redemption. The rags-to-riches plots and romantic love stories discussed earlier, along with gothic novels, saints' lives, and other similar genres, all dramatize and reinforce this belief. So do our major religions. As Carol Ochs argues in *Behind the Sex of God*, the central stories of Judaism and Christianity—Abraham's willingness to sacrifice Isaac and God the Father's willingness to sacrifice Christ—dramatize the healing power of martyrdom.[1]

If love for one's child is great, sacrificing that child is the ultimate sacrifice, greater even than dying oneself. Taken metaphorically, the willingness to sacrifice one's "child" also may represent a movement beyond the narcissistic egocentricity of the Orphan that requires us to learn to give and care not only when it is easy but also when it is hard, when it feels as if giving is at one's own expense.

Sacrifice and martyrdom have received much bad press lately, whether in the male or female mode, yet there is hardly a soul who does not believe in it in some form. At its base is a recognition that "I am not the only person in the world." Sometimes I choose to do something not so much because I want to, but because it will be good for someone else or because I believe it to be right. Some sacrifice is necessary in order to interact lovingly with other people.

Sacrifice as Self-Abnegation

There are two major reasons for our distrust of martyrdom—besides the basic human distaste for suffering. Most of the martyrdom we see around us is at a very rudimentary level of development— pseudo-martyrdom, really. The stereotype of the American mom or the Jewish mother reflects in exaggerated form the destructive effects of being prematurely assigned to the Martyr role with no permission to find oneself or to fight for what you yourself want. Its results are bitterness, manipulation, and a general sense of guilt and dis-ease.

Women are particularly suspicious of the glorification of sacrifice because they have done more than their rightful share of it, to the exclusion of their growth in other areas. At some point the culture's tasks became divided up. Men were expected to compete in a marketplace metaphorically envisioned as a "jungle" and to fight when necessary to protect hearth and home. Women were expected to create a world marked by care and gentleness in the home. The creation of the private sanctuary from the storm was dependent upon sacrifice—not only the necessary sacrifices required by raising children, but more than that. Because men had opted out of the world of care for the world of conquest, women were expected to supply the care for both of them.

The sacrifice of women's development in this scheme until recently has been seen as redemptive for both men and women. Of course, this arrangement has been crippling to women because, instead of sacrifice being just one developmental task, it has defined their whole lives. Furthermore, the mythos of love and sacrifice has been used to *keep* women in traditional and limited roles. Consequently, the women's movement has not been very respectful in its rhetoric towards sacrifice; yet martyrdom has informed much of the behavior in the movement—just as in many other revolutionary movements.

For example, Eleanor Smeal, president of NOW, said in an interview in the *Cincinnati Enquirer* (3/18/83) that she understands the workers in the women's movement because she is one of them: "I know why people make the 100,000th phone call even though they're so tired they want to drop. I know about loyalty. I know why this movement was their life and is their life. The 'oomph' in the movement is people caring. When that stops, the women's movement will stop." The reporter notes that something about this woman with a "perpetually tired voice touches people."

What we see here is women sacrificing in a Martyr mode that is more typically male—working tirelessly and at whatever cost to one's health or happiness for one's country, company, or cause. And, of course, women run the risk of experiencing the same problems men have, of giving for a cause or an abstraction without specific attention to the impact of their actions on individuals. For instance, a parent works all the time to provide a good future for his or her child, but never really knows the child; a politician works for "the people" but really has contempt for ordinary people who do not have power and connections.

For women in our culture, sacrifice has been accorded a value in itself. It is not just sacrifice for someone or something, but suffering itself, especially for love, that is redemptive. Traditional literature has encouraged this attitude. Chaucer's Patient Griselda of the *Canterbury Tales*, for instance, is portrayed as a perfect medieval wife. She continues to be loving to her lord (her husband) even when he sets her aside, brings in a new wife, and pretends to have killed her children. Throughout all this she patiently serves him. He finally sees her worth, proclaims her the ideal wife, sends away the other woman, brings back her children, and they live happily ever after.[2]

For many people in real life, however, sacrifice is not rewarded in this storybook way. The wife may sacrifice continually, hoping to win the approval and love of her husband or children, yet find she is taken increasingly for granted. The employee may give up his weekends and evenings to the company without any reward. Indeed, often people watching a Martyr cut into themselves to do for others assume they have no self-esteem and treat them accordingly.

Many religious people try to be really "good" to please God. They assume that if they do so they will be spared the trials and pains other people experience in their lives. When this turns out not to be the case, they may become disillusioned and lose their faith—declaring that God is dead—or instead intensify their efforts, trying to convert others, to stamp out sin within and without—all in the hope of finding for themselves some exemption from life's suffering. Martyrs have learned that more is required of life than waiting passively for rescue. They believe that salvation must be earned by suffering and hard work. In this initial way, Martyrs work very hard to please God, their employers, their mates. What they want is love and esteem. Their efforts are a conscious or unconscious attempt to earn whatever they so desperately need. When they feel this way, it never occurs to them that they may deserve to have love and respect simply by the fact of their being alive, so they bargain. The contemporary film *Amadeus* illustrates this tendency in pathological extreme. Salieri, the protagonist of the film, bargains with God while a boy, saying he will give his industry, obedience, and chastity if God will make him a great composer. He becomes a good composer and is very pleased with himself and with God—until he meets Mozart. Mozart is disobedient, disrespectful, undisciplined, and certainly not chaste, yet when he composes he does not even have to make corrections. Salieri concludes that God has made the infamous Mozart into a divine instrument instead of the virtuous Salieri. The injustice is too much for Salieri to bear, so he declares war on Mozart and on God.

This mentality, which informs the first stage of martyrdom for most people, is really pseudo-martyrdom. The actions are sacrificial, the form is right, but the goal is the same as the Orphan's—to find a way to be saved. In this mode, Martyrs not only feel deprived most of the time because they are sacrificing parts of themselves in an effort to get validation from God or from other people, but, like Salieri, they often also are angry. It is essential to them that other people follow the same rules they have bought into because they cannot fully believe their sacrifices will work for them unless the same system works for other people. They need the unmarried pregnant woman to suffer (they may outlaw abortion, for instance) or their chastity will seem less virtuous; they need welfare chiselers to be punished or their hard work seems meaningless. Their worst fury, like Salieri's, goes toward those who flout the rules and still seem to flourish. And they make it their business to see that they do not flourish long. At this level, they need to see others punished to believe that their goodness will bring an exemption for them.

Even worse, martyrdom often is used to camouflage cowardice. Martyrs can hide behind this mask of being good and unselfish as a way to avoid taking their journeys, finding out who they are, or taking a stand. Much of the appeal of traditional sex roles, especially as they act themselves out in marriage relationships, is that the partners need not know who they are. Moreover, since the roles are so completely elaborated culturally, it is not necessary to become truly intimate and know one another. It is all very good and safe, and quite deadly to the process of individuation.

The reason martyrdom is such a trap for women is that it gets them off the hook on the issue of personal growth and of making a significant contribution to the world. When they fear they are not good enough or that they will be punished by the culture for having the audacity to declare themselves heroes with journeys to take, women can take refuge in the apparent virtue of self-sacrifice.

If a woman is having trouble in her career—if she fears failure, for instance, or if she has trouble with the Warrior culture she finds in the male work world, or if she is exhausted because she is doing all the housework in addition to her career—she has the option of a seemingly virtuous escape and may decide to quit and stay home with her children. While in some cases it certainly is appropriate to decide to stay home with a child or to take care of elderly or infirm people, it is not honest to use them as excuses for the fear of failure, for not asserting one's own needs and values in the workplace, or for not insisting that one's partner or family share responsibility for domestic tasks. Similarly, in Washington, D.C., these days virtually every man who resigns from high office announces he wants to go back to private life to spend more time with his family. While in some cases this may be true, it also is true that this "mom and apple pie" statement frees him from having to declare the real reasons he is leaving, whether they be political disagreements with the White

House, disgust with a situation, or failure to assert that men in government also have the right to time with their families.

Transformative Sacrifice

Sacrifice is not always a way to manipulate God or other people into giving you what you want or a way of avoiding challenge, risk, and pain; it also can be given freely as an expression of genuine love and care. At a higher level, the Martyr is not trying to bargain to save self but believes that the sacrifice of the self will save others. This is what the Christ story is about: sacrificing to save others. Accordingly, God so loved the world that Jesus—God's own son—was sacrificed in a most brutal way to atone for human sin and to open the gates of heaven to us. Similarly, the proponents of modern existentialist thought, finding no inherent meaning in life's suffering, often urge social action and putting aside instant gratification of whims in favor of working to make the world a better place for us all. This same impulse is there in parents who see little hope of improving their own lives but who then sacrifice to make a better life for their children.

The decision to care, even at the cost of self-sacrifice, is a choice here for life and against despair. It also is the dominant spiritual lesson people have been working on for thousands of years and, as we have seen, it is the essence of Christianity and Judaism, as well as much of leftist and liberal politics.

I was talking recently with a friend about this book, and he said that to him the hero is someone who has endured life's trials and tribulations. When pressed, he explained he meant something more than that. Heroes, he continued, not only endure hardships, they maintain their love of life, their courage, and their capacity to care for others. No matter how much suffering they experience, they do not pass it on to others. They absorb it and declare: Suffering stops here.

For some people, the movement from gratuitous suffering to sacrifice in the name of care provides a major sense of pride and self-esteem and is the transition point out of the Orphan stage. A woman might explain to herself or to others that she would not have abortions, leave her children in daycare, or neglect her husband to selfishly pursue a career; her husband might explain that he does not run around on his wife like other guys, cheat in business, or neglect his children, even though in doing so he has lost many opportunities for fun and profit.

In the primitive Martyr's morality, it is appropriate for mothers to sacrifice for their children. Their daughters, in turn, will sacrifice for theirs. Fathers and sons are expected to give their lives willingly, if called, for their country. Everyone sacrifices themselves to God, or more precisely they sacrifice those parts of themselves that are seen as wrong or sinful in the service of good. There is nothing much going on but sacrifice. It has become an end in itself and, hence, does nothing to improve the world. Indeed, it usually adds to the world's cumulative pain.

Such is the situation in Joseph Heller's *Catch-22*. Yossarian, the central character, comes to see the social system he lives in (the army during World War II) as defined entirely by suffering and with every victim victimizing someone else: "Someone had to do something sometime. Every victim was a culprit, every culprit a victim, and somebody had to stand up sometime to try to break the lousy chain of inherited habit that was imperiling them all."[3] Although he has been told he is flying bombing missions to save home and country, he comes to recognize that he is really doing so to save Milo Minderbinder's international business interests. So he stops flying. Yossarian knows that he cannot necessarily be free, since the army can court-martial him. However, instead of the meaningless affliction of flying more missions, this refusal can have some positive effect. At the very least, he is living by his own values and has regained his integrity. At most, other people may refuse to fly more bombing missions too. Then the chain of suffering may be broken.

Yossarian comes to understand that the sacrifices he has been forced to make not only are not transformative, they are actively destructive to himself and to others. As long as he keeps flying bombing missions, he complies with the forces that are killing people needlessly on both sides. The choice to say "no" also requires sacrifice—perhaps of an honorable discharge and hence of respect and career opportunities back home; yet this sacrifice *is* transformative because it is an appropriate and courageous response to the actual needs of his specific situation.

Such is the transformative sacrifice of our great political and religious martyrs, who genuinely give their lives to make the world a better place. Equally ennobling are acts by which people risk their own lives to save others. For example, a few years ago a passenger on an airliner that crashed into the Potomac in a snowstorm stayed in the water and helped save the lives of several fellow passengers. He eventually succumbed to exhaustion and hypothermia and drowned.

We see this kind of ennobling sacrifice not only in people who die to save others but also in those who spend their whole lives helping them. I think of famous examples, such as Mother Teresa of India; but I also think of the many people who take jobs that in our society are not very rewarding in terms of pay or chance for promotion, simply because they care. They may be working in day-care facilities, in homes for the aged, in community organizing, or in many other places that make such a difference in the lives of people. Few may know who they are, but they daily make the world a better place to be in.

Although rewards may not translate into material wealth or power in the world, genuine sacrifice is tranformative and not maiming. How can you tell whether you are giving appropriately? When you are, doing so feels compatible with your identity, an outgrowth of who you are. Ultimately, we know who we are by what we would die for. Great martyrs like Martin Luther King, Jr., for instance, so believed in themselves and their cause or principles that they knowingly risked death rather than the soul-harming living death of being less than they could be. So, too, Mother Teresa. She works with the homeless and dying because that is who she is. For many of us, making decisions about when and how much to sacrifice helps us learn who we are.

Sacrifice and Identity

The capacity to sacrifice, like any skill, always needs some fine tuning. It is one thing to sacrifice briefly one's sleep to comfort a child with a bad dream; it is quite another for a mother to sacrifice her whole career for a child. It is one thing for a father to sacrifice his desire to go fishing today because he needs to go to work to feed the family; it is quite another to work for forty years at a job he hates. There are, of course, times, places, and situations in which such extreme sacrifices are called for—and when (rarely) they are genuinely necessary, they can be ennobling. But often such massive sacrifice, if not a result of cowardice, comes from an inability to discriminate between giving that is necessary and life-giving and giving that brings death to the Martyr and hence to those around him or her.

There is a thin line between giving and unhealthy "enabling" (i.e., supporting someone else's dependency or irresponsibility). Sometimes we persist in giving to people who use our gifts and energy only to help themselves continue in a destructive pattern. This behavior is demonstrated most clearly by an enabler-addict symbiotic relationship in which one person seems totally selfless, helping the other, but actually is making it possible for the other to persist in a deadly habit such as a chemical addiction or other self-destructive actions. This also may be the case in less extreme form with parents who continue to support children financially long after they should be supporting themselves. Enabling is evident in the oft-repeated situation of the housewife who takes care of everything so her husband can continue his workaholic behavior. It also is characteristic of traditional husbands who discourage their wives from working or even driving—promising to take care of them and hence stunting their development.

An easy litmus test can determine whether one is giving or enabling. If, when we give, we feel either used or smugly superior, it is time to look at what really is going on. Healthy giving is respectful of both the giver and the receiver. If Martyrs do not acknowledge that other able-bodied adults are capable of taking care of themselves, they are crippling them. If they use giving to feel superior, then they really are masking their own sense of inadequacy, something that must be attended to. Otherwise they will have a vested interest in keeping other people dependent for the satisfaction of feeling needed and important. And, finally, if Martyrs think giving is more virtuous than receiving, they are likely to give inappropriately and also to block the gifts they do receive, so they always feel shortchanged.

At best we do not sacrifice ourselves for others; we help others and we sharpen and define ourselves as we make choices. We sacrifice some things we could be for other things, and in this way create, carve out a self, an identity. If I go to the store and see something that both my friend Elissa and I would like and buy us both one, that is giving but it is not sacrifice. But what if I have only enough money to buy one? Then I am faced with a hard choice. Will I sacrifice my own longing for it and buy it for Elissa, or will I buy it for myself? Either way I have to give up something—either the item or the experience of pleasing my friend. Making a choice in a situation of scarcity—whether of money, goods, or time—helps me define what is most important to me at the time and hence to know more about who I am. In that sense, I win whichever way I choose, if I choose honestly and not out of a sense of what I ought to do.

Many concepts about sacrifice in our culture are confusing because our language and our attention focus on the outer forms of things. Consider two mothers who decide to forgo their careers to devote themselves to raising their children. On the surface, both seem to have sacrificed a career to motherhood. But when we look deeper we learn that the process was very different for each of them.

Suzanne was a statistician. She loved her work and was just beginning to develop her skill and her reputation. When she found herself pregnant she was torn because she believed a mother should stay home with her child; but she really wanted to work. In the end, she decided to choose the child's welfare over her own and stayed home, all the while longing for the time when she could go back to work.

Madeleine, on the other hand, was a big-time journalist. People were amazed when she gave up a thriving career to stay home with her son. The truth was that she felt she had *done* journalism, that she had learned all she could there for now. Indeed, in her way of looking at things she had developed her "masculine" side, and she wanted to develop her "feminine," nurturing side. She was, she noted, really tough. Now she wanted to learn to be more gentle. A few years later when she went back to work her stories had a new depth to them, and her toughmindedness was mixed with a fuller humanity, a greater depth of compassion.

It is clear, here, how Madeleine's relatively painless sacrifice is congruent with her individuation process. However, so is Suzanne's.

She discovers in this more painful way that she is a person who believes staying home with one's children is more important than having a career. If she takes responsibility for this choice as her own, it also can be a big step forward in her life. Or if she later discovers that it was not a free choice but simply a conditioned one, she will have learned and can make new choices. However, if she does not take responsibility, in either case, for her choice and for its consequences, she may become destructive to herself and others by becoming bitter, by blaming her husband (instead of taking a stand with him if necessary to support her new choice), or by blaming her child. Then both pay.

Appropriate sacrifice gives Martyrs a deeper knowledge of their values and commitments to work and to others and hence makes them more, not less, themselves. Conversely, inappropriate sacrifice makes them lose touch with themselves and with the capacity for love, intimacy, or the joy of connection. The result is a tendency to vicarious experience, to substitute someone else's identity for their own. Thus, it becomes critical that the other person live up to their expectations.

For example, parents who give up their lives for their children almost always demand tribute—that the child give his or her life to validate or justify the parent's sacrifice by being successful, dutiful, attentive. Children then are not allowed just to be themselves. But if the parents' giving has been appropriate, reflecting what they also needed to do for themselves, then they do not need tribute, even though they undoubtedly will appreciate their children's love and gratitude.

I remember a newspaper story not too long ago that moved me profoundly. A couple had lost their adolescent son. When interviewed, they emphasized not their incredible loss, but their gratefulness at having had him for sixteen years. They did not have to see him grown and successful to feel their efforts and probably appreciable sacrifices had "paid off." The experience of parenting him was its own reward.

Similarly, I was talking recently with a friend who is a massage therapist. She said she became aware that she had been sending out signals to people that she wanted them to show appreciation for her work by telling her how great she was. She felt she was giving so much to her work that she wanted something back beyond the fee she charged. Then it came to her that she loved her work. It was the work of her heart. Doing massage was its own reward. Later she came to see that she also had a perfect right to want and get praise. As her self-confidence grew, she found appreciation all around her. It was her original fear that she would not be cared about that caused her to try to control the outcome of her efforts. When her faith in herself and the universe grew, she could both give for the sake of giving and know she always would have everything she needed— enough money, friends, love, and appreciation.

When we look at the profound impact martyrs like Christ or Gandhi have had on the world, it is understandable that some people respond by glorifying martyrdom itself. At a more complex level of analysis, however, one need not conclude that their example requires the rest of us to be martyred. There are many different missions, many different paths. For Christ, dying freely for love's sake was a fulfillment of his life. For another person, martyrdom might be an escape from the tough demands of life. The beginning of wisdom is being able to distinguish between transformative sacrifice and mere suffering caused because we are too cowardly or too unimaginative to think of a more joyous way to live.

Some sacrifice is required for life. The birth of every child is attended by pain. For the mother, it is the pain of labor; for the child, the torturous journey through the birth canal into a strange world. We cannot become adults without leaving behind childhood, and we cannot move beyond this world without dying. The price of making a commitment to another person, a cause, a work is a loss of freedom of all the other possible choices you could be making. As Janice Joplin sang in "Me and Bobby McGee": "Freedom's just another word for nothing left to lose." The only way to be totally free is not to commit, but then we have nothing.

Behind much of asceticism is a superstitious belief that if we do not really live this life, we will not have to die. Beauty, sensuality, passion, all are suspect because they seduce us from focusing on the timeless beauty of God by enamoring us with earthly beauty. Ascetics and all the rest of us who have fears about fully experiencing life, then, fail to receive it and hold ourselves apart from its blessings. Deep in the human psyche is the fear that we will pay dearly for our pleasures. This is blatant, certainly, in fundamental Protestantism and Catholicism, in which pleasures of the flesh potentially can result in eternal damnation!

We have been taught that we must give back, and give back in predetermined ways. Or we fail to take in all that is given to us because we have defined giving as virtuous and taking as selfish and Orphan-like. Our self-esteem comes from being virtuously altruistic, so we block out our awareness of how much we receive daily. To give well, we also must receive well. We cannot have one without the other.

Once we define ourselves as the giver in a particular situation or relationship, we may not notice how much we also receive. This is particularly true for parents. I remember one day I had gone over my limit giving to my daughter. I came home from a particularly intense day at work, made her a quick bite to eat, and rushed to get her and her friend to their gymnastics lesson. The lessons were too far from home to come back, so I waited, hungry and tired, for an hour and a half, bit my tongue when she fooled around after practice, rushed home, got her bathed and dressed for bed, and read a story. I still had not had time to eat or change out of my business clothes.

When she then demanded in a rather whiny voice that I also sing her to sleep, I said rather crossly, "I'm tired. You have to think of me sometimes, too." As she turned over to go to sleep, she reached over, touched my cheek with her little hand, and said, "Mom, I always think of you." There was such love in her voice that I felt fully seen and loved by her. Certainly that was as great a gift as my taking her to her lessons and making her dinner. But had I been attached to the idea of my martyrdom as a mother, I could not have let in her love and her simple, honest way of giving it to me. Then I still would have felt depleted instead of suddenly quite full.

Bringing her up, too, I have reconnected with the little girl in me, learned to play again, and experienced daily delight and love. When I fully let that in, I know that she has brought at least as much to me as I have shared with her. Very few of our relationships really have to be one way. Therapists learn from their clients; teachers learn from their students; ministers learn from their congregations. When the energy is not flowing both ways, something is wrong. If the giving and receiving happen with no blocking, then both receive more than they give—for the process intensifies and enriches the energy exchanged. Learning to give or to sacrifice appropriately is certainly as hard as learning to play baseball. Our first attempts are always very clumsy. People misinterpret and think we want something in return. Or, like the mother who gives up her career or the father who works in a field he hates to support his family, we overdo it. As we become better at it, our giving and receiving take on the effortlessness of real pros playing catch. It all seems easy—throwing and catching and letting go again.

Our first sacrifices seem wrenched from us, as if we gave up primary parts of ourselves. Later we learn that it never is appropriate to give up what is essential to us. The things we appropriately sacrifice always should be the things we are ready to let go of. For most people, sacrifice is painful because they feel they have to control or manipulate everything if the ball is ever to come back to them. And, if they think that having thrown the ball to first base they have to get it back from first base, they may be sorely disappointed. But sooner or later—from third base or left field—the ball returns. Indeed, when they let go of notions about the particular form blessings must take, affirming instead that they will have what they need, they find themselves besieged with balls.

The more we give in this kind of free way, the more we get—because nature abhors a vacuum; it fills us up. That is, it does unless we have misunderstood sacrifice and see the state of emptying out as a static good rather than only a stage in the process. Then we get what we asked for—emptiness, depletion.

When we learn both to take and to give, we can move into a flow of giving and receiving that is love's essence—reciprocity. In this way, the flow of energy does not go just one way, but both. I give to you and you to me and we both fully receive the energy. Christ said to "love your neighbor as yourself." Sacrifice, however, has been misinterpreted as loving your neighbor *instead* of yourself.

For sacrifice or anything to be transformative, it must be let in. That is why Christ asked his disciples before the crucifixion to celebrate communion "in remembrance of me." That also is why the Hebrews were enjoined to eat special Passover foods to celebrate the Exodus from Egypt. Eating is a powerful symbol for taking a gift in, for no gift truly is one until it is received.

Like giving, receiving takes some skill and discretion. Some people block their gifts even though they are besieged with them because they do not know that they have volition about receiving. They think just because something is offered to them, they must take it, so they feel safer in ignoring it. Sophisticated receiving raises the hard issue of choice, and of taking responsibility for having chosen to let in one thing and not another. Yes, I will marry you, but not you. Yes, I will work with you, but not you.

Sometimes we are not able to receive gifts because we are afraid that in receiving them, we have obligated ourselves to pay the giver back. This kind of contractual giving may be a form of manipulation. We can use our intuition and turn down gifts with inappropriate strings attached, but we also should be aware that sometimes we simply project our fears onto the giver.

Communication in relationships vastly improves when we make our expectations explicit to our loved ones. Because almost everyone gives what they would like to receive without realizing that the other person may want something very different, it is most useful to talk about those expectations. I once was in a relationship with a man who felt I did not really love him because I did not do little things for him like sew buttons on his shirt. When he told me this I got angry because I thought he was being a male chauvinist. Later, I realized that it was not so much that he wanted me to be conventionally female but that his idea of how you show love was doing little things like that for one another. Because my idea of how you show love is to say, "I love you" and share the secrets of one's heart, I felt unloved by him—not recognizing that he showed his love for me by returning my overdue library books! To stay together we would have had to learn each other's giving vocabulary.

Commitment

For many, even the thought of making a major commitment to someone else raises major fears. For example, it might be nice to marry this person, but what if I find someone later whom I like better? Or what if he leaves me? What if he is unsuccessful? What if she turns out like her mother? What if she gets cancer and I have to take care of her? To commit is to risk the unknown, but even more than that, it is saying, as George implicitly tells Martha in Edward Albee's *Who's Afraid of Virginia Woolf?*, "Yes, this will do."[4] It is sacrificing the idea of the perfect mate for a real, flawed human being. When we do so honestly and freely, out of clear preference, the result can be transformative. If the commitment is reciprocal, it can make for a magic relationship of closeness and joy. If it is not, it still can be personally transformative because through it we learn the skill of loving fully and not holding back from that experience. And we learn we can survive the loss of what we love most.

So, too, with life. Commitment to living this life means giving up rigid ideas about what the world should be and loving what it is. That, of course, does not mean that we do not work to make the world a better place or that we do not work on our relationships. It means that we can give up the pose of being disappointed idealists and let ourselves know what a blessing it is to be incarnated on this planet. We allow ourselves to let it all in. It also means giving up the notion of scarcity: that there is not enough to go around and that I am not enough, you are not enough, and the world is not enough. In accepting life, we can believe that there is plenty of love, goods, room to be happy.

Ability to Give Away

When we learn to give and receive appropriately and skillfully, the result is miraculous. I had the opportunity a couple of years ago to participate in a Native American Give-Away Ceremony that allowed me to see how the process of letting go of what you no longer need and of giving to others what they need can come together magically and painlessly. We had been told before the ceremony to bring something that was very valuable to us (it need not have monetary value), something that we also were ready psychologically to give up and move beyond. We were to place this item on an altar. Then we all were to walk by and take whatever item beckoned to us. The miracle, we discovered as we discussed it later, was that everyone received just the right gift. What I learned from this experience was that miracles of synchronicity (meaningful coincidences) do occur— regularly!

We all can have enough if we do not hoard. Our job is to appreciate thoroughly and treasure whatever we truly want that we already have, and at the same time to give up anything we no longer need. *Our capacity to give away speaks to the universe of our willingness to receive.* We do not have to hold on to things, protecting ourselves against a rainy day. If we freely give away, we also will freely receive *just what we need.*

In the early 1970s, a scarcity of gasoline was threatened. Gas was perceived then as scarce even though there still was an adequate supply. People were stocking up out of fear. The fear that there would not be enough, ironically, was a self-fulfilling prophecy. When people believe there is enough and hence share freely, there *is* enough. What Franklin Roosevelt said in 1933 still is true: "The only thing we have to fear is fear itself."

Our capacity to receive life fully is psychologically related to our willingness to give what it requires of us: to love as fully as we can, even though we know that doing so opens us up to pain and sorrow; to live our vocational purpose, to do our work, even though we risk failure, poverty, or receiving little or no appreciation; and ultimately to die, for that is the price we pay for having lived.

Acceptance of Mortality

The Wanderer, the Warrior, and the Magician learn increasingly sophisticated lessons about ways to control their lives and destinies. Ironically, it is only when this control is achieved that the hero can let it go and learn the final lesson of martyrdom—the acceptance of mortality. Death is basic to nature. The leaves fall off the tree every autumn and make possible spring blossoms. All animal life, including humans, lives by eating other life forms. As much as we try to deny it, humans are part of the food chain. We eat plants and animals and excrete substances that fertilize the soil so that more plants can grow. Every life breath depends upon our symbiotic relationship with plants, with whom we exchange oxygen and carbon dioxide. In death, our bodies decay and fertilize the soil. This is the wisdom that fertility religions teach us.

This cosmic dance of birth and death, love and sacrifice, has little to do with ascetic practices that remove us from life. It speaks to us of Eros—passion. What it requires of us is abandonment of our fears of loss (including our fear of death) into the ecstasy of life and living. Aphrodite, Eros, Dionysus require of us our lives, but they offer earthly pleasure as well as divine, sexual as well as spiritual, and temporal as well as timeless. In this fertility drama, all our loves, even our lusts, are part of the process of cosmic transformation and rebirth. The gods love us not despite our mortality but, passionately, because of it.

Our lives are our contribution to the universe. We can give this gift freely and lovingly, or we can hold back as if it were possible by refusing life to avoid death. But no one can. How much worse to die, never having lived! The final lesson of the Martyr is to choose to give the gift of one's life for the giving's sake, knowing that life itself is its own reward and remembering that all the little deaths, the losses, in our lives always have brought with them transformation and new life, that actual deaths are not final but merely a more dramatic passage through into the unknown.

Until we are willing to give our lives to life, we always will be possessed by martyrdom. We may reject sacrifice philosophically, but we will find that inevitably we martyr ourselves to our wandering, to our warrioring, and even to our magic-making. The more freely and fearlessly we give, the less it feels like sacrifice and the more it feels simply like an expression of who we are. That is how we learn that, ultimately, we all are one and that what binds us together is love.

Chapter 6

THE MAGICIAN

She was the single artificer of the world
In which she sang. And when she sang, the sea,
Whatever self it had, became the self
That was her song, for she was the maker. Then we,
As we beheld her striding there alone,
Knew that there never was a world for her
Except the one she sang and, singing, made.
—WALLACE STEVENS, *"The Idea of Order at Key West"*

Every culture has a story about creation. A goddess lays the cosmic egg, or a god speaks the magic words, creating light. The archetype of the Magician teaches us about creation, about our capacity to bring into being what never was there before, about claiming our role as cocreators of the universe. This role, however, does not make us special or unique, since we share it not only with the gods, but also with the lowliest human, with plants, animals, mountains, stars—with everything and everyone. Yet however much our cocreation is interdependent with all these other cosmic actors, ultimately we do create our world and we are, therefore, responsible for our own lives.

When we enter the terrain of the Magician in our journey, after we have begun to take responsibility for our own lives and for our impact on the world, we discover that the Magician is not a shaman, witch, or wizard who sings a sacred song or concocts a sacred brew, whereupon a person is healed or killed, the war won or lost. That is a Magician from the Orphan's point of view. The Magician is not other, we discover, but ourselves. At this point, heroes come to believe that the universe is not a static thing. It is in the process of being created all the time. All of us are involved in that creation, and thus all of us are Magicians.

We cannot *not* be Magicians. We cannot live without ordering and arranging life. Yet, until we relinquish the Orphan's notion of the Magician as someone who does magic for you or someone who is evil and likely to victimize you, we cannot take responsibility for creating our lives. Until we grapple with our identity and vocation issues, there is always the danger that we will use our power destructively. And until we resolve our warrioring issues, we run the risk of using the power of the Magician to demonstrate our superiority or to try to control other people. The seductive idea that we can solve our problems by magic instead of taking our journeys has given the New Age movement (which has articulated widely the Magician's way of seeing the world) a bad name with some people— mainly because of a few folks associated with it who latch on to some of the Magician's concepts without understanding them fully. For instance, they misuse the notion of our responsibility for our lives by equating responsibility and blame, and then blame others for their problems. Some are developmentally at the Orphan stage, but seize on Magician concepts, hoping to escape, instead of to further, their journeys.

If we have not resolved our Martyr issues fully, it will be hard to experience fully the Magician's power, because doing so requires us to give our lives fearlessly to the universe, trusting that our gifts are the right ones, that we are what is needed by others, by the universe, and by ourselves. If we do not know this, we always will be mucking up the works by giving the wrong gifts, based not upon who we are but on some idea of who we should be.

As Orphans, Wanderers, Martyrs, and Warriors, we find our identities in opposition to a world imaged as hostile and dangerous. As Magicians, we claim the universe as home, a friendly, inviting place to be, and in doing so, we reclaim innocence. Our relationship with life, we learn, is like that with a potential lover. We move toward the relationship walking on the edge of our fear—Will I be safe? Will I be loved? Am I making a mistake? Is this the right one?— until little by little we discover that it is safe to trust and to let down our guard, to do the dance of life together.

The Magician learns that we are not life's victims; we are part of the unfolding of God. The resolution of the Warrior/Martyr duality, according to which we either take from life or give to it, is the understanding that each of us contributes to the unfolding of God, not by holding back our natures to live up to some ideal of perfection, but by allowing ourselves to be who we are, to love who and what we love, and to do the work that brings pleasure to our hearts and minds.

This means, however, giving up the illusion that we can force life to fit our own scripts, that we can shape up other people to match our idea of the perfect mate or friend or employee, or even that we can make ourselves fit our own images of what we should be. For Magicians and for Wanderers, life is an adventure of discovery. But Magicians take responsibility for the world they make, even inadvertently, blindly, by simply living their lives.

They are tough on themselves, but theirs is not the toughness of the Warrior. Warriors learn to force themselves to do what they are afraid of doing and they struggle against great odds. Magicians discover that, at a deeper level, force does not work, that if they are not flowing with the universe, but rather are struggling against it, no amount of perseverance, skill, courage, or wit will help them get what they want. They see that a new kind of discipline is required here, the clarity and strength of will to act always in accordance with their deepest, wisest self.

The discipline required to stay in touch with themselves at that level is certainly no less than that required by Warriors. Yet, this discipline operates in a context of humility and a certain positive fatalism. No matter what we want, if it is not to be, it will not be. Magicians know that they are not the center of the universe; yet that knowledge does not distress them. They know they are important, that their individual choices and acts accumulate to codesign the universe, and like the Martyr, they know that it is only in giving their unique gift to the universe that true happiness and satisfaction can be found.

While Warriors learn the rules of cause and effect, Magicians learn those of magic. Magic works acausally. We understand when the physician prescribes medicine to fight an infection, because it is a clear example of cause and effect and also because we know and believe in the archetypal slaying-the-dragon plot. But we do not necessarily have a conceptual framework to understand so readily the Magician who, like Christ, simply says "take up your bed and walk." The Martyr, the Wanderer, and the Warrior often are suspicious of such healings, and perhaps that is why spiritual or faith healing often has been avoided and even disdained by respectable people (except, of course, by great saints, who usually are appreciated only after they are safely dead).

Magic is dangerous at certain levels of consciousness because it panders to the Orphan's desire for a quick fix and for rescue from without. The Martyr, the Wanderer, and the Warrior have different ways of learning that they must do something to be healed. They must suffer, search, and work hard, respectively.

But the Magician understands grace—not as an unusual occurrence, but simply as one kind of energy available to us. There are times when our energies flag, when our skills fail (as with Tom Brown on his fast), or when the normal, everyday ways of solving problems are of no avail. Doing so requires the ability to stay in balance with the ultimate energy source of the universe. Religious people might call this living in harmony with God. More secular-minded people merely would say they learned to get rid of their internal static so they could be receptive to and tap into energy outside themselves. There are many names for such energies. In the movie *Star Wars*, it is called The Force. Some people do not think about it as anything magic or mystical, but do know those moments when they feel as if they are flowing with the universe and everything rather magically is going right.

Magicians strive, then, to live in harmony with the supernatural and natural worlds, and doing so requires wholeness and balance within. Magicians must have apprenticed not only with the Magician archetype, but also with all the others discussed in this book. Most critical is a resolution of the Orphan dilemma, which allows Magicians to trust in and submit to a power greater than themselves, saying, "Thy will be done." Of course, Magicians understand this at a level different from that of Orphans. Orphans assume that doing God's will means giving up their own, which is defined as being self-centered and ignorant and in opposition to God's plan. When we achieve a deeper level of self-knowledge by having resolved many Wanderer issues, we are less dualistic. Because we are part of God, our will and our good at the deepest level are part of the unfolding of God.

While Magicians have a kind of humility in understanding that we are only a small part of the great ongoing activity of creation, claiming cocreation with God is an act of great self-assertion. Because none of us is perfect, we run the risk that instead of improving our lives, we inadvertently will bring more pain and suffering into them and into the lives of others. Taking responsibility for cocreation of the universe requires that we also take responsibility for the apparently undesired outcomes. Even God, according to Genesis, created Satan in the process of making the universe, and subsequently sent his son to mitigate the results. Such apparent mistakes are an inevitable part of creation. Although we may posit that the gods know what they are doing in the process of creation, often *we* do not, and so may call forth monsters, which we finally recognize as our Shadow.

Naming the Shadow

As we have seen, the movement from Orphan and Martyr to the Wanderer requires heroes to stop blaming themselves for their problems and to see the Shadow as outside themselves. Paradoxically, the movement from Warrior to Magician requires heroes to acknowledge their responsibility for the Shadow—to see that it is, indeed, part of themselves. However, this recognition does not require blame or require them to slay or repress that part of themselves.

Magicians move beyond dualistic, static notions of good and bad to seeing life as a process. The part of ourselves that we have repressed and not allowed to flourish and grow is stunted and manifests itself as negativity or even evil. People who are arrested in the beginning Orphan stage, for instance, may become habitual criminals or victims because their positive qualities cannot find ways to develop. Or, in the case of the Warrior or Martyr, some qualities are allowed to flourish at the expense of others considered weak or selfish, and the result may be one-sided, unbalanced personalities.

These undeveloped qualities can possess us in monstrous form. For instance, our culture is just moving out of puritanism to deal with the Shadow of sexuality. Hence, it manifests itself often in perverse yet extremely powerful forms. Sex is used in advertising to sell everything from cars to power tools, either by subliminal means or by scantily clothed women standing by the object being sold. Such juxtaposition makes no logical sense unless we understand that we are quite simply possessed by our repressed sexuality. And often our sexuality emerges in twisted and perverse ways. In contemporary movies (and in contemporary life) sexuality often is accompanied by violence. Rape, violent seduction, molestation of children, pornography, the rise of sado-masochism all speak to the reality of our culture's Shadow possession, as does the more subtle but even more pervasive image of sexual relationships in which one (or both) of the parties is objectified.[1]

People in a Warrior mind-set assume that the answer to this dilemma is to slay the dragon—to get rid of the sexuality within and without, to ban it. What happens then, however, is more repression, and the dragons get bigger and the possession more pronounced. When the Warrior/Martyr resolution is achieved, we learn to face the dragon and to recognize that it is dangerous—to ourselves and others—but then to transform that monster by affirming it and acknowledging it as our own.

Violence is caused in large part by the repression of assertiveness. We learn to be nice, to give in, that we do not have a right to ask for what we want. Many of us are not taught skills for recognizing and asserting our needs. Consequently, emotions build up, like an internal time bomb. The result is an explosion—anger and perhaps emotional or even physical violence inflicted on ourselves or another person. Paradoxically, the antidote to violence is not self-control and repression, but self-knowledge and skills of self-expression and assertion.

Magicians understand the courage and audacity involved in asserting themselves and their will on the universe when they themselves are not yet whole. To do so means letting loose their demons upon the world. Actually, because we all are cocreators whether we want to be or not, we run this risk all the time anyway. However, Magicians take responsibility for this process and basically trust it. If dragons are but their Shadows, their unnamed, unlived, unloved parts, then the only way to transform them is to act, and by acting bring them into the light of day.

Yet some discretion is required in the scope of their action to avoid calling forth demons too great for them to handle. In *A Wizard of Earthsea*, Ursula Le Guin's Sparrowhawk believes, in his youthful arrogance, that he is powerful enough to call forth the dead. He succeeds, but in doing so lets loose a monster from the underworld powerful enough to destroy the world. Youthful and inexperienced though he is, Sparrowhawk understands that it is his responsibility to track down this demon and to confront and disarm it. He spends years on this lonely journey. When he finally tracks him down and faces him, he understands that the way to gain power over him is to speak the demon's real name. Facing him, he calls him Ged (Sparrowhawk's real name), and in acknowledging his Shadow as a Shadow, the two parts of himself are unified and the threat is no more.

Le Guin writes, "Ged had neither lost nor won but, naming the shadow of his death with his own name, had made himself whole: a man who, knowing his whole true self, cannot be used or possessed by any power other than himself, and whose life therefore is lived for life's sake and never in the service of ruin, or pain, or hatred, or the dark." After this triumph, Sparrowhawk sings a sacred song that celebrates paradox: "Only in silence the word, only in dark the light, only in dying life: bright the hawk's flight as an empty sky."[2]

The Magician comes to understand the precious balance in the universe and how individuals help to either foster that balance or disturb it by the choices they make about their lives. In *The Farthest Shore*, the third in Le Guin's Earthsea Trilogy, Sparrowhawk rights the balance again. Cob, a great mage gone evil, has decided to use his power to conquer death and give people immortality. The result, of course, is that people have become possessed by Death's Shadow. Everywhere Sparrowhawk finds the walking dead: alienated, listless, many addicted to drugs, no one taking pride in their work or loving one another.

He explains that what has caused the problem is that people desire "power over life," which he calls "greed." The only power worth having, he notes, is not "power over," but "power to" accept life, to allow it in. The result of the desire to control life and death in order to attain immortality creates a void within. Sparrowhawk explains to Cob that "Not all the songs of earth, not all the stars of heaven could fill your emptiness," for Cob, in going for "power over," has lost himself and his true name.[3] Magicians, then, allow life in themselves and in others.

Magicians also are namers. As a rule, psychological and cultural balance and stability are maintained by keeping much of reality out of our field of consciousness. When an individual or society is ready to grow, the Magician's task is to destroy unhealthy stasis by allowing in previously repressed or denied elements. Doing so is anarchistic and creates chaos. Culturally, the 1960s was such a time. Our major cultural theorists all upset the cultural applecart in such diverse areas as music, sexuality, race relations, and even America's very image as a peace-loving, just society. Sometimes Magicians respond to the chaos other people have created but for which they will not, or cannot, take responsibility. Magicians then restore the balance of the psyche or the society by *naming* the new reality and domesticating or transforming it. They also encourage the ongoing evolution of the universe by helping others find their true names (i.e., their identities), for that is how the universe evolves—by our all becoming increasingly more ourselves and more willing to take responsibility for the world we are creating together. This is why, in the seventies, our major thinkers focused on issues of consciousness and personal growth as ways of integrating new material into our psyches. (The reappearance of conventionality in the eighties may be needed to reassert cultural balance and to provide a time for individuals to assimilate the cultural changes of the sixties and changes in consciousness experienced in the seventies.)

Many people, especially if they are in or moving into the Warrior stage, are afraid of honest naming, whether it is naming of denied cultural realities or our own repressed and denied qualities. For the Warrior, the naming of the dragon as the villain is a prelude to attack. To be honest is to make oneself vulnerable in the pecking order. Especially because people usually are trying to seem more than they are so they may rise up the hierarchy, honesty is very threatening. It means having one's failings exposed. But in a Magician's hands honesty can be transforming.

In Philip Ressner's wonderful children's book *Jerome the Frog*, a playful witch tells Jerome she has turned him into a prince.[4] He still looks like a frog, but townspeople begin sending him on quests just in case he really is a prince. He has several successes, so finally they send him to slay the dragon, who is always breathing fire and destroying villages. Jerome finds the dragon and draws his sword, but the dragon asks why. It is, after all, his nature to breathe fire and burn villages. Jerome ponders this and they discuss things awhile and finally come up with a solution agreeable to all. The dragon will burn the town garbage every Tuesday and Thursday, and lie around and tell lies the rest of the week. Jerome does not try to convert the dragon or convince him to be "good," but instead helps him to be more fruitfully who he is, since dragons not only love to breathe fire and burn things up but also like to be admired and appreciated.

Jerome's kind of victimless, villainless problem solving is predicated on the assumption that none of us is wrong or bad. We may, however, be repressing who we are and acting out of our Shadow, or we simply may lack skills to assert ourselves in a socially responsible manner. When either of these is true, we may cause difficulty for ourselves and others. There is nothing inherently wrong with dragons when their true natures are discovered, developed, and usefully channeled!

It is not just honesty, then, that is important, but the energy that surrounds it. If honesty comes out of a desire to cut down, it can be very destructive. However, enveloped in love, it has quite a different effect. The hero's goal is not to slay, but to *name* the dragon—to reinstate community through communication.

Madeleine L'Engle's children's story *The Wind in the Door* illustrates this point nicely. The hero of the story is Meg, a young adolescent daughter of a feminist family: Both her parents are prize-winning physicists. The problem is that her beloved younger brother, Charles Wallace, is dying. Her mother has discovered that something has gone wrong with his farandolae. Inside every human cell is an organism with its own RNA and DNA called a mitochondria, without which we could not process oxygen. Inside the mitochondria, Meg's mother posits, is a farandolae that has the same relationship to it as the mitochondria has to us.

The vision of interdependence of all life runs throughout the novel. Meg is visited by people from outer space and by a cherub, who explains that size makes no difference. Everything in the universe is just as critical as everything else, and everything is interconnected. They also explain that she can save Charles Wallace, because she is a *Namer*. A Namer, it turns out, is someone who names things, who helps them know who they are. They explain that Meg's friend Calvin is a Namer to her because she feels more like herself when she is with him than at any other time.

The source of the problem is the Echthroi, the "Unnamers," who are responsible for black holes in the universe, alienation, despair, crime, because they try to keep people, stars, trees, etc., from claiming their real identities and, therefore, from making their contribution to the universe. After practicing naming on a few people, Meg goes down into the mitochondria and talks with the farandolae. It turns out that the Echthroi have been there and convinced the farandolae that they need not take their journeys, that they are the greatest thing that exists. When the farandolae take their journeys, they sing with the stars. If they do not, the whole organism they are a part of dies.

Meg succeeds in naming the farandolae but then realizes she must face the Echthroi themselves to free herself and her friends. When she does so, she does not try to kill them as a Warrior might. Instead, she begins a litany of naming, ending with:

I hold you! I love you, I name you. I name you, Echthroi. You are not nothing. You are. . . . I fill you with Naming. Be! . . . Echthroi. You are named! My arms surround you. You are no longer nothing. You are. You are filled. You are me. You are Meg.[5]

In this view of the world, the job of heroes is to enlighten the world by loving it—starting with themselves. Their task is not to slay the dragon—within or without—but to affirm the deepest level of truth about it: that is, that we are all one. Such dragons are only our Shadows, our unnamed, unloved parts.

There is an inevitable conflict between the Magician's evolving notion of the universe and the Warrior's perfectionism. We live in a culture that does not trust process and is intolerant of diversity. Therefore we all are expected to be perfect, and beyond that, to be perfect in similar—if not the same—ways to one another. We are supposed to "live up" to standards of virtue, achievement, intelligence, and physical attractiveness. If we do not, then we are expected to repent, work harder, study, diet, exercise, and wear better clothes until we fit the prevailing image of an ideal person. Thus, our unique qualities are likely to be defined as "the problem" that we need to solve to be OK. In this case, the Magician's role is to name and acknowledge those differences as sources of our individual and collective strength.

One of the best examples of a hero who comes to understand this is Sissy Hankshaw of Tom Robbins' *Even Cowgirls Get the Blues.* Sissy was born with oversized thumbs. Virtually everyone sees her as handicapped, but she tends to resist this way of looking at things. As a young teenager, however, she stands before the mirror and realizes that she is beautiful. If she were to have plastic surgery to reduce the size of her thumbs, she could lead a "normal life." As she contemplates this alternative, her thumbs begin to twitch and urge her to "live life at some other level . . . if she dared."[6] Instead of having plastic surgery, Sissy goes on to become the greatest hitchhiker in the entire world. She is so good, she can call cars on the other side of a four-lane highway to pick her up. In fact, she takes hitchhiking to the level of a Zen experience.

Like everyone else, however, Sissy has her moments of self-doubt, and during one she marries and gives up "her career." When she frees her husband's pet bird, however, he takes her to a psychiatric clinic. One of the psychiatrists (the namesake of the author) understands her. He explains to Dr. Goldman, a Freudian psychologist, his enthusiasm for Sissy by telling him how impressive it is that she has become the best hitchhiker in the world. She truly has found the life she was meant for. Dr. Goldman, missing the point entirely, asks if he means she has transcended her affliction. Dr. Robbins says no. He explains that transcendence smacks of hierarchy, the class system, of a way of thinking that cannot see Sissy's innate value. He continues:

The trick is not to transcend but to *transform* them. Not to degrade them or deny them—and that's what transcendence amounts to—but to reveal them more fully, to heighten their reality, to search for their latent significance. I fail to detect a single healthy impulse in the cowardly attempt to transcend the physical world. On the other hand, to transform a physical entity by changing the climate around it through the manner in which one regards it is a marvelous undertaking, creative and courageous.[7]

Sissy so changes Dr. Robbins' life that he "calls in well" and never returns to the clinic.

In this view, all people are heroic, and all are essential to human evolution. Our task is merely to affirm completely who we are. We do not have to spend all or even any of our time trying to prove we are OK. That is why the "black is beautiful" campaign is so critical to black Americans. That is why affirming femaleness is so transformative for women. And that is why good mental, emotional, and physical health for everyone requires learning to love oneself fully and unconditionally.

The Rainmaker

Instead of struggling against powerlessness, loneliness, fear, or pain, the Magician accepts them as part of the fabric of life and hence opens up to discovering the lessons they bring us. The image of God the Creator speaking into the void to create life is a profoundly active image of creation, which at least seems to imply that the act of creation is totally under conscious control. The image of the Goddess giving birth often is closer to what creativity is like for many people. When the Goddess creates something out of nothing, her creation comes out of her body, not her mind. When we create in this way, we may labor long to give birth to something, not being quite sure what we are birthing. The creation may seem to us not so much something we chose as something that has chosen us, and we may fear that the baby will be born dead or deformed. There are few certainties about it. And, once the process is under way, it takes on a life of its own. We stop it only at risk to our own life.

At the basis of life is eros, passion, sexual energy. Creation comes from opening up to that energy and allowing the natural process of spontaneous creation to occur. To do that, we need to be courageously open. Sometimes, though, we get hit with genuine tragedies. To continue the metaphor, the new birth begins not with love, but with events that feel more like rape. While the pain and suffering involved is not invited or deserved—it simply may be the price we all pay for living in a world still at a very primitive level of development—even such catastrophies can be used by the psyche for growth, and hence eventually to bring us treasures—if we allow the resulting growth to take place.

May Sarton's Joanna in *Joanna and Ulysses* comes to understand this when she chooses to celebrate her thirtieth birthday by going off by herself for the first time in her life. Although she always has wanted to be an artist, she is a clerk, and she leaves for the island of Santorini from Athens in the hope that she will be able to paint. Her goal is to really *see* objects as they are, so that she can paint them. The surprise to her is that in doing so she breaks through her denial systems and sees more than she is conscious of asking to see. On Santorini, she makes friends with a small boy who asks her why she never married, and in answering she tells a story she never has told anyone. Her mother had been a resistance fighter. Captured by the Fascists, the mother was made to watch while guards stuck cigarettes into her son's ears until he was made deaf. All the time the son shouted, "Mother, don't talk." Then they tortured her until she died, but she never talked.[8]

The son was released and told the family the story. Joanna put off her hopes of becoming an artist and took care of them all. Her father sat alone much of the time in a darkened room, and she took a dull job. They all went through life numbed by the tragedy and putting one foot forward at a time. At thirty, arriving on Santorini, the first thing she sees is a donkey full of sores, piled high with baggage and being beaten. This scene is the last straw for her. She cannot stand any more inhumanity, and she runs up screaming for the donkey's owners to stop, but they explain they are poor people and do not have the luxury of coddling animals. They just want the donkey to get to the top of the hill before he dies. Finally, in exasperation she buys the donkey at a ridiculously inflated price and begins her vacation, leading a dying donkey, whom she christens Ulysses.

Ulysses represents to Joanna the part of herself that is an artist, the part that has been starved, neglected, and mistreated. She calls him Ulysses because she recognizes her potential for heroism, but she also chuckles that her Shadow would take the form of such an ignoble beast, especially since she sees her aspirations as so ridiculous that she is afraid to speak of them.

As she begins to paint, she nurses Ulysses back to health. When she tells the young boy her story, she expects him to be shocked or grieved, but instead he reacts with exultation, saying, "I am so proud of your mother. I am so proud of your brother." His response surprises her into seeing things differently, into remembering how passionate her mother was, how she loved flowers, and how she loved freedom enough to die for it. Actually telling the story and hearing the boy's liberating response makes her feel as if "she were being brought out at last from a dank, dark cell where all she could think of was suffering, the endless chain of suffering."

Later, in Athens, when Ulysses, whom she has hidden in the base-ment, chews through the rope and surprises her and her father up-stairs, she and her father talk honestly for the first time since her mother's death. She shows him her paintings; they talk about her mother, and she exclaims: "If you shut out pain, you shut out ev-erything, Papa! . . . Don't you see, how everything stopped—my painting became trivial, my life too. I could not remember Mother as she was. We shut her out . . . like shutting out life itself!"

To deny the pain was to hold on to it. Only by going through it, allowing it, feeling it, speaking aloud about it, could she learn from it and go on to feel joy and power in a new way. The hero who can do this is rewarded with much more *life* than the stoic macho hero who rides off into the sunset or, more classically, retreats into the "power over" position of king and never knows the intensity of real human vulnerability and love.

Equally important to Joanna's honoring and affirming both the pain and the joy is her commitment to her art and what that art means to her. It truly means to learn to see the real, for how can the Magician help along the balance of the world if she is not willing to see what that balance is, or (to use Madeleine L'Engle's metaphor) to hear the song of the stars? Besides the fact that repression takes away our lives, it also traps us into our illusions so we cannot know what is real. Joanna gives the gifts of the artist both when she shows her father her paintings and when she explains to him what she has learned. By expressing her truth, she changes not only her own real-ity, but his. She is a Magician, indeed.

Magicians must be part artist in their commitment to seeing, hear-ing, and in every way knowing the real; they also must be part fool. In ancient times, the king always was complemented by the fool, who not only joked around and kept the king honest by pointing out his foibles, but even more important, kept a kind of cosmic balance in the kingdom. As William Willeford wrote in *The Fool and His Sceptor*:

The babbling fool is one prototype of our relationship to numinous powers. . . . The fool stands beside the king, in a sense reflecting him but also
suggesting a long-lost element of the king that, we may imagine, had to be
sacrificed at the founding of the kingdom, an element without which neither
the kingdom nor the king is complete.[8]

The transformation from Warrior/King to Magician is accompanied
by a return to innocence, embodied in the image of the fool. When
we embark upon the journey, we leave innocent simplicity behind
to gain the skills required by a tough world. The innocent, trusting
self we left behind seems foolish and is to be avoided, but in some
ways it is always with us—whether we listen to it or not. The more
rationalistic we are, of course, the more foolish and babbling fools
will seem to us. Yet it is the reappearance of the Innocent that often
makes it possible for us to act like Magicians when rationality sees
no way out of a dilemma.

In Joseph Heller's *Catch-22,* Orr, who is seen by everyone as a
grotesque, giggling fool, shakes Yossarian out of his paralysis when
Yossarian hears that Orr has gone AWOL and has rowed to Sweden.
Even though the claim that Orr has done so is absurd, Yossarian
determines on its basis to take a leap of faith and refuse to fly any
more bombing missions.[10]

The Magician's view of the world is quite simply absurd from any
conventional, linear, cause-and-effect way of thinking; to the ordinary
mind, Magicians seem to be fools. And so they are, in the most
classic sense, for it is the wise fool who, as Willeford argues, is our
link to numinous powers. Claiming such magical thinking for oneself, then, often is accompanied by a laugh and a profound sense of
lightening up.

At this point the Magician learns that life need not be so hard.
For one thing, when people have integrated most of their Shadows,
they spend less energy repressing and denying their internal reality.
For another, they spend less time fighting external battles because
they don't so often project their Shadows onto others.

They are like Claremont De Castillejo's rainmaker in *Knowing
Woman.* When a village in India experienced a drought, they would
send for the rainmaker. Rainmakers do not do anything to make the
rain happen; they just come to the village and stay there—and the

rain comes. They do not make the rain come, they allow it or, more exactly, their inner atmosphere of allowing and affirming what *is* creates a climate in which what *needs to be* happens. Perhaps you have known people like that. It is not that they make the sun shine, the rain fall, or people work harder in their office, but when they are there, things work right—and apparently effortlessly.[11]

Being a rainmaker requires great faith. Sometimes after great effort, Magicians need to be reminded that they are not struggling alone to right the balance of the universe. For instance, Morgaine, the hero of Marion Zimmer Bradley's *The Mists of Avalon*, gives her whole life to trying to preserve goddess worship in England during the time of King Arthur and the Round Table, as a growing Christian influence undermines the position of women and declares the masculine aspect of God to be the only true divinity.

Near the end of her life, she feels that both she and the Goddess have been betrayed by King Arthur, and fears they have lost the battle with history. She visits a convent in England near the historical Avalon (where she had trained as a priestess) and witnesses young girls worshiping in a chapel to St. Bridget. She realizes that Bridget is not really a Christian saint at all; the statue there is of the "Goddess as she is worshipped in Ireland." Morgaine sees that "even if they think otherwise, these women know the power of the immortal. Exile her as they may, she will prevail. The Goddess will never withdraw herself from mankind." Morgaine asks the Goddess for forgiveness for her doubt and bitterness, saying, "I thought I must do what I now see you can do for yourself." She understands that not everything had been in her hands, so she can let up on herself: "I did the Mother's work in Avalon until at last those who came after us might bring her into this world. I did not fail. I did what she had given me to do. It was not she but I in my pride who thought I should have done more."[12]

Morgaine recognizes that she had been trapped in the Warrior's grandiosity. She did not need to do it all, only her small part. In doing that, she was not all-important, but a cocreator with the Goddess of her own destiny and the world's.

Magicians gain great faith in themselves, in God, in the universe. That faith makes it possible sometimes simply to wait for clarity when bad things appear to be happening.

"Ask and Ye Shall Receive"

In *Collections,* Shirley Luthman ponders the question of what she would do if she discovered she had a brain tumor. She would be quite shaken up, obviously. Nonetheless, while allowing those feelings, she maintains that she would not do anything until she could focus inward and get clear enough to understand what was going on. Had her being decided that it was time to die? Or, if not, what was the tumor trying to tell her? Only when she was clear about where she was going would she decide what to do. That might mean deciding it was time to die. It might mean finding some alternative treatment.[13]

Fundamental to her approach is a strong belief that at some level of our beings, we choose what happens to us—which includes choosing our illnesses and our own deaths. We make these choices, she says, not out of masochism, but because they will teach us what we need to learn. It is, therefore, important to honor everything that happens to us as a way of honoring our choices as the teachers of needed lessons.

Now, the Orphan cannot hear this because for her, choice means blame: If I choose to be a battered woman, that means I am to blame for my own suffering. But to the Magician blame is irrelevant, and the search for a culprit is a useless diversion. The useful questions are not "who is to blame?" but "what can I learn from this experience?" *and* "given the wisdom I have gained from it, what do I want to choose now?"

Looking back from the vantage point of the Magician, a woman may recognize that she had long had a batterer in her own head, telling her she was too fat, too selfish, too pushy. By getting into a situation in which she is physically or emotionally battered by someone else, she finally comes to the point where she says, "Enough: I may be bad, but I am not bad enough to deserve this kind of treatment." So she finds help, gets out of the relationship, and eventually works on her self-esteem to the point where she does not spend so much of her time at the mercy of her internal batterer. Although the external situation was painful, it produced a crisis that forced on her the opportunity to opt for growth, change, and eventually less pain in her life. In that way, attracting a battering relationship in the long run brought her health.

In an autobiographical chapter, "My Own Journey—New Life," in *Energy and Personal Power*, Luthman tells about her pain when she lost her husband. They had had a deep and fulfilling relationship, and when he died she was grief stricken. In spite of everything else she believed about life and how we choose what happens to us, she felt herself to be a victim. Later, she confronts her own belief that "on a deep level of my consciousness I may have known I was marrying a man who was going to die and leave me, even though I had no cognitive awareness of such a possibility." Then she opens up to ask herself why she would do that; she gets two answers:

I reached a depth with my husband on an energy-consciousness level in which I felt one with him without losing my own identity and sense of self. . . . If our relationship had continued to expand in that depth and intensity, I would have attached my ability to have such an experience to him and to that relationship instead of to me. What I have experienced since then has taught me that I create the form into which someone comes along who fits me on the level I am capable of experiencing. My ability to be alive, intense, and to relate deeply is connected to me and not dependent on a particular person or place, on anything external to me.[14]

Magic is based upon a synchronicity of the macro- and micro-world. *Synchronicity* is a word coined by Carl Jung that means "meaningful coincidences" or acausal connections.[15] As the Warrior learns the lessons of causality, the Magician learns about synchronicity. You know those times when you go to a bookstore and just the book you needed (but had never heard of) practically falls into your hand? Or when you run into just the person you need, seemingly coincidentally? Actually, many truly miraculous "coincidences" have happened in my life, but I will share here a very ordinary, everyday example of a seemingly accidental fortuitous event.

While contemplating leaving a relationship, I took a walk early in the morning and was reminding myself of something I had told others, but often did not fully believe myself. That is, like money, wealth, and time, love is not scarce. If we open up to allow life, we can open up to an abundance of health, prosperity, time, and love. As I walked along thinking that but really feeling quite lonely and fearful that I always would be alone, a man walked up and chatted with me for about a minute and then left. In that instant I realized that, while I certainly did not want that particular man to stick around, his affable presence had given me exactly what I needed in that moment. In doing so, it had made real to me what my need was telling me but the rest of me was resisting: I would always have the relationship I needed. I would not need to hold on to an inappropriate one out of fear of being alone.

Now, if no one had ever suggested to me that it is perfectly reasonable to expect the universe to provide what we need (and often even what we want), he might have come up and chatted pleasantly, and I would not have noticed the gift. If I were in my Orphan space, I might see his quick departure as an omen that everyone always would leave me. If I were feeling like a Martyr, I might feel sorry for myself, that even when I was on a walk, trying to sort out major issues in my life, someone always wanted something from me. In my Warrior mode, I might even get affronted that a strange man had the audacity to accost me on the path! We get little gifts all the time, but we receive them differently.

In some ways, the Orphan, the Martyr, and the Warrior live in similar universes because each believes in scarcity. In contrast, the Magician experiences a world in which it is possible for all people to have everything they need, for there is enough.

One good way to think of synchronicity is as mirroring.[16] The world outside mirrors our world inside. Partly, as we have seen with the example of the battered woman, the external world tends to dramatize what is going on in our internal world so that we notice it. An example: One day last year I was heading out of town. It had been a very busy week, and I was rather proud of myself for getting everything done and still having time for a quick jog before heading for the airport. I started running near my home, congratulating myself on my pace, which, considering I had not run in a week, seemed pretty good to me.

All of a sudden, the mail carrier, who was waving in a friendly fashion, yelled, "You can do better than that! You're hardly moving!" Well, I immediately felt awful. I kept running, aware of how angry I was about this fellow's ruining my fine mood. However, I figured he probably was trying to make a connection but lacked skills, so I rounded the block and came back to where he was munching on a sack lunch. I stopped and said, "I know you probably meant that comment to be helpful, but I was running at the right pace for me. Your comment felt like a real putdown. I hope you don't do that to your wife or girlfriend." He replied in a rather crestfallen manner, "Maybe that's why I don't have one."

Treating him as a potential friend was only part of my task, a part that enabled him to respond with honesty and vulnerability. The other was to check out whether this incident could be mirroring something inside me. Going inside to change clothes, I thought about his comment and realized I had had a tape in my head all week, saying "Hurry up, you aren't going fast enough." I didn't notice my tape, but I sure noticed his comment! Hearing it and getting angry helped me to recognize that I did not need to pressure myself that way either. I had been going at a good pace, for me, all week. No need to push further or judge that effort.

Mirroring also works the other way. That is, often when I change my inner world, the outer one changes as well. For example, I know women who see men as either potential rescuers or villains, so most of the men they find usually fall into the latter category. The women want to be rescued because they do not know they can rescue themselves. When they take their journey and develop what they and the culture see as their more masculine side (i.e., self-sufficiency and courage), suddenly they discover men who are neither rescuers nor villains but just people like themselves, and rather nice people at that! Put another way, when women develop and make friends with the man inside them, then, as if by magic, the external equivalent appears—although sometimes there is a time lag! Similarly, when men fully allow and integrate their own intuition, vulnerability, and need for love and intimacy, they often are astounded by how many interesting and thoroughly admirable women suddenly appear on the scene.

When we are in the Wanderer stage, the world is full of suffering; when we move into the Warrior stage, the world miraculously changes with us, and confronts us not so much with catastrophies as with challenges. As we enter the Martyr stage, we find ourselves surrounded by people needing love and care at every turn.

When people pronounce that everyone is out to get them, watch

your pockets when you are with them! Some people are always talking about how hard life is and, sure enough, they have one catas-
trophe after another. Or, conversely, sometimes we attract to us what
we are denying. So someone walking around with rose-colored
glasses all the time may attract certain problems so as to grow in
awareness. Someone in the Warrior phase may believe that life is a
battle or contest. They view any other way of seeing the world as
escapist or naive. Try to tell them about abundance, sharing, and
love, and they think you have lost your marbles. Because they believe
that and hence live it, everything in their life *is* a contest or battle.

Often the people we have the most difficulty with spark a Shadow
side of ourselves. If we cannot abide political "hawks" or Pentagon
generals, we may find that the vehemence of our feeling declines as
we take a strong stand fighting for a world free of nuclear threat. If
our teeth are set on edge by dependent, whiny people, we may find
that as we acknowledge our own dependency and sense of powerlessness, we can be more empathetic with them. As we expand our
own repertoire of behaviors and allow ourselves to be more whole,
we attract to ourselves more interesting people—or we are able to
understand how interesting other people have been all along. Many
women, for example, socialized to be competitive with other women,
think that other women typically are competitive, backbiting, and not
to be trusted. As they begin to find value in their own femaleness,
most of the women around them seem suddenly and quite miraculously to have become sisterly and honest. If this does not happen,
they might then take the responsibility for attracting Shadow-pos-
sessed women, asking "What is this mirroring in me?" The negative
qualities associated stereotypically with men and with women are
examples of what happens when we do not allow our full femaleness
or maleness, and become possessed by the Shadow of our sexual
identity.

Sometimes we also cannot abide people who display the qualities
we are just moving beyond. When we move out of the first stages
of Martyr, for instance, we usually want to be done with sacrifice.
Our feelings of irritation and anger at people who still are maiming
themselves for others motivate us to explore other, more assertive
archetypes. Ultimately, however, Magicians recognize that when a
manifestation of the archetype so hooks them, they have more work

to do with it. The strength of our revulsion to such a manifestation of any archetype is itself a call to the quest to understand it at a different level of truth. Ultimately, all the archetypes bring us treasures, just as do all the experiences of life—good and bad—if we hang in there and learn from them.

As Martyrs learn to allow pain, Wanderers loneliness, and Warriors fear, Magicians come allow faith, love, and joy. The more they let in, the more they attract to themselves. Matthew Fox, in *Whee!, We, Wee All the Way Home,* argues that the ultimate prayer is to receive life fully:

A friend who gives me a record is pleased when he learns of my delight at playing the record. After all, my delight was the very goal he intended in giving me the gift. The Creator can be no different. Our thank-you for creation, our fundamental prayer, therefore, is our enjoyment and delight in it. This delight is called ecstasy when it reaches a certain height, and it is also prayer. Like all prayer, it touches the Creator and we are touched by the Creator in that act of ecstasy and thank-you.[17]

The Magician's process is not simply passive receiving, however. It is a matter of asking, too, and sometimes rejecting. The Christian Scripture that most resonates for the Magician's consciousness is Matthew 7:7–9:

Ask, and you will receive; seek, and you will find; knock, and the door will be opened. For everyone who asks receives, he who seeks finds, and to him who knocks, the door will be opened.

A novel that exemplifies the Magician's process is Margaret Drabble's *The Realms of Gold.* Its central character, Frances Wingate, thinks back over her life with a humble sense of wonder at all she has received. Frances has a rather unusual capacity to trust herself and her vision, and the result is that she habitually has asked for what she wanted . . . and gotten it. She is aware that she never has made things happen; they just have happened. She is an archaeologist who became quite famous when she discovered the ruins of an ancient city in a desert. Actually, one day in an airport she simply knew where it was. Of course, this intuitive knowledge was grounded in all her study of the ancient culture of the Phoenicians, but it was the intuitive flash that made the difference. Furthermore, she unquestioningly followed her hunch and found and then excavated the site. She wonders:

If I hadn't imagined it, it wouldn't have existed. All her life, things had been like that. She had imagined herself doing well at school, and had done well. Marrying, and had married. Bearing children, and had borne them. Being rich, and had become rich. Being free, and was free. Finding true love, and had found it. Losing it, and had lost it. What next should she imagine?[18]

The enormity of the power frightens her. She worries that she might imagine something frightful and that would happen, too. Accordingly, she comes face to face with her sense of responsibility for her own life and her contributions to the world. It also is true that Frances is looking back over her life with the Magician's consciousness as she ponders. Events do not feel so fortuitous and easy as they happen. Yet had she not learned the lessons of the Warrior, she could not so confidently have followed up on her hunch, organized an expedition, and proceeded to dig. Similarly, she would not have had the independence of mind and courage to take her career seriously at a time when women were not expected to be able to combine career with a husband and family.

Her life is an interesting example of the Magician's consciousness, and a very human one. She is not "perfect." In fact, she drinks too much and in other ways is prone to self-indulgence. But that is part of the point: She is *not* better than other people, and she *is* a Magician. She visualizes what she wants and takes action to get it with a simple, relaxed confidence that it will happen, without falling into denial or escapism. For example, she sends a postcard to a lover from whom she had parted, saying she wants him back. The postcard is delayed in reaching him, and her response when she does not hear from him is puzzlement. After all, he always said he would come back if she asked him to, and she believed him. Finally, he receives the postcard and runs to her side, and she has her wish—a truly satisfying, intimate relationship.

I have a friend who recently became interested in affirmations. As Orphans we learn, as we face our helplessness, to pray for divine intercession and/or to ask for people to help us. As Magicians we retain this important lesson but add something to it—the ability to affirm good as existing in our lives *right now*. We do not need to plead or even ask for the things we need to thrive, we only need to open up to them. Everything we ever could choose is already in the universe: pain, hardship, loneliness, joy, ease, love. By affirming that we have what we want, we call it to us. My friend gave me a "perfect happiness" affirmation (from a book by Marion Weinstein called *Positive Magic*),[19] and explained to me that I could affirm just about anything, like prosperity, the perfect lover, or one's true work, but that I never should ask for someone else's money, joy, husband, or lover. That is, I never should affirm anything at anyone else's expense. To help me stay in that mentality, she reminded me of the abundance of the universe and that I never need to take from another in order to have what *I* need.

I tried affirming perfect happiness and initially I felt ridiculous and presumptuous. First of all, saying affirmations—how silly! Beyond that, who did I think I was, affirming happiness? Wisdom, maybe. Strength. Compassion. But happiness seemed so selfish. Then I thought that through and realized how the ripple effect works. If I am unhappy, look dour, act grouchy, I certainly pass that attitude on to my children, my husband, my friends, my students, and my colleagues. If I am happy and smile at them, the people around me are likely to smile back and carry that smile on to their other interactions during the day. Happiness breeds more happiness, so that happiness—like prosperity and love—can radiate outward to benefit others.

Affirmations are but one of many strategies to open up and choose the good, the beautiful, and the true. In making such choices we become rainmakers, allowing what should be to come to us and helping it come to those around us as well. If what we really need for our growth is to develop warrioring skills, we will attract a great challenge; if we have not fully learned the lessons of martyrdom, we may invoke the chance to give a great gift or to learn to accept a great loss. Perfect happiness is always getting what we need to grow. However, what we need will *always* include a good percentage of joy, abundance, and prosperity if we stop fighting life and instead open up to the full range of human experience.

It also is critical to remember that we always have choices. Saying yes to life is meaningful only to the degree we know we can say no.

Sometimes we want to say no to what someone else may intend to be a gift to us. Sometimes people give us gifts as a way of manipulating us, or they give to us out of a sense of duty when it does not genuinely fit for them to do so. Or it may fit for them to give to us, but not for us to receive it.

Accepting such gifts may cause both persons harm. In the familiar story of "The Frog Prince," a young princess drops her golden ball into the pond and is inconsolable. A frog appears and says he will get it for her if she promises that she will let him eat from her bowl and sleep on her pillow. She agrees, and he fetches the ball. Then, to her horror, her father insists she keep her word. In the version I heard as a child, the frog turned into a prince when she kissed him. Lots of jokes have made the rounds about how many frogs women kiss, hoping one will be transformed into a prince, but little attention has been paid to the princess's suppression of disgust. The princess feels repulsed by the frog, and implicit in the story is a message that the proper young princess should repress those feelings.

A contrast with a similar story is helpful here. "Beauty and the Beast" is a prototypical Magician story. Here, too, the Beast is transformed into a prince by the princess's kiss, yet the circumstances are quite different from those in "The Frog Prince." The Beast acts quite princely to Beauty: He is always kind and generous to her. True, he asks her to marry him every night, but she stays with her feelings and always says no. He respects her right to do so even though he knows it means he may stay a beast always, because only love will undo the spell and make him human. And finally, when Beauty agrees to marry him, she *does* mean it. She *does* love him. Then, and only then, is he transformed.

"Beauty and the Beast" suggests that we can transform not only ourselves but others by loving them just as they are—especially if they let in that love. "The Frog Prince," however, is a different story. The frog takes advantage of the princess, and she is emotionally younger and not so wise as Beauty, not so able to love the frog as a frog. Madonna Kolhbenschlag, in *Kiss Sleeping Beauty Goodbye*, however, pleased me very much when she explained that in the original version of the Frog Prince story, the frog was transformed not by a kiss but only when the princess acknowledged her disgust, picked him up, and threw him in the fire.[19] (I like to think she shouted "Yuck!" as she did so.)

Wise Love Transforms

I certainly have known people who have been transformed because someone loved them just for who they were, warts and all. But I also know that in our culture, love often means indulging people, allowing them to mistreat you. I have seen more men changed, I think, when their wives stopped putting up with their chauvinism than through their acceptance of it. I have seen children change when their parents thought enough of them to demand that they act in keeping with their inner wisdom, or at least common sense. In fact, I do not think this is a dualism. I think love, wise love, sometimes demands a transformative toss into the fire, rather than the reinforcement of beastliness or froggishness in people. The toss into the fire also was a statement of self-respect for the princess. She had enough respect for herself not to force herself to kiss frogs—no matter *what* her father said! No matter what she had promised!

The Beast is transformed through the love of Beauty, and the frog is transformed only when he is thrown into the fire. What that means is that both women are Magicians when they fully trust and assert their own integrity. Now, this is not the Warrior's view of integrity—which requires keeping one's word, whatever the cost—but integrity that means living fully in keeping with one's deepest self. (Although keeping one's word is important to Magicians, too. They will not trust their capacity to name and to cocreate if they speak carelessly.) The young woman princess in "Beauty and the Beast" turns the Beast down night after night as long as it does not truly fit for her to be his bride. She does not force herself to do some goody-goody rescue number. What saves him is the genuineness of her love, just as the frog is so much better off after knowing the princess's honest disgust.

I often have been surprised at people who assume that, because I am for women's liberation, I hate men. I tell them that if a woman is standing there and a man is stepping on her foot, the proper thing to say is, "You are standing on my foot." If he does not move, then it makes sense to say, "Get off my foot!" Once he is off, and her foot no longer hurts, they can proceed to have a cordial conversation. If, however, (as women are encouraged to) she continues a cordial—perhaps even flirtatious—conversation while he is standing on her foot, pretty soon she is in fairly serious pain. That is when she starts hating herself and him. And that hatred blocks the love. Just as fear is a gift, so too is anger. It teaches us what we need to change to free ourselves, what we need to change to feel more love.

Being ladylike or gentlemanly and denying one's anger simply results in unconscious sabotage of the relationship. Allowing one's anger is transformative because it allows for a true and open, honest relationship. It allows, therefore, for love. Margaret Atwood writes in *Lady Oracle* about a protagonist who lives several lives, all versions of the roles she has been taught to play. It is only the explosion of her anger at the end of the novel that makes any real relationship possible. She hits a reporter over the head with a wine bottle (mistaking him for her husband). Visiting him in the hospital, she notes they have become great friends. He is, after all, the only person who knows anything about her.[21]

One of the best things men and women can do for each other today is the liberating (metaphorical) whack on the side of the head that forces them out of playing tired, worn, old sex roles into finding out what it really means to be male or female—or human. If we try to adopt the Magician's outlook without ever having learned the Warrior's lessons, we inevitably will think that the Beauty and the Beast transformation can happen by an indiscriminating judgment, which does not show much self-esteem. It certainly would not transform Beast if Beauty's acceptance of him was a result of a belief that she did not desire anything more than beastliness. Nor would it serve if she simply thought that everything in life was wonderful and she loved everything equally. Being open to life and to love does not mean giving up the capacity to choose whom you wish to spend your time with and what you wish to do. The Magician is not sentimental or romantic. The goal is to recognize what is true about yourself and others. While at the root we are all one in love, there are many layers above that reality—layers it may be inappropriate to overlook.

It takes so much courage and discipline to live with true integrity moment to moment that we cannot do it without having gone through the stage of being a Warrior. We all have learned well the lessons of acting nice or manipulating so we can control the situation. Being honest and open in the moment is being profoundly vulnerable. It does not allow for manipulation and control, but it does allow for intimacy, for love, and occasionally for magic moments of transcendence.

This is what Anne Wilson Schaef calls "living in process," being absolutely true to your being in the moment.[22] It is a kind of heroism that is not available to persons in the stage of proving their worth, because they always will be straining to be better than they are and hence always will be just a little dishonest. Being able to "live in process" requires a view of the world in which everyone and everything is peer, because everyone is crucial to human evolution.

Because women so prize affiliation and intimacy and because they usually have been socialized to be open, affirming, and receptive, they take to the Magician stage like ducks to water (that is, *if*, and only if, they have dared first to claim their identities as Warriors).

For men, the situation is more complicated and less obvious: terrified of intimacy and believing in their superiority, they feel they have much to lose in being merely peer. They may be loath to leave the warrior stage because it is equated with their masculinity.

What am I, a male may ask, if not man the hunter? And often in the transition from Warrior to Magician, a man may be alienated temporarily from (at least traditional views about) masculinity and focus on developing his more caring, affiliative, sensitive side. Yet, in doing so, he may feel a profound loss, and wonder about what it means to be male. That is where pioneering men like Tom Brown (in *The Search*) are so important, redefining what it means to be a hunter, taking us back to the ancient love of the earth, pride in oneself, yet with the knowledge that being a hunter does not mean superiority—hunters also are prey.

Some men are coming to see that if it is their nature to hunt, they should hunt. If it is their nature to protect, they should protect. Doing so will not mean they cannot also nurture or be sensitive and empathetic. To put this in Jungian terms, after they integrate the anima, they need to circle back and integrate the animus, their deeper sense of masculinity. In the resulting androgynous state, however, masculinity no longer is macho: One can be male and fully honor women, giving up the illusion of superiority for the reality of human community. Most men who have done so find that to be no hard bargain.

So, too, some women set aside or repress their major focus on nurturance and affiliation in the service of acquiring qualities of independence and assertion. Later, when they have claimed their power and their autonomy, they may feel that something is missing, and as a result once again allow in themselves the qualities associated with femininity that truly fit for them. Inevitably, femaleness at this juncture comes to mean something much more powerful and exciting than conventional femininity.

Each sex begins by defining his or her sex role in opposition to the other, repressing the qualities they associate with the opposite sex. In developing these banished qualities—and integrating the anima and animus, respectively—there is a temporary flip-flop in which the old sex role is rejected in the interest of new growth. Finally, as an individual becomes more and more androgynous and as both sides are allowed, maleness and femaleness are redefined. And, as heroes repress fewer and fewer qualities, they become clearer and more balanced and thus more capable of transforming their worlds.

Shug in Alice Walker's *The Color Purple* is a powerful example of an androgynous Magician who lives with almost total fidelity to who she is. As a result, she transforms a patriarchal, power-over environment in which there is little or no love or happiness into a true community. She does not set out to change things. They change because she is who she is—which includes qualities of independence, assertiveness, gentleness, and care. Celie, the main character in the story, begins as a molested and battered child, married off to a man who does not love her but just wants someone to care for his children. He beats her because of his rage that she is not Shug, for he loved Shug although he did not have the courage to marry her. Celie knows about Shug, knows how free and honest she is, and instead of being threatened by her, gets courage just from seeing Shug's picture.

Celie had already gained some self-esteem from a choice she made for martyrdom when, as a teenager, she dressed up to attract her father so he would not also molest her little sister. She chose to sacrifice her own body for her beloved sister. Later, from Shug she learns to stand up for herself. Shug at first is hostile to her because she is married to Albert, but after Celie nurses her through an illness,

Shug comes to love her. In this beauty and the beast situation, Celie comes to value herself because Shug cares about her, and eventually they become lovers. Shug helps Celie learn to love and value her own femaleness and to find her own gifts: She makes wonderful, custom-made comfortable pants. Finally Celie learns to love without dependence when she discovers she can survive and be content even when Shug leaves her.

Albert's fate is more like the frog's. First Shug confronts and rejects him when she learns he has beaten Celie, and then Celie confronts and leaves him, cursing him all the while, saying that everything he has ever done to her will rebound karmically on him. He is healed, however, by the love and care of his son.

By the end of the story, all three—Celie, Shug, and Albert—care about one another. Albert has given up his pretensions to being the patriarch and Shug has returned to Celie. When the women claim their lives, they create a nurturing and empowering community with one another. The men are left to console one another. The result is that the men, too, choose to give up their illusions of power and open up to caring for each other. Their reward is to be let into the loving community.

Ultimately, Shug, the Magician, redefines not only human community but spiritual reality as well. Patriarchal religions have defined God the Father as "up there" and people as a ladder with a white male god at the top. Shug explains to Celie that God is not male and not white. God, she says, is an It and you do not need to placate and please It. God really is in everything, including Celie and herself. Rubbing Celie's thigh, she explains:

. . . God love all them feelings. That's some of the best stuff God did. And when you know God loves 'em you enjoys 'em a lot more. You can just relax, go with everything that's going, and praise God by liking what you like. God don't think it dirty? I ast. Naw, she say, God made it. Listen. God love everything you love and a mess of stuff you don't. But more than anything else, God love admiration. You saying God vain, I ast. Naw, she say. Not vain, just wanting to share a good thing. I think it pisses God off if you walk by the color purple in a field somewhere and don't notice it. What it do when it pissed off? I ast. Oh, it makes something else. People think pleasing God is all God care about. But any fool living in the world can see it always trying to please us back. . . . Yes, Celie, she say. Everything want to be loved. Us sing and dance, make faces and give flower bouquets, trying to be loved. You ever notice that trees do everything to git attention we do, except walk?[23]

What we see here, so elegantly explained by Shug, is a new spiritual paradigm. Magicians do not try to appease God, envisioned as above them, and they do not try to work hard to be like God either. There is no need to because God is not envisioned as better. Without a God up above and a devil down below, there is nothing to prove and no guilt to atone for. People are expected just to *be* people the way flowers are flowers—and nothing else. Our job is to live and be both fully ourselves and in loving relationship with one another, the earth, and with God.

For many women and some men, the religious paradigm Shug describes is easier to envision when they imagine not God, but a Goddess. Women are not expected to be superior or have power over us, so the image does not evoke such judgmental implications as a Father God. Because the image of a male deity also has been used as an apology for male dominance, and because some women experience a deity as Other—as not female—it often is empowering for women to image a Goddess. The Goddess is like us. The image also helps us understand and honor the divine in ourselves. Other women may not evoke the image of a Goddess, but will emphasize the feminine attributes of God.

The same is true for some men, because they identify a nonhierarchical affiliative way of seeing the world as female. The Goddess, or androgynous ways of imaging God, then, can facilitate their claiming the parts of themselves that prefer loving to conquering. Hence the Goddess often presides over the transition from Warrior to Magician and the attendant integration of "female" love and nurturance with "male" courage and discipline. It is important to recognize, however, that although men have preferred warrioring and women loving, the Magician is an androgyne who has integrated both.

Movement into the New World

Just as there are levels of truth experienced by the Martyr, the Wanderer, and the Warrior, there are stages of being a Magician. The Magician's journey actually begins with the archetype of the Innocent in the magical thinking characteristic of children. In our culture we discourage such thinking to foster more rationalistic ways of seeing the world. As we begin our journeys, we do need to learn to distinguish fact from fiction and what we make up from what we actually experience, and we need to learn not to expect magical solutions. Yet even having been taught at an early age to distrust such thinking, most people have had some experience that feels magical—E.S.P., a moment of grace, or that time they just knew to get off the road. But most people compartmentalize those times as being outside the category of the real, separate from the rest of life. Actually, none of these phenomena—including synchronicity and mirroring—really are magic. They operate by laws as demonstrable as causality or gravity. The Magician simply learns these other laws in addition to those of cause and effect and thus assumes a new way of seeing, quite different from the consensual reality of our culture.

Historically, only a few people in the culture have moved to this stage. At present, however, large numbers of people in the New Age movement, the feminist movement, and liberation movements within Christianity and Judaism are thinking in these ways. Many others simply live as if such ideas were true. The transition to this stage for many depends upon people knowing it is there, just as the Martyr is unlikely to imagine what it is to be a Warrior unless she actually has seen people who went after what they wanted, fought for it, and won.

The Magician's power, however, should not be used until the lessons of the Martyr, the Wanderer, and the Warrior have been learned. Without the desire to use one's power for others as well as for oneself, without a commitment to one's own integrity, and without the courage and discipline it takes to assert one's own truth in the world, the Magician's power inevitably will be misused. It may be used to gain an exemption from pain, to help others when helping really is meddling, and most often, to gain one's own egocentric ends. That is why it is just as well that most people do not believe in that power. And that is why many people refuse to believe in it, even when they have experienced it. They know they would misuse it. The idea frightens them.

For most people, then, the first stage of magicianship will be separated from the rest of their experience and for some time will have little or no effect on the ways they see the world. Like Shug's impact on Celie and Albert, the Magician's way of relating to the world can begin to influence one's life if one meets a Magician or reads books that make that worldview accessible. The next step may be simply to begin noticing synchronistic events or to look back over one's life, asking, "What if I chose (at my deep soul level) everything that has happened to me? And what if I have faith that I chose rightly?" The result will be to understand that, even without knowing it, we have been cocreators all the time. The final stage is to make that process more conscious, to take responsibility for creation as a conscious as well as an unconscious process. Doing so requires the audacity and confidence of the Warrior to name and confront dragons. Doing so responsibly and well requires the Martyr's ability to let go and love the universe, affirming dragons as Shadows. Paradoxically, as Magicians both take control and let go, they open up to the adventure of going where they have to go and want to go, in faith and in joy.

In practice, this means having the faith that, when they are ready for a new love, they will have one. When they are ready for a new job, it will be there. They will live in as transfromed a kingdom as they are ready to live in. When they are ready for something new, it means visioning what they want, asking the universe for it, yet also knowing that if they do not get what they ask for, their deeper, wiser self may be putting in yet a different order. Often when they do not get what they want by envisioning it, it is because they need to be developing skills associated with some of the other archetypes. Maybe they need to assert themselves more in the world. Maybe they need to learn additional lessons about giving or exploring.

Sometimes they also need to remember interdependence. Their capacity to get what they need is dependent not only upon their own development but upon that of other people.[24]

When asked if it is true that people choose their own parents, Starhawk (author of *Dreaming the Dark*) said, "Yes, but it is a little like ordering a Japanese car. Supplies are limited. You may not be able to get the style and color you prefer." In other words, the world out there is not illusory. You cannot have what you ask for unless it exists—or you are willing to invent or create it.

If what you want does not exist yet or is in very short supply, you may need to invent it or just wait. Sometimes the partner you want is there but not yet at the right place in his or her journey to meet you. Maybe the culture you live in does not have a standard form of employment to match your vocation. One woman I know felt very aimless and went to a psychic, who told her her problem was being by nature a temple-keeper in a world with no temples. There are no ads in the paper for temple-keepers. Obviously, the answer for her was to build temples, or to redefine what it means to be a temple-keeper in today's world. What is helpful to remember here is synchronicity. Rarely are persons so far ahead of their culture that they are not, at least in some ways, a microcosm of it. Temple-keepers need to find out what they revere as holy and then keep those things safe.

Recognizing our interdependence can feel limiting because we can go only so far into a new world or new age by ourselves. However, first it is important to recognize how profoundly our lives can be changed even in the present society. I have noticed people in the same country who seem to be living in very different universes. There are those whose lives are defined by a sense of scarcity, lack, loneliness, fear, poverty (of spirit, which makes even people with wealth feel poor), and ugliness; and there are those who are surrounded by love, beauty, and abundance and who feel befriended, prosperous, and happy. Similarly, some people are living in the nineteenth century while others are living in the twenty-first century. In many ways, we truly inhabit different worlds.

The Warrior believes we have to force people to move into the new world, but the Magician knows that we only need to be presented with an option. People are attracted to increased life. Left to themselves, they will gravitate to it. And so much more is out there and available right now than most of us ever will have a chance to enjoy fully. There is now more than enough, and as more people become freed up to be more creative, there will be more and more all the time.

Mary Staton's science fiction classic, *From the Legend of Biel*, describes a civilization that slowly grows to encompass most of the universe, yet never fights a battle. The civilization is peaceful, egalitarian, and complex. Other groups join them, not because they are forced to, but because their curiosity always eventually leads them to it. When they get there, they find themselves in the Hall of a

Thousand Chambers, where they experience many adventures. In doing so, they evolve and discover who they are on a deeper level. In the process they move from a primitive, linear, dualistic, hierarchical, patriarchal consciousness to a more complex, multidimensional, and egalitarian way of seeing the world.[25] When they have advanced to that level, they cannot imagine going back to their former ways of doing things. That would be like crawling after they had learned to walk—or fly.

Magicians do not try to force social change, because they recognize that people need to take their journeys in order to be able to live in a humane and peaceful world. On the other hand, they recognize that there is so much in the culture that artificially retards people and keeps them unnecessarily stuck. Magicians act as magnets who attract and galvanize positive energy for change. They can do this by identifying the places where growth can occur for individuals, institutions, or social groups, and then by fostering it. Although they may or may not be the leader in a particular political, religious, or intellectual movement, they act as rainmakers. When they are there, growth occurs.

Because so much of what we believe about the world really is projection, Magicians are able to inspire hope in others because they *know* it is possible to have a peaceful, humane, just, and caring world: They have learned to be peaceful, caring, and respectful of others and themselves! Further, they attract what they are, so they also have many areas in their lives in which they experience such a world as their reality.

They know that when we open our hearts, we always have enough love. When we stop hoarding—talents, ideas, material goods—we always are prosperous. They know we create scarcity through our fears, but when we fully give the gifts of our lives to the universe and each other, we find our true work, or true loves, and experience the fullness of our true nature—which always is good.

Thus Magicians come to believe that life can be joyous and abundant, from the actual experience of their lives. Shevek in Ursula Le Guin's *The Dispossessed* speaks out of the Magician's consciousness when he says, "You cannot make the Revolution. You can only be the Revolution."[26] The Magician knows that when you do so, your world changes—as if by magic.

Chapter 7

THE RETURN

It takes
So many thousand years to wake,
But will you wake for pity's sake. . .?
—CHRISTOPHER FRY, *"A Sleep of Prisoners"*

At the beginning of the classic hero myth, the kingdom is a wasteland. Crops are not growing, illness is rampant, babies are not being born, alienation and despair are pervasive. The fertility, the sense of life, has disappeared from the kingdom. This dilemma is associated with some failure on the part of the king, who is impotent, or sinful, or despotic. The more youthful challenger goes on a journey, confronts a dragon, and wins a treasure, which may be riches or a more clearly symbolic object such as the grail in the Grail myths or a sacred fish in the Fisher King myths.[1] When the hero returns, he (and, as we have seen, it was classically a he) is made king, but more important than that, upon his return the kingdom is magically transformed: It rains, crops spring up, babies are born, the plague is cured, and people feel hopeful and alive once more.

Heroes, then, are not only people who grow and change and take their journeys but also ones who help transform the kingdom. In *The Hero: Myth/Image/Symbol,* Dorothy Norman maintains that "Myths of the heroes speak most eloquently of man's quest to choose life over death."[2] Joseph Campbell, in *The Hero with a Thousand Faces*, defines the hero as "the champion not of things become but of things becoming; the dragon to be slain by him is precisely the monster of the status quo: Holdfast the keeper of the past."[3] The hero's task always has been to bring new life to a dying culture.

Heroes in this new age have just the same function. They differ, however, in the essentially equalitarian nature of the quest and of the kingdom. Instead of one person—and that person usually a white man—taking the quest and bringing a new truth or reality into the kingdom, we all need to be doing so. Heroism for this age requires us to take our journeys, to find the treasure of our true selves, and to share that treasure with the community as a whole—through doing and being fully who we are. To the degree that we do so, our kingdoms are transformed.

If you read the newspapers, it may appear to you that little is changing—or that things are getting worse, not better. Indeed, in times of massive social transformation like this one, things always get better and worse simultaneously. The seeds of the new world are sewn in the ruins of the old, but it is still the old world that makes the headlines. In such a time of transition, there really is not one kingdom, but an infinite number of kingdoms. It is a highly experimental time until a new consensus is formed.

In the meantime, the outward appearance of the transformed kingdom has little to do with who is president or what laws Congress passes (although these activities certainly are important, for good or ill, to the quality of life of most people in the country and absolutely critical to people living on the margins). While the macrocosmic community clings to the old ways and responds to growing fragmentation by trying to enforce them on others, microcosmic communities are changing: workplaces, neighborhoods, associations, networks. The political processes of the environmental, peace, and feminist movements, for instance, are radically different from that of conventional politics; similarly, the assumptions behind practices in the wellness movement and alternative education are light-years away from those of mainstream health care and education.

We now have choices, in many areas of our lives, about what worlds we wish to inhabit. When we take our journeys so that we know who we are and what we think and feel, what our values and convictions are, we begin to put ourselves out there and be seen. When we do so, we attract to us people like ourselves who want to live in the same kind of transformed kingdom. We form mini-kingdoms, communities of like-minded people who experiment with new ways of being and growing in the world. This process feels miraculous—like the miraculous transformed kingdom at the end of the hero's journey.

In most cases, we did not even know that all these other people, these movements, these books—right on our own wavelength—existed. It is like learning a new word. You never were conscious of it before, but after you learn it, you hear it all the time. It always was there, of course, but not for you. You did not notice it because it did not exist in your world. Similarly, early in our quest we feel lonely and alienated, assuming that to fit in we have to conform to what we believe to be "reality." As we change, however, reality changes, too. The more we have the courage to be ourselves, the more chance we have of living in communities that fit for us.

Another archetypal way of looking at this progress is to think about the classic plot in which the hero is an orphan, or is oppressed and unappreciated in the family, and searches for his or her true home. As we become more and more who we are and hence link up with others with whom we feel a deep connection, we have more, and more satisfying, intimacy with others. The reward for the hero's inevitably solitary journey, then, is community—community with the self, with other people, and with the natural and spiritual worlds. At the end of the journey, the hero feels and *is* at home in the world.

This does not mean an end to problems. Taking our journeys does not exempt us from life; illness, mortality, disappointments, betrayals, even failures are part of the human condition. But if we have faith in ourselves and in the universe, they are much easier to bear. Further, because heroes confront their terrors, they are not limited so much by their fears. We can act without the continual tape questioning whether we are doing the right thing, whether someone else will not approve, or whether someone else is out to get us. As Gerald Jampolsky explains in *Love Is Letting Go of Fear*, it is all these layers of fear that keep us from experiencing the love underneath. The more we are able to let go of our fears, the more we can tap into the life force. When we are continually afraid we are not OK, we cannot tap into the basic spiritual energy available to each one of us.

If we fear nature and see it as inferior to spirit, if we see it as a place of danger where wild animals or bugs will devour us, we will not be able to be nourished by it. If we fear other people (that they will reject, ridicule, or harm us), we will not be able experience deep love and commitment to and from them. In short, we take our solitary journeys so that we can live in love and harmony with ourselves and others, and so that we can be bathed in the flow of loving energy that is always around us. It comes from inside ourselves, from other people, from the natural and spiritual worlds. It is always available. The heroic task is to develop enough of a self to receive it without being afraid of getting lost in it or overwhelmed by its power.

In the old classic context, the hero became king—or queen. While in an equalitarian heroic model this is not likely to be the case, we might note that we do not find grails or sacred fish either. Perhaps what it means to become a king or a queen is that we take responsibility—not only for our inner reality, but for the way our outer worlds mirror that reality. We take responsibility for being kingdom rulers. That means, too, that when our kingdoms feel like wastelands, we know it is time to hit the road and continue our quest. We may have become too comfortable and stopped growing.

As James Hillman explains in *Re-Visioning Psychology*, our journeys and especially our encounters with the archetypes are about "soul-making."[4] We take our journeys to develop our souls. Collectively, we are making a world soul. The macrocosmic kingdom we live in reflects the state of that world soul. Whatever else we do to try to improve the world we live in, our fundamental duty is to take our journeys. Otherwise, instead of bringing more life into the world, we become like black holes, voids that take from life, and no matter how much we try to give, we sap the life energy of those around us and leave our worlds diminished and less alive.

The hero's journey is not a linear path but, as I suggested earlier, a spiral. We keep circling through its archetypal manifestations at different levels of depth, breadth, and height. It is not so much that we go anywhere, but that we fill out. You know how some people feel shallow to us, as if there is not much there. Their souls are thin, anorexic from lack of nourishment. The journey fills us out and gives us substance. People who have taken their journeys feel bigger— even if their bodies are thin or they are small of stature. We feel the size of their souls.

As we move through the spiral, the "stages" of our journey become flowing parts of a process of interacting with the world. Every time we experience something that makes us feel disillusioned and/or powerless, we put to use the lessons we learned as Orphans—we mourn our loss and, recognizing that we do not have the skill or knowledge to deal with a situation entirely ourselves, we seek help. When we feel alienated, we focus inward and ask ourselves, who am I this time? We must take the time we need to keep up with our changing identities.

When we feel threatened and angry, we know that we are not living exactly the way we wish to or believe in. We then assert ourselves and our values, taking the risk to step off the edge of conventionality to live the life of our choosing—and to take the consequences of that choice. When we feel maimed by giving too much or inappropriately or feel put upon by other people's demands, it is time to explore what gifts are truly ours to give. We must ask, what do I really need to give to this life, and what is just placating others?

Finally, when we feel doubt and fear, that is when we open our hearts in faith and love to enfold and affirm the shadows that creep at the edge of our lives, thus expanding the boundaries of the place that seems safe and joyful to us. *This is how the Magician merges with the Innocent, and how we fold back to where we began*, only more conscious and thus able to make freer choices. Now Eden is so much more inclusive and not so limiting. There is room there for more truth about ourselves and about our worlds.

The first swings through the spiral take time and energy. They are experienced as hard work. It is a bit like riding a bicycle, however; once you get the hang of it, it comes quite naturally. As we learn the lessons that are the gifts of each archetype, they become a natural part of who we are. It's not so much that we leave the hero's journey, but that it becomes so much a part of us that we no longer are conscious of it. Our focus is on the next challenge—journeys that may be quite different in substance and in form from the hero's.

Although the hero's journey, as described here, is typical, it may or may not describe any given individual's experience. While schemes such as this one serve as a general, generic map for our journeys, ultimately each one of our journeys is different. Because there are no maps to show us the way, we must trust our own process totally. Whatever path you choose, as Don Juan has explained to

Carlos Casteneda in *A Separate Reality*, it leads nowhere. It is no disgrace to try one as many times as you need, for there is only one test of a true path—that it brings you joy.

Your quest may or may not follow the pattern of this one. Follow your own path, whatever it may be. For one thing, the hero's journey is only one possible path. You may need to explore another journey first, or you may have finished with heroism as a major focus of your development, at least for the time being. I have been asked what happens after the hero's journey. Of course, that subject is outside the province of this book, but suffice it to say that heroes become kings and queens, taking responsibility for their kingdoms. And/or they become lovers and study at the feet of Aphrodite or Eros. And/or they explore the way of freedom and spontaneity with the archetype of the fool.

Whatever journey you are on, trust it absolutely, for the archetypes are here to help you. Open up and let them in.

Chapter 8

HOW TO USE (AND NOT USE) THIS BOOK

If I speak in the tongues of men and of angels, but have not love, I am a noisy gong or a clanging cymbal. And if I have prophetic powers, and understand all mysteries and all knowledge, and if I have all faith, so as to remove mountains, but have not love, I am nothing. If I give away all I have, and if I deliver my body to be burned, but have not love, I gain nothing. . . . . So faith, hope, love abide, these three; but the greatest of these is love.

—1 Corinthians 13: 1-3, 13

It is important to use all knowledge ethically, humanely, and lovingly. This book is written to help people by naming for them many of the patterns that may underlie what they experience as their "problems." Because of the assumption in the culture that we "normally" should be functioning just fine, smiling, well-adjusted and happy, people feel terrible about feeling terrible. In addition to suffering from the pain and confusion in their lives, they feel a sense of inadequacy for having the difficulties in the first place. Or, at the very least, they feel they should be able to cope with them better.

When we see our difficulties as parts of a developmental journey, then some of the pain can be lessened. We can respect the process and honor ourselves as evolving beings, rather than fearing there is something wrong with us for our discontent. To the degree that we can honor ourselves and our journeys, moreover, we can move along more easily and with a greater sense of adventure and excitement in the process. It certainly is more dignified when one is going through a hard time to think of it as one's heroic "road of trials," an initiation of sorts, rather than proof either of one's general ineptitude or of how miserable and unfair life always will be.

Therefore these theories should be used with respect for the individual journey, whether it is yours or someone else's. They never should be used to censor someone else for being, for example, at the "wrong" place on the journey. It would be better for you not even to have read this book than to use it as more ammunition with which to clobber yourself or others.

Ethical issues related to possible cultural biases are important. A number of my colleagues and students read this book in manuscript form and raised questions about the extent to which taking one's journey might be a nice expectation for privileged people but possibly irrelevant to the less fortunate. I have some problems with this. Soul-making is not just the province of the well-to-do. Indeed, the relationship of human development to questions of class, race, etc., is quite a complex one.

I know people with more money, privilege, and access to education and career success than most of us ever will have, but their spiritual poverty is so great that they do not develop. So, too, in the poorest, most depressed black or Hispanic neighborhoods and on Indian reservations, inevitably you will find old men and women who are as wise and fully developed as you will find anywhere. My claim is not simply that individuals can triumph over odds (or resist growth in the best of circumstances); it is also that affluence is not just a matter of wealth and power. There is a tendency among white middle-class people to see the worth of our own materialistic culture but not of the many subcultures in our midst, especially where those cultures are not materially successful.

Alternatively, we sometimes romanticize minority cultures and thereby escape having to acknowledge the genuine barriers to growth resulting from debasing and crippling poverty, dependency, and alienation from a society that does not respect or cherish one's individuality or culture. This is most blatantly true for Native Americans, but also to varying degrees for all oppressed groups, whether that oppression is based upon race, ethnicity, sex, sexual orientation, or class.

Oppression tends to lock us into the Orphan mode, since the more oppressed and mistreated we really are, the more oppressed we feel. We do a disservice to ourselves and others when we gloss over these realities. Particularly if we internalize in ourselves or reinforce in others the societal myth that everyone has an equal chance to compete in the society (and conversely that we are then to blame for our failure to succeed), we keep ourselves and others from recognizing and accepting the pain of our oppression. Seeing the world as it is and mourning its inhumanity is a prerequisite to moving on to other paths.

Similarly, we should not romanticize privilege. Many upper class white men have been allowed to grow up in such a self-centered way that their development is arrested in the Innocent stage. Without acknowledging both the ways that they, too, are limited and how their advantages are won at the expense of other people, they cannot progress very far along their journeys, either.

There are no true hierarchies in soulmaking. The evolution of the collective human soul depends equally on each of us, and none of us is more important than anyone else. There are many paths, and not all of them are heroic ones. Some people you meet may even be exploring their dark side—a path many would disapprove of. Who is to say their soulmaking is less important than the heroic path described here? Indeed, some reconciliation with and affirmation of the Shadow is necessary to travel the Magician's path.

Accordingly, these ideas also never should be used for manipulative purposes. It is true that your business might be more profitable if your employees were at the Magician stage, but that does not give you the right to try to force them there. I recently heard of a very well-meaning man who was playing tapes with subliminal messages in his place of business so that his employees would learn, subliminally, to trust the universe and believe in prosperity and abundance. He does not need to violate people this way. Instead, he could become a Magician himself, and he would attract plenty more persons like himself.

The description of a progression here is only that—not a prescription. It should not be used to design experiences that try to help people move lockstep through the same stages. Although the patterns, I believe, hold up in general, individual psyches are very diverse, and their autonomy and uniqueness need to be respected. These patterns can help you along, because as you can name the experiences that you or others are going through, you can hasten learning and make the experience easier and less threatening. They should, however, never be seen as normative, as stages one *must* go through or be forever inadequate.

In short, as long as you remember that what is important is the individual journey—not any theories about it—feel free to be as creative as you like in devising ways to use the ideas in this book. They are meant to give people comfort on their journeys and to remind us all that questing is a sacred function. It can be described and encouraged but should not be unduly contained and certainly not manipulated, forced, or rushed. Often, the best path may be a winding one, and we may appear to be heading quite the opposite way from where we ultimately will perch. Journeys are not efficient, predictable, or linear.

Archetypal psychology carries with it an approach to life that values most of all the development of the individual soul. To attempt to contain that development within some preconceived idea of virtue, mental health, good adjustment, proper functioning, or what is necessary to succeed in a materialistic culture is to do evil, to add to the walking death in the culture. It is not that mental health, virtue, achievement, and material and social success are not important; they simply are not absolute values. Certainly, they are not worth sacrificing individuation, individuality, and the development of a unique soul for. There are times when people need to go crazy, to be poor, alone, or bad, for their development. While it is critical that we provide help for people when they are in trouble in these ways (and protect ourselves if doing so is required), we do so best when we help them learn the gift, the lessons they can gain from each state, and not make them act a certain way that fits our images of how they should be.

The uniqueness of each individual complicates the issue, but it does not absolve us from the responsibilities that come from knowledge—even quite limited knowledge. On the one hand, it is not ethical to try to manipulate or force growth. On the other, when we understand the importance of soulmaking and of some generalizations about the patterns of our interactions with the gods and goddesses who help us with this task, we are responsible for being midwives to each other's development in every way that we (respectfully) can.

Many of our institutions and our personal relationships hold people back from their journeys. Business, through advertising, plays on human insecurity and fear in order to sell products. Educators, ministers, and psychologists often fail to teach us the skills we need to develop on our own because they need us to come back to ensure their livelihood. An unhealthy dependency thereby is maintained. Lovers, spouses, friends, and parents many times discourage change and growth when they are fearful of being left behind.

We are responsible for dealing with our own fears—that no one will buy our product if we do not create an artificial need for it, that no one will come to us for services if they learn self-reliance, or that no one will love us if they are not dependent upon us. It is not ethical to slow down other people's growth because we cannot or will not deal with our fears. If we do not, in truth, have anything to offer that anyone wants or needs, it is time to take our own journeys and get a clearer sense of our vocation and of the identity of the lovers, friends, or jobs that are appropriate for us.

With knowledge comes the responsibility for creating environments that encourage growth and development. Those of us who are political, intellectual, or organizational leaders easily can see that we are responsible for the environment in our organization. However, everyone helps create environments. No leader does it alone. At the very least, if you feel powerless at work, in school, and in most of your institutional environments to set a tone, you still have a substantial role in the creation of an atmosphere in the family, in your daily interactions with coworkers, and with your friends.

People need environments that are safe and supportive, in which they feel valued as unique individuals, in which their souls are honored and they are not seen as objects to be used and tossed aside. These environments also must provide a realistic level of challenge—enough so that people will not be bored or stay stuck in their ways but not too much so that success is impossible. Furthermore, people grow in places where honesty can be counted on and where integrity and appropriate assertiveness are expected and rewarded. And people need to be cared about enough that they will not be allowed to get away with being dishonest, manipulative, irresponsible, or passive-aggressive. Healthy environments include caring but firm confrontation and consequences for behavior that is harmful to others or to the group.

Finally, people need environments characterized by a shared commitment to personal growth and that provide ongoing education and discussion. Who, watching a man drown, would not throw him a rope? Who would watch a woman overpowered by a rapist and not intervene or get help? No one with any integrity and compassion!

People are drowning in their ignorance and are overpowered by the destructive stereotypes and myths they have internalized. If you are a therapist, responsibility means not always being a fence post. Sometimes people need to be educated about other ideas and ways to think about things. If teachers, leaders, and employers have all the answers, students, group members, and workers will not learn to find their own. Alternatively, leaving them to struggle entirely alone is irresponsible; they may not survive the challenge. People need help, and the most pressing need they have is for their souls to be recognized and honored.

If you feel you have progressed to a point where you wish to think about how these ideas can be used to help others (rather than simply pulled out if the need arises), and especially if these ideas have relevance to your work, you may be interested in the brief hints that follow to practitioners about how to use the concepts in this book in your work.

Suggestions to Practitioners

If you are in the helping professions, you can use this book as a diagnostic tool to help identify where your clients, parishioners, or students are, and to formulate an appropriate intervention to enhance their growth and effectiveness. It also can be used as a bridge between different schools of thought. For instance, political conservatives tend to imagine the poor as Wanderers (that is, if they do not see them as scoundrels) and hence assume the best approach is to leave them alone. Liberals are more likely to think of the poor as Orphans who *do* need help. Either could be true in a particular situation. The task is to find out what approach is needed with different individuals or groups based on where they truly are. Such recognition could help articulate policies that enable people eventually to become productive, happy, and prosperous citizens.

Different approaches to faith development also are appropriate to various stages. It is useful to tell an Orphan simply to pray and have faith in Jesus, but to someone just entering the Warrior stage, it makes more sense to encourage spiritual discipline (possibly meditation, study, even fasting) and/or to work hard to get what he or she wants. It is not until someone has developed some discipline and assertiveness that it makes much sense to talk about claiming abundance here and now.

It is useful to have people tell their life stories to you at any of these stages, but what they highlight at different times will reveal what skills they are mastering. For example, the first time people tell their story they may emphasize their victimization; later they may highlight their sense of isolation; still later, they may talk about how much they have accomplished and what a struggle it all has been. Then, these same individuals—though after years of therapy or analysis—may focus on all the gifts they have been given and how fortunate they have been after all.

People at all stages need to be encouraged to experience their feelings fully and learn the requisite lessons from them. Yet the feelings themselves will change, even about the same events in their lives. Many people who struggle to confront and allow their pain, grief, and fear may find to their amazement that they have the same trouble fully feeling their joy.

We run into problems in our culture because our minds are cut off from communion with our souls. To get back in touch with our souls we need to clean out old, repressed, compacted feelings that block access. Anne Schaef's process therapy is the most effective form of cathartic therapy I have yet found that helps people clear away blocks so they can be open to truth from their beings. It is even more effective when combined with body work to release emotions held in our bodies. Some people learn to listen to themselves through meditation, or analyzing their dreams, or through art therapy. The form can vary, but the goal is the same—connection with our inner being. Others who are not as damaged as most people in our culture can do so just by learning to pay attention to their minds, bodies, and dreams if they are taught the skills to do so.

Different forms of therapy are best for people working with particular archetypal patterns. For instance, people entering the Warrior phase need assertiveness skills and other behaviorally based strategies to learn to act effectively in the world. They also need to process their anger. Wanderers benefit from analytic and emotionally cathartic strategies to clear out old patterns and find out who they truly are.

People ready to enter the Magician stage can be held back by rational, analytical forms of therapy that may see the Magician's interest in transcendent reality, intuition, and alternative realities as escapist, if not downright crazy. To be effective with this group, therapists must be Magicians as well or they will not be able to help in this process. Guided fantasy work, dream analysis, meditation, and other techniques that can help clients gain direct access to the voices from their own souls are key here. This is the point at which people begin to take conscious responsibility for their own evolution, and doing so requires this kind of direct access to messages from our beings.

The creation of rituals can be facilitative here, too. Most of our lives are weighed down with personal and institutional rituals, habits, and conventional ways of doing things that are anachronistic and, when unexamined, weigh us down. Developing communal and individual rituals that emerge out of the spontaneous present needs of our souls helps us reprogram our conscious minds to live our soul's purpose. Such rituals can include spiritual ceremonies, or the ways we interact in our workplaces or families, as well as what we do when we get up in the morning or when we first get home from work. It matters whether our coming home ritual is to rush in and yell at the kids or to give them a hug and sit down and find out about their day; whether we throw dinner together or are conscious of cooking as a sensuous process; or whether we take some time for ourselves to get centered or just fix a strong drink to calm down. All these are ritualized habits that inform the daily quality of our lives, just as surely as religious rites we practice or invent.

When people are learning to embody the Magician archetype, they are ready to take the kind of conscious responsibility for their lives that means making conscious choices about their rituals and habits.

Fortunately, whether teachers or therapists, we tend to attract people similar to ourselves, and we usually are best at helping people through whatever stage we are just leaving. Noting whom you attract and what their issues are is a good way of identifying the passage you are getting ready to complete. We do, inevitably, teach what we are trying to learn.

Teachers, employers, and group leaders can use their knowledge of these archetypal patterns to be more effective in the classroom, workplace, or organization. For example, Orphans need rules, regulations, structure, and a sense that someone cares about them. They also need strict enforcement of these rules and accountability. They benefit from team situations in which they are motivated to be responsible by care for others (or simply by peer pressure).

People who are habitually responsible and who do their work as they promise no matter what the cost to them have proven they can be trusted. They may, however, become confirmed Martyrs unless they are encouraged to be more autonomous and to make original contributions to learning, the organization, or the group. Martyrs need to be encouraged to become ambitious and to climb the ladder of success. (This is especially important for women, who often get stuck as the faithful, long-suffering, but unfulfilled employee or club member, or the dutiful, conscientious, but unimaginative student, because no one has expected more from them.)

Wanderers, on the other hand, should not be pressured into team work. They need latitude to find their own vocational voice or to study what interests them. When they do find something they can get excited about, it is helpful to get them warrioring, i.e., selling their idea (or teaching it) to others.

Warriors respond to risk and competition (which may put off people in other stages), but at some point they may get burned out if they are not exposed to any other way of doing things. The energy of people in the initial Warrior stage can be harnessed to work together against a common enemy or competitor. This keeps them from turning their anger on one another. Later, however, this group can benefit by learning listening skills, mediation techniques, and other strategies to help solve problems collaboratively, and also from sharing feelings, fears, and vulnerabilities as well as their thoughts with their colleagues. If you can get them to learn to be candid and to act on their own convictions while also respecting others, your business, organization, or classroom will flourish. It also is at this point that nonhierarchical and alternative structures can work well.

Finally, if you want your organization, business, or classroom to be magical, encourage all involved to listen to their inner voices about what they and the group should do, and you will be amazed at the results. When everyone shares his or her wisdom and insights freely with one another, it is possible for you all to be more sane, happy, wise, and prosperous than you imagined possible.

If we are aware of these archetypes in raising our children, moreover, we can encourage development in all relevant learning tasks early on. At present, society actually retards development by formulating questions dualistically (dependence versus control; nurturance versus autonomy and freedom) and by providing cultural images only of the more primitive modes of the Martyr, Wanderer, and Warrior archetypes. Moreover, we fail to teach children that they can be Magicians. They see no Magicians except in escapist fiction, which we take great pains to explain away as fiction, not fact. Providing children with images and stories of the more highly developed and sophisticated modes of all the archetypes can help them waste less time. I suspect the next generation need not go through all the stages of growth within each archetype. They could benefit from our journeys and have a significant head start into a saner, healthier world.

Because this journey is not really linear, we *could* develop all these skills concurrently. The hero within is not just a Magician, but someone who has learned fully the lessons of all the archetypes described here. The ultimate gift of each of the stages helps the hero live in loving relationship with all things. As we experience the lessons of each archetype, we learn many skills that help us in this regard: to ask respectfully for what we need, from God, each other, and the natural world; to give away to each other and to the universe as a statement of our willingness to receive; to choose and value ourselves, for until we do that, loving our neighbor as ourselves means little; and to fight for ourselves, our loved ones, the species, and the planet against anything (or anyone) that threatens to lessen life and vitality for all of us. Finally, when we learn to celebrate and affirm all we are, and all we daily are given, to love ourselves, each other, the planet, God, and the potential of life in the universe, we move into the new age.

EXERCISES FOR
*THE HERO WITHIN**

In response to queries by readers of the first edition of *The Hero Within*, the following exercises have been provided to help you gain access to the heroes that lie within you and to reap the rewards of encountering each of these archetypes at different levels of sophistication and depth. Many of the exercises are designed for journaling, so it would be helpful before beginning them to secure a journal or notebook. Write answers to the questions in it, and use it to record your experiences doing the more experiential exercises. If writing is not a preferred means of expression for you, you may wish instead to answer in pictures, through movement, by talking into a tape deck or directly to a friend, or any other means that comes more naturally to you.

Other exercises are designed to be shared with a friend or confidant. It would be ideal if two or more of you agreed to do the same exercises and to share with one another. Failing that, however, it would work perfectly well to share with someone who is not also completing the exercises. Some people prefer to share with their therapist, minister, rabbi, or some other professional rather than simply a friend. That's fine, too. Or, if you do not want to share, complete the journal assignments, the daydreams, fantasies, and meditations, and those activities that can be adapted for individual use. Or, you can share with an imaginary friend, as many children do.

In doing the fantasies, daydreams, and meditations, find a place where you can be comfortable and uninterrupted for about thirty minutes. Sit in a comfortable chair or lie down. You may wish to have quiet music in the background or complete quiet. Take some time

* It would be impossible to acknowledge or even trace all the people, books, and workshops that have influenced the development of the exercises included here. However, I want to thank especially David Oldfield, Director of the Midway Center for Creative Imagination at the Psychiatric Institute Foundation of Washington, D.C., whose Creative Imagination Methods course greatly influenced these exercises. I would also like to thank participants in the certification course I now teach through the Midway Center for their feedback on the exercises and their general support and encouragement about the importance of this approach.

to breathe slowly and deeply, and then relax your body by sequentially tensing and relaxing each part, starting with the toes and progressing to the scalp. When you feel completely relaxed, read the exercise through until you remember its main points. Be as creative as you wish in doing the exercise. It's fine to take liberties, and you will definitely need to fill in details. When you have completed the exercise, spend a few minutes in deep, unprogrammed relaxation before going back to daily activities.

Most of the activities included (whether to be done alone, with another person, or in a group) are for people at any level of development. Each section, however, includes one advanced activity designed only for those who have developed all six archetypes to some degree and are quite highly developed in the archetype in question.

Some readers are already discussing *The Hero Within* material in classes or small groups and might find it useful to try doing the exercises together. Other readers may wish to form Heroes Within support groups, groups of three to seven members who pledge to provide support for one another's heroic journeys. The exercises that follow can form the basis for the experiential components of such groups. If you wish to start a Heroes Within support group, it is ideal to invite others—people you would like to spend time with— to meet with you. Tell them what you plan to do—and whom you plan to invite. Make it clear whether you plan to lead the group or whether you expect rotating leadership (each person leads for a session) or shared leadership (some or all the members share responsibility for keeping the group healthy and on the agenda). Useful guidelines for group members are included at the end of the exercises (see Appendix A).

Whether you do the exercises alone or with a friend, a professional, or a group, the goal is to help you gain the treasure associated with each of the six archetypes described in *The Hero Within*. Feel free to modify exercises or to add or substitute others. There is no need to do them all. Do the ones that appeal to you. The issue is not to follow the directions exactly but to gain access to your inner heroes.

Innocent

Journal Exercises

1. Make a list of people and things you depend on and trust—those who do not, generally, let you down. The list may include providers of basic services who tend to get taken for granted (such as the postal service and the postal 'carrier who consistently delivers mail on time), as well as the friends, coworkers, family, and others who are close to you.
2. Where and with whom do you feel safest?
3. When and where are you most dependable and trustworthy?
4. Think back over your life to times that felt almost idyllic. For people from happy families, this might include their early childhood years. It might also include a time you spent with a lover. It might have been a therapy situation or personal growth experience that seems especially safe. Or it might be time shared with a friend, the excitement of a new job, or just being alone in a favorite place. Describe one or more such incidents in your life.

Daydream I

Nap Time

Imagine you are a young child—say in kindergarten—getting ready to take a nap. You may dawdle a bit—color, play—until the teacher insists you lie down. Like most young children, however, you resist sleeping and begin fantasizing about the great things you are going to do and be and experience when you grow up. As if you were a little child, do not censor your imagination because you think something is inappropriate or impossible. If you want to daydream about running off to join the circus or anything else, indulge yourself. Just be certain to allow the daydream to be as rich and detailed as it can be.

Daydream II

The Perfect Childhood

In your daydream allow yourself to experience a perfect childhood where you have everything you need: love, possessions, security, stimulation, encouragement to your growth in every possible way. Allow yourself some time to process your feelings. Be aware that no matter what the reality of your actual childhood, you can give yourself a perfect childhood anytime you wish in your fantasy life.

Fantasy

My Safe Place

Imagine yourself traveling through time and space, taking whatever form of transportation appeals to you—a horse, a camel, a car, a spaceship. Allow yourself to imagine yourself traveling. Notice your surroundings and notice yourself and what you are wearing and how you look. (You may take on any form you like.) Your destination is a totally safe and secure place. When you get there, notice what your safe place looks like. Be aware (in fantasy) of how it feels and smells, and of any sounds there. Notice if you are alone or with other people or animals. If others are there, who are they? Take a few minutes to enjoy being in this place. When you are ready to leave, travel back the way you came.

Once you have discovered your safe place, you can go back anytime you wish. You may wish to do so, at first, only when you are alone. In time, as you grow proficient in getting there easily and quickly, you can go there in situations and in times in which you feel threatened.

Meditation

The Beauty of Creation

Meditate on the beauty of creation. Open up to remembering the miracle of a mountain stream, a soaring bird, an innocent young child. One by one, allow yourself to focus on what to you is beautiful, inspiring, and joyous.

Activities

1. Share the above exercises with others.
2. Often we simply assume that others should be fair, kind, competent, and even generous. When they aren't, we are very disappointed. To move your focus onto the positive element of life and away from life's disappointments, stop taking the positive for granted. Make a habit of saying thank you for things you might otherwise take for granted. Thank the salesperson who smiles at you for his cheerfulness, the waitress for serving you, your coworkers for work well done, your spouse for being supportive. Reinforcing positive behavior not only encourages more of the same in others, it also focuses your attention on the positive aspects of life.
3. In the same spirit, remember to thank yourself for all the things you do that are right, competent, kind, etc. Thank yourself in advance for the good things you plan to do. When you mess up, do not berate yourself. Thank yourself for your good intentions. Think through how you might do better the next time and then thank yourself for taking the time to think how you might improve.
4. Go to the zoo or park, fly a kite, blow bubbles, buy an ice cream cone, sing silly songs, play childish games and pranks, and generally indulge in any other activities that pleasantly remind you of the innocence of childhood.
5. With a partner, do a trust walk. Close your eyes and allow your partner to lead you by the hand. The other person is charged with being certain you do not trip or run into anything and otherwise ensuring that you are safe and unharmed. The guide can also create pleasant experiences, such as putting rose petals in your hand to feel. Such experiences should be designed to enhance the sense of safety and support.
6. Play games, such as Simon Says or Follow the Leader, where everyone unquestioningly does what the leader says to do. (Remember, it is the leader's job to be trustworthy.)

Advanced Activity

Imagine that you live in a perfect world and all difficulties, all evil, all pain are really illusionary—that the human species has created them just to provide drama and interest in life. You can, if you choose, decide to return to Eden and live in a world where everyone and everything is safe and can be trusted. This does not mean walking in front of a car or jumping off a cliff. Even in Eden, natural laws need to be respected. It does mean that you choose to move to a deeper level of functioning where you recognize that everyone, at the deepest level, strives to do good and to be loving. For this reason, spend a day in which you refuse to judge anyone or anything by its surface appearance of threat. Respond on the deeper level of loving connection rather than on the level of appearance and see what happens.

Orphan

Journal Exercises

1. Make a list of people and things (beliefs, causes, organizations, institutions) that have betrayed, abandoned, victimized, disappointed, or hurt you.
2. Where and with whom do you feel most powerful? Describe the situation and how you feel.
3. Make a list of people who have felt that you betrayed, abandoned, victimized, disappointed, or hurt them. Would you agree with them?
4. When and where have you betrayed, abandoned, victimized, disappointed, or hurt yourself? For example, when have you failed to live up to your own ideals or values? When have you chosen not to follow your own heart? When have you been unwilling to get help when you needed it? When have you used drugs, alcohol, relationships, food, etc., abusively?
5. What are your addictions or obsessions? Any behavior that diverts us from confronting an unpleasant circumstance, awareness, or emotion may be addictive or obsessive, especially if we feel little or no control over that emotion. Most people are aware of drug and alcohol addiction, and many are also aware of relationship and food addictions. However, shopping, worrying, nonstop talking, overwork, and even virtuous activities like giving and meditating all can be addictive or obsessive behaviors if they are used to avoid feeling pain, depression, or anger. List any behaviors you have that you believe have an addictive or obsessive quality.
6. When and where have you reached out for help? What happened when you did so?
7. Itemize the way the world around you is unsafe and/or unfair. Note the threats you see to your own well-being as well as to society as a whole.

Daydream

Rescue

Allow yourself to indulge in fantasies of rescue, whether it is "someday my prince (or princess) will come," or dreams of the perfect therapist, the great boss, or the political leader who will restore Camelot. Allow yourself to experience being taken care of by this caring, benevolent, and powerful person. Then imagine yourself becoming like that person. What does that feel like for you?

Fantasy

Revisioning the Past

Imagine a huge rainbow coming into the room where you are feeling totally relaxed and calm. You are so relaxed you feel light as a feather, and you begin floating up into each color of the rainbow so that you are completely bathed in turn by red, then orange, then yellow, then green, then blue, and finally purple light. The rainbow softly deposits you on a white cloud, on which you can travel through time. Go back to some incident in your life during which you felt orphaned, abandoned, victimized, betrayed, or otherwise hurt. Stay a bit distant, if you can, as if you were watching a movie, but be free to identify with the main character (you) and feel sympathy (which may lead to crying or otherwise expressing empathic emotion).

Then, when you have finished, imagine you have just been empowered to reshoot the movie and to update the plot. This allows you to reshoot the movie the way you wish it had happened. Change anything you wish: how you acted, how other people acted, and so forth. It is perfectly fine to invent a figure to rescue you. Keep reshooting the movie until you are completely satisfied with it. Then go to the place where movies are stored and throw away the earlier version of the film and substitute your new film. Return via your cloud and the rainbow, only this time allow each color to flow through you, healing any residual pain you might feel at the initial memory. As you proceed through purple, blue, green, yellow, orange, and red light, allow the healing to be total.

Once you have completed this exercise, remember you are free to return and watch this new film anytime you like. Anytime you feel tempted to go back over the earlier, painful version, remember that it has been replaced with an updated version and watch that one instead. Remembering past disappointments, over and over, reinforces negative beliefs about the world. In shooting a new "movie" you are creating alternative mental circuitry and hence new beliefs about the world and what it might offer you. You may wish to repeat this exercise with a different memory, but do not do so more than twice a week.

Meditation

Turning Life Over to a Higher Power

Reflect on your sense of powerlessness—all the things you have tried that have failed; the times you have been let down or let yourself down. Let yourself really feel and acknowledge the extent of your vulnerability and helplessness. Then imagine there is some higher or deeper power in the universe. Let yourself open up to the image that is satisfying to you. If it is more satisfying to you to have that image be old and male, let it be old and male. If it is more empowering to imagine this force as female, then let it be female. If you'd rather it have no gender or no personified presence, imagine it as an energy force, as nature, as a scientific force such as evolution, as anything that feels right and believable to you. Some may even prefer to image this power as their own, inner, higher, or deeper self.

Imagine that this higher or deeper power has wisdom far beyond your own or any human's. Therefore, if you feel any anger against this power, simply let it go, knowing you do not know the deeper reasons behind events. Finally, recognizing the greater wisdom and power of this higher power, allow yourself to turn over control of your life to him or her or it and to rest in the security of knowing that your life is now in the care of a higher, wiser, more powerful being than your ordinary conscious self.

Activities

1. Share the exercises above with one other person or a group.
2. Anytime we feel orphaned we need support. Many support

groups exist for problems related to ways we have been orphaned or have orphaned ourselves. Examples include twelve-step groups (such as Alcoholics Anonymous, Al-Anon, Adult Children of Alcoholics groups, Overeaters Anonymous, Emotions Anonymous, Parents Anonymous), women's consciousness-raising groups, men's groups, or therapy groups. Research the groups that might be available in your area to provide you with the support you need. Join the appropriate group for you and allow yourself to have the help each one of us deserves in working out our problems.

3. The twelve steps, which were originally designed for alcoholics, work very well with all kinds of issues related to feeling powerless over one's own behavior or that of others. See the copy of the twelve steps reprinted in Appendix C. In step one, which tells you to admit your powerlessness over alcohol, substitute for alcohol the word that best describes what you feel powerless over. Do the meditation above to help you find your higher power, if you do not subscribe to a particular religious belief system. If your higher power is not a "he," substitute the appropriate pronoun. Then follow the steps as indicated, remembering that with the twelfth step, which calls you to reach out to others in need, you would be reaching out either to anyone in need or to others who feel vulnerable and powerless in the same way that you do. If your sense of orphaning is very great, it is best to do this with the support of a group, where possible.

4. Whatever else you do to deal with your sense of powerlessness and victimization, it is essential to really feel and express your pain, disappointment, and anger. One of the most effective ways to do so is direct catharsis. You can do this alone, but most people feel safer with at least one other supportive person to encourage the process. Find a private, safe place and simply allow your emotions to be expressed. Sometimes just allowing yourself to breathe deeply (since most of us repress our feelings by some level of holding our breath) is enough to get us in touch with our feelings. Feel free to sob out loud, to yell, to beat on pillows or a bed. Do whatever you need for catharsis

(as long as you don't hurt yourself or someone else). Let the pain out and take as long as you need to do so. Let yourself experience more than one emotion if your first feeling leads to others. (Caution: Be sure the person or people with you as you do this cathartic exercise are not those whom you feel caused your pain.)

5. Express your pain and rage through some kind of artistic expression: a poem, a song, a picture, a weaving, a sculpture, a well-crafted journal entry, a dance, or whatever means of creative expression comes naturally to you.

6. Role play—with your group, one other person, or alone with a mirror—ways to confront someone who has hurt you or let you down. Try to find ways to express how bad you feel without being blaming. (Not "You are bad. . . ." but "When you. . . . I feel. . . .") Allow yourself to benefit from feedback from the individual or group or your own observations as you watch in a mirror. Keep repeating the role play until you feel satisfied with what you are saying and how you are presenting yourself. Then you may wish to confront the actual people or person who mistreated you. (Note: It is much easier to confront someone who has hurt you, appropriately or directly, if you first take the time to express your pain fully as described in the third activity and then take time to do a role play.)

7. This exercise is best done only after several of the preceding activities have been attempted, so that it is not simply a way to bury your pain. After you have expressed your pain and found constructive ways to grapple with the situation that caused the pain, this final exercise provides a capstone cathartic experience.

Narrate the incidents that caused you such a sense of pain and victimization as funny stories or anecdotes. Tell friends, your group, your journal, or yourself in the mirror. If it is hard for you to do this, you may not have fully expressed or dealt with your pain, so go back to some of the previous exercises. If it is relatively easy for you to do so, allow yourself to laugh out loud and to enjoy the absurdity of the story as you tell it. The essence of humor is often the simple absurdity of being merely human, fallable, and vulnerable. Laughing at ourselves is one way we learn it is okay to make mistakes or to be vulnerable in what is sometimes a very difficult world.

Advanced Exercise

As you move through the world notice times that you close off to the suffering of others—blaming them, for instance, for their own plight. If you find yourself doing so, it is a clear sign that you are still repressing to some degree your own inner Orphan. Go inside and see what is there that mirrors the person you are having difficulty accepting into your heart. The sign that you have adequately acknowledged your inner Orphan will be a softening toward that individual or type of individual. (Note: This does not mean that you will not exercise reasonable limits with this person, and it does not necessarily mean that you need to feel an obligation to help him or her. It does mean that you will restore your ability to feel empathy and compassion in the situation, and it will allow you to determine whether it is necessary or appropriate for you to help.)

Wanderer

Journal Experiences

1. When and where do you feel alienated and lonely? Describe this as fully as you can, looking to understand what part of you feels shut out of that situation or interchange.
2. Where, when, and with whom do you hide or deemphasize aspects of who you are? What are you hesitant or afraid to have people know you? What do you imagine happening if you allowed those aspects to emerge in that place, at that time, or with those people?
3. How do you explore the world and your options in it? Do you travel, do you read or study, do you "interview" others? What are you seeking to learn?
4. Are there people and situations in your life right now that you should leave in order to be true to who you are? If so, what are these situations and who are these people? How are they limiting or harming you?
5. The initial dawning of what is right for us often comes from recognizing what is not right. What do you know about the options that are wrong for you? List as many as you can. Then try listing the opposites, or the most likely alternatives to things that are wrong for you. For example, if you have listed smoking dope as wrong for you, you might write a drug-free life as its opposite. However, if you have listed traveling to Europe as wrong for you, you might want to write either staying home or traveling to Asia or somewhere else. When you have completed the second list, check as many of the opposites or alternatives as seem genuinely right for you. With those that do not feel right, play around with other alternatives—even if some of these seem absurd or unusual—seeing if you can find one that fits. If you cannot with reasonable ease find an alternative that fits for you, leave the task, recognizing that this area may be one of the question areas in your life. Or, sometimes, we need to let go of things without substituting anything

else, and in this way create more space and openness in our lives.

6. Make a new list of everything you know about yourself—what you like, what you enjoy, and what you are yearning or striving for.

7. Notice the addictive or obsessive behaviors you identified while doing the Orphan journal exercises. Many times our addictions or obsessions give us hints in symbolic form of what quest we may be avoiding. For example, alcoholism and drug addiction are calls to take a spiritual journey and may well also call one to integrate the Dionysian element appropriately into one's life through finding healthy ways to get high, such as long-distance running, meditation, ritual, dance, or drumming. Workaholism is a call from the self to stop working more and enjoying it less and to find one's real vocation. Love or relationship addiction masks a call from Eros and Aphrodite to become priests or pristesses of love and to channel love freely, especially, initially, toward oneself. Obsessive talking calls one to the journey of finding and expressing the deeper truth of one's heart and as part of that process to begin to genuinely listen to what one is saying. Free-associate about your addictive or obsessive behaviors to see if you can gain clues about what quest calls you.

8. Make a list of things you have always wanted to do. Pick out one or two to focus on and elaborate. How do you imagine it would feel to do these things?

9. Do you believe it is okay to be special, unique, important? If not, what would have to change to make it all right?

Daydream I

My Perfect Life

Imagine a perfect day or hour or week sometime in the future when you are doing everything you would love to be doing. Imagine the setting, the company, and your activities. Imagine what you look like, how you are dressed, and how you feel. Be as specific as you can, and include as much sensory data as possible (what does it look like, feel like, taste like, smell like, sound like?).

Daydream II

Questing in the Twentieth Century

Begin by imagining that you are a modern knight going on a quest. However, everything needs to be updated, since modern knights do not usually wear armor, carry swords and shields, and ride trusty steeds. Indeed, few even publicly acknowledge that they seek the grail. However, recognizing that you are, in essence, a questing knight in modern dress, let yourself daydream freely about what might constitute your armor. What do you use for a shield? What do you use for a weapon? For example, you may use a certain way of dressing as armor, or you may shut off emotionally and armor yourself. Your weapon may be verbal, or you may use the law or rules or a tendency to blow up. Your shield could be a certain social role or job that asserts your status and identity in the world and protects you from attack. Some people even use their infirmities as shields or defenses to keep off others' demands.

What is your steed? What supports and aids your quest? You may answer this in a very literal way—a car, a plane, a motorcycle, for instance. Your answer might also take metaphysical forms; perhaps you are supported in your travels by riding a particular belief system or career path.

What is the grail you are seeking? Imagine what it looks like. Is it wealth? Success? Inner peace? A stronger sense of identity or vocation? What is it for you? Allow yourself to imagine the attainment of your grail. Let yourself see it, hear it, feel it, taste it, smell it— to know on the most sensory level what it would feel like to find your grail. After having done so, you may wish to swear fealty to your quest and to searching faithfully for the grail you desire.

Fantasy

The Call to the Quest

Imagine yourself in an ordinary, everyday environment going about your work when suddenly you experience a "call to the quest." Perhaps as with knights of old, a grail appears and no one can see it but you. Perhaps you hear the voice of a deity speaking to you. Maybe you experience a call from an animal (which could be your totem animal), a person (who could be your guide or mentor on the quest), or anything at all. Whatever form the call takes, allow yourself to imagine that you leave everyday reality and move into an imaginary world where spirits and totem animals and dragons and grails are real and you can see and hear them. Let whoever or whatever calls you show you the way there and follow it. Be aware if you are called to the mountains, the seashore, underground, to a forest or castle, to outer space, or to any other place or time. Be as focused as you can so that you attend to and recognize the landscape. Explore as much as you wish, but when you return be careful to leave the way you came and to take nothing with you.

Meditation

Heeding the Call of the Gods

One respectful way to respond to any of ones's pathologies (physical and mental illness or limitation, addictions, and obsessions) and to any of the tragic events of life (deaths, abandoments, misfortunes) is to see them as calls from the gods to begin a new quest. Take a few minutes, in quiet meditation, to open up to awareness about the pathologies, tragedies, or other wounds in your life and how they might be calls from the gods. Ask the god or goddess who called you in this way to speak to you and to provide wisdom about the path you need to take to find yourself and your identity at a deeper level.

Activities

1. Share the exercises above with an individual or group.
2. Go back to your list (journal exercise no. 8) of things you've wanted to do but haven't. Begin allowing yourself to do some of these things. Take that trip you always wanted to take. Sign up for that course that seems inviting. Try out new ways of interacting with others.
3. Begin weeding out objects, people, and activities from your life that no longer fit you. Create room for more genuinely fulfilling and satisfying possessions, lovers, friends, work, or hobbies.

4. Allow yourself to find out more about yourself. You might wish to keep a regular journal, to sign up for personal growth and exploration workshops, to develop the habit of taking long walks, practicing meditation, or otherwise gaining quiet for self-contemplation. You might find it useful to take one or more of the many psychological tests that help you learn about your psychological type preferences, your career interests, and so forth.

5. With a companion, play the mirror game. First, standing face to face, you move and your friend acts like a mirror, trying to move exactly as you do—down to the smallest nuance. (Don't try to trick your friend. Keep movements relatively slow so they can be followed.) Second, reverse. Let your friend move and you be the mirror.

6. This time be a mirror to your friend with words. Try to tell your friend as many positive things as you can about what you see about him or her. These can include physical, emotional, and mental qualities or behaviors as well as the quality of his or her interaction with others. It can also include what you think he or she might be striving or hoping for—what his or her quest is about. Your friend can respond with acknowledgment, a thank you, or a query but is not allowed to say it isn't true or to say anything that is self-critical. Let your friend respond and then switch roles. Let your friend tell you what's right about you.

7. Decide to the best of your ability what you want in your life right now and share that with an individual or group. Ask them to brainstorm and help you think of ways to get what you want. Resist any desire to play "Yes, but" and simply take in their suggestions and ideas. Follow up on any ideas that you wish to put into practice.

Advanced Exercise

This exercise is for people who have a strong sense of identity and vocation and wish to refine and deepen their awareness of what is really theirs to do at this time in their lives. Spend some time contemplating the simple truth that if each of us does what is really ours to do, no one will have to work so hard. If we tap into our deepest wisdom, we will know what is essential for us to do and what is work that belongs to others (whether or not they are doing it). We cannot compensate for people who are not being true to their inner selves, and hence—however hard they may be working at other tasks—not making the contribution that would be uniquely theirs. We can only do our part. If this truth resonates for you, choose a certain length of time that you are willing to commit to this experiment—at least a day and perhaps a week. With each possibility for acting during this period, take a moment to reflect, "Is this mine to do?" If it is, do it. If not, resist the desire to act. Or, if you know whose work it is, you might gently alert them of the opportunity.

Warrior

Journal Exercises

1. Outline your current goals and objectives for your life. What do you want to achieve and, practically, what do you need in order to succeed in reaching your goals?
2. Note what or who feels like an opponent, an obstacle, or a dragon in your life. Might these obstacles, opponents, or dragons keep you from achieving your goals? How might you overcome these obstacles, opponents, or dragons? What strategies might you use that would enable you to proceed toward achieving them?
3. Do you have any inner resistance to asserting your own will, values, and desires or toward striving to get what you want out of life? If so, what is the nature of these inner dragons or obstacles? What strategies might you use to slay or tame them?
4. In what situation or situations are you struggling or fighting? How does it feel to you? Are you challenged or frightened, or is some other emotion called up in you?
5. Whom or what are you trying to rescue by your behavior? Is it someone else or a part of yourself? Why does the rescue seem necessary?
6. For what or whom are you willing to fight? Is it easier for you to be a warrior on your own behalf or to fight for others?

Daydream

Winning the Goal

Imagine something of great value that you want very much. It could be an object, a person, an honor or position, or anything that has a strong attraction for you. Imagine yourself mounting a campaign to get it, using all the firepower you can muster. Your firepower might be guns and tanks and grenades or it might be words, the wielding of political influence, making others feel guilty, etc. Whatever your means, imagine yourself fighting as long and hard as you need to attain that goal. If you feel resistance to such no-holds-barred fighting, remember this is only a daydream, not reality. When you have succeeded in attaining your goal, take time to let yourself really enjoy it and to process whatever feelings you may have about doing so.

Fantasy

Confronting Your Dragon

Return to the heroic landscape you discovered in the Wanderer Fantasy: The Call to the Quest. It is best to go there and to return by the same route you did before, unless you feel a particular call to another mode of travel or another route. In this landscape you will confront your dragon, but first you need to be aware of what weapon and shield you carry and what kind of armor if any you are wearing. Take some time to shore up your courage and your resolve.

When you are ready, be aware of your dragon, ahead in the distance. Take note of the dragon's appearance—size, shape, color. As it comes nearer, be aware of its sounds and smells and its feel, and look carefully for some sign of vulnerability. Then, gathering together all your courage and skill, proceed to confront that dragon and to slay it or in some other way render it harmless. Take all the time you need. Since dragons almost always guard a treasure, look around after you have confronted your dragon for the treasure that is there for your taking. The treasure may be a traditional one—jewels, a pot of gold—or something very different. Whatever it is, you may take it back with you as you return to ordinary reality. If you fail to confront your dragon in a way that satisfies you, return another day. Keep trying (with time in between) until you feel good about what happened in your fantasy.

Meditation

Righting Wrongs

Spend some time meditating about the great social problems, such as the threat of nuclear war or environmental hazards or alienation or world hunger or whatever is a major problem in your eyes. Then be aware of what seem to you to be the major problems for your own community, for the organizations with which you are associated, and for your family and friends. Then consider these three questions: (1) If you had the power to act to do something substantial to help find a solution to even one of these problems, would you do so? (2) Is there something you could be doing that might really make a difference? (3) If so, imagine a workable strategy for doing so.

Activities

1. Share the above exercises with an individual or a group.
2. To learn to feel a Warrior stance in one's body, it is helpful to do Warrior in some physical way. Try one or more of the following as a way to build your orientation to strength, confidence, courage, and achievement: Take up a competitive sport like tennis, football, baseball, softball, wrestling, volleyball, or track; adopt a competitive attitude toward your daily exercise— whether jogging, calisthenics, or yoga—by setting goals for yourself and marking your achievement; or study a martial art like judo, aikido, or karate.
3. Integral to the Warrior spirit is the urge for self-improvement. Decide on goals in some part of your life and set up a plan to achieve them. This can mean a diet, a plan for career development, or a disciplined strategy to break a bad habit. If possible, enlist the support of a friend, a professional, or a group in helping you monitor your progress.
4. Play chess or other games of strategy with a friend, your family, or your group. Develop strategies at home or at work to get what you want. You may wish to read books that focus on issues of strategy (in sports, military action, careers, politics).
5. Develop the habit of self-assertion. Notice how often or how rarely you speak and act in ways that assert what you want, what you believe in, and what you value. Role play with an individual or group to sharpen your assertiveness skills. Remember to make good eye contact, adopt a strong body posture, and clearly state what you want from the other person as concisely and directly as possible. If you have difficulty with assertiveness, sign up for an assertiveness training class.

6. Make a point for a designated period of time—perhaps a week—not to let slights or wrongs go by. If you are wrongfully issued a traffic ticket, fight it, don't pay it. If you are slighted, stand up for yourself. If you see someone else being insulted or mistreated, don't just stand idly by, do something. If it is safe to do so, intervene. If not, take action to see that appropriate authorities are called in. Write a letter to your state or national representative. Organize neighbors or coworkers to redress a wrong. Begin with a small, easily attainable stand and move up to ones that require more courage and risk. Enlist the support of a friend or a group in your efforts, either simply to monitor your progress or to actually help you achieve your goal.

Advanced Exercise

Indentify someone in your life who seems like an antagonist, perhaps even an enemy. Ideally this should be someone you have not learned how to deal with effectively. Ask an individual or group to help you empathize with this person, to fully experience his or her point of view, thoughts, and feelings. Then clearly state your position, feelings, thoughts, and, most of all, what you would like to have happen with this other person. Then, together with the individual or group, brainstorm possibilities for win-win solutions that are not based upon compromise.

A true win-win solution is found when both people get what they want by moving to a deeper level of awareness of what their real needs and desires are. For example, Nan was new in her executive position and was trying to prove herself. Hank was feeling threatened by the attention she was getting and began attacking her to make himself look good, since he was bucking for a promotion. Nan's group helped her find appropriate strategy to get them both out of this bind. They also helped her find language that Hank could hear. She tried it and he bought it. Instead of competing with each other, Hank and Nan remembered they were on the same team and would concentrate on achieving the team's goals. This meant that Hank would help her learn the ropes, and while he would continue to debate with her on issues, he would do so in ways that suggested his respect for her abilities. Nan, in turn, while she continued to debate issues with him, agreed to treat him with the respect due a senior colleague. The win-win here is that both got more than they would have with their initial strategy of conflict, which was undermining team morale and making them both look unprofessional.

Undertake an experiment for no less than a day and no more than a week in which you strive for genuine win-win solutions (not simply compromises) in every situation in which conflict presents itself.

Martyr

Journal Exercises

1. How much care and responsibility do you have in your life? Whom do you take care of? Do you feel genuinely responsible for some people? If so, who are they? Are there people you choose to give to or take care of? If so, who are they? Do you sometimes give just because someone asks for something?
2. What were you taught as a child about care and sacrifice? What messages do you receive now from parents, children, friends, your partner, your work environment, and the culture at large? What messages do you give others about giving and sacrificing?
3. Have any sacrifices you have made felt maiming and harmful to yourself or others? Have any felt good, transformative, or clarifying? Describe both with the goal of identifying what circumstances produce which result.
4. What or who is worth your sacrifice? How much sacrifice is appropriate for you to give? In what situations does sacrifice seem warranted?
5. Are you able consistently to say no to requests from others that do not fit for you? Are you able consistently to take responsibility for choosing to give or sacrifice, so that you do not feel put upon and do not need to make others feel guilty? Are there changes you would like to make in regard to the way you give to others? What are they?
6. Are you able to acknowledge and accept gifts or even sacrifices from others when they are offering (with no strings attached) something you genuinely want or need? Are you able to decline gifts and sacrifices that you either do not want or that come with inappropriate and unwanted strings attached? Are there changes you would like to make in regard to your response to gifts and sacrifices offered to you? If so, what are they?

Daydream

Plenty to Share

Imagine that you had infinite resources to share: time, money, wisdom. You do not have to work, so you spend your time wandering through the world helping anyone in need. Imagine the situations you encounter, the help you provide, the gratitude of the recipients of your generosity.

Fantasy

Giving Your Gift

Find your way back through what is now your habitual way to the heroic landscape you discovered in the Wanderer and Warrior fantasies. This time you feel very at home in this world and safer because, after all, you have confronted your dragon. Take time to look around and to notice any changes in the landscape or in your own garb or general demeanor. This time you will be meeting someone old and very wise. Open up to finding this guide and to knowing where he or she resides. Let yourself be aware what this creature looks like, sounds like, smells and feels like. This ancient being feels compelled to tell you that you have a particular gift to give that is important to the well-being of the planet. In some way, she or he will communicate—perhaps in words or symbols or a gift or some other manner—what it is you will need to give or contribute. When you have received the message, return to ordinary reality the way you came.

Meditation

What I Would Sacrifice For

Meditate, as you did with the Warrior, about the major problems around you—those of the planet, your country, your community, organizations with which you are associated, the people you love. If any of these problems could be solved by your making a major sacrifice—of your life, your time, or your possessions—would you be willing to make that sacrifice? Consider seriously what sacrifices might appropriately be asked of you and which of them you would be willing to make if you were relatively sure they would have a genuinely transformative, positive effect.

Activities

1. Share the above experiences with an individual or group.
2. Organize a give-away ritual as described on page 113 of the Martyr chapter.
3. Become active in a church, temple, charitable organization, or other group striving to do good in the world through giving to others.
4. Practice asking for what you want from others, being willing to take no for an answer. If you have been sharing these exercises and activities with an individual or group, start asking for what you want there. Also, enlist the individual or group's support in helping to clarify what it is you want and in learning to ask in a nonmanipulative, clear way.
5. Practice taking responsibility for your giving and sacrificing. Give and sacrifice only when it feels appropriate to you and when you feel it will actually be of help. This means gaining skills in saying no to others' demands that don't seem appropriate and also in saying yes without any strings attached when you do, genuinely, want to help someone else. Again, ideally you can begin with the individual or group you have been sharing with and can enlist their support in helping you to extend any new behaviors to the larger world.

Advanced Exercise

With another person, with a group, or by yourself, think seriously about what you want to give and contribute to others or to the larger social good. Let yourself know what sacrifices (of time, money, etc.) might be involved, and whether you care enough about this issue to make such sacrifices. If so, plan what you need to do and carry out your plan.

Magician

Journal Exercises

1. Write a brief description of your life right now and how you, out of the wisdom of your being, have created this life. If you don't like certain elements of your life, describe the good that will eventually accrue from even these less desired parts of your reality.
2. What is your Shadow? You can get a clue by what qualities drive you crazy in others. What might you do to begin to integrate the Shadow into your psyche?
3. When have you experienced synchronicity (acausal but meaningful coincidence) in your life? What did you tell yourself about such events? Have you been willing to talk to others about these events? If not, why not?
4. Describe a time in your life when you had a vision or image of what you wanted to happen and you got it without your having to make it happen. What did you tell yourself about this event? What did you feel?
5. Whom and what do you love? What makes your heart sing? What do you find hard to love in yourself or others? Are there any ways that you would like to expand those limits?
6. If you were completely authentic and true to your deepest or highest feelings and perceptions in every moment, would you act in any way different from how you are acting now?
7. If you were completely faithful to your dreams for your own life and those around you, what would you do?

Daydream

Creating My Own Life

Imagine you had a magic wand and could change anything in the world you wanted for yourself and others. Allow yourself to imagine what you would change, and, staying in a dreamy state of mind, allow the drama to unfold in your mind so that you witness the effects of your magical work. Allow yourself some time to process the results—to enjoy your successes and to regret any miscreations.

Fantasy

Gaining Magical Powers

Once again return by your usual route to your heroic landscape and pay attention to your surroundings and to yourself. Have either you or the landscape changed since you last visited this world? This time you will be visiting a great Magician who will teach you magical powers. You need to learn them because you will be sent to free a kingdom from an evil curse placed on it by a wicked sorcerer. As a result of this curse, the kingdom is a wasteland: Crops are not coming up, babies are not being born, people feel alienated and dispirited, and the economy is in shambles.

Allow your imagination to run free. Imagine the Magician's castle or tower or hut. Imagine what he or she looks like. Imagine what and how the Magician teaches you. Finally, let your fancy have free reign as you experience your own journey to the wasteland kingdom and watch the way you undo the wicked sorcerer's curse. Allow yourself to feel your frustration with any initial setbacks, and to enjoy your ultimate success. Then return back to normal reality by your usual route.

Meditation

Creating Your Life

Imagine yourself being totally true to your deepest desires and in the process creating magnetism that draws everything you need to you. Allow yourself to watch as you let go of addictions as well as superficial or lesser desires to make room for your deepest longings. As your fidelity to your deepest yearnings grows, imagine the change in your actions and presence and what you attract in the process. If any fear, despair, or cynicism emerges during this exercise, just let it go to make way for your more genuine sense of empowerment. Open up to receiving more cosmic support for everything you do. Finally, envision your changes as having a positive impact on those

around you, and before returning to normal consciousness ask yourself this question: Would I be willing to be completely true to my
deepest, wisest self if this or something better would be the outcome?

Activities

1. Share the exercises above with an individual or your group.

2. Create as clear and detailed a vision as you can of what you
   want to manifest in your life. Share this vision with a group.
   Ask if they can entirely endorse that vision. If not, find out
   why not, and make suitable adjustments if they seem warranted.
   When everyone can agree to support that vision for you, ask
   the entire group to strongly imagine your attaining that vision.
   In case the universe has in mind for you something even better
   than what you have envisioned, it is generally best to say, as
   you strongly image what you desire, "This, or something
   better." Then give thanks together that you, at some level, have
   already brought forth that vision.

3. Keep a clear vision before you of what you want to manifest
   in your life. Representing it in some concrete form—a picture,
   symbol, or metaphor—as well as imaging it in your mind will
   make it more real. Then begin giving thanks daily that you
   have manifested the vision. Do not worry at all if there are no
   tangible signs of it in your life. By affirming that you already
   have what you need, you instruct your unconscious mind to
   begin attracting the vision for you.

4. Enlist an individual or group to help you work on your Shadow
   issues. After having identified your Shadow by noting what you
   abhor in others, begin by opening up to appreciate those qualities, to see what others might get out of them. Then consciously send love to people who act that way and to the repressed Shadow part of you. Be open to witnessing and
   honoring the transformation that will result. Reciprocate with
   others.

5. Begin listening to your internal conversation. If you note yourself making negative comments about yourself, others, or
   events, stop and turn the statement into a positive one. For
   example, if you find yourself thinking, "I'll never attract the

kind of person I want to love; I'm short, fat, and not that bright," turn the statement into, "I'm attractive in mind and body, and I attract to me people equally as attractive." Allow yourself to feel the negative emotions that surround the first statement and the positive ones that surround the second one. If at first you are too skeptical to have good feelings about your positive statement, play around with it until you find a form that does make you feel good. For example, if you are not ready to see yourself as attractive yet, you might say, "I eat small amounts of healthy food and I study good books, so I am attracting love from people who also care about health and intelligence."

6. Give an individual or group permission to challenge you if it appears you are using the Magician's tools for ego aggrandizement or to avoid other parts of the journey. Listen closely if they challenge you and assess whether what they perceive might be true. Always be ready to bow to greater wisdom without in any way moving away from your own power.

Advanced Exercise

Create a ritual to celebrate your commitment to expressing your full power and creativity in the world in the next phase of your life. You may wish to do this ritual alone, but ideally it would involve others, partly because collective ritual is more powerful and partly because it helps galvanize the support of others for your new mode of being. Trust your intuition to let you know what should be included as part of the ritual. There are no rules. Do what seems right to you.

Appendix A:

Self-Test

Discover the Archetypes Dominant in Your Life

Indicate how frequently the following statements reflect your attitudes by scoring them from 0 to 4: Never = 0; Seldom = 1; Sometimes = 2; Frequently = 3; Always = 4. After taking the test, see columns below that categorize the statements into archetypes. Total your score in each category. Nine or more in each suggests that the archetype is active in your life; fifteen or more suggests it is very active.

1. ____ It's important to be careful. Other people will cheat you when they can.

2. ____ I find that when I change my attitudes my environment changes.

3. ____ Most important to me right now are identity issues. I'm not sure who I am.

4. ____ I push hard to prove myself and to succeed.

5. ____ The world is good and I am safe and cared for.

6. ____ I feel very alone, but it gives me satisfaction to see that I can make it on my own.

7. ____ The most important thing is loving.

8. ____ I often feel disappointed in or betrayed by other people.

9. ____ All seeming problems really are illusions. I can assert God's love/the perfection of the universe and once again see that all is well.

10. ____ I am very competitive and really enjoy winning.

11. ____ Times have been rough, but I've learned to cope.

12. ____ I find out about my own shadow self by what upsets me in others.

13. ____ I use drugs/alcohol to get high and feel better. (Or: I use shopping, work, or frantic activity to divert myself from problems.)

14. ____ I expect people I meet to be trustworthy.

15. ____ When challenged, I stand up for myself and, if necessary, fight to defend myself.

16. ____ I'm in a new job/doing my job differently/undertaking a new course of study.

17. ____ I expect to be loved and cared for.

18. ____ I struggle hard for the causes/ideas/values I believe in and against those that are wrong or harmful.

19. ____ I frequently give people more than I get back.

20. ____ What I really want is someone to take care of me, but there is no one who will/can really care for me.

21. ____ When I am betrayed or unjustly treated, it reminds me to take pains to be fair to others.

22. ＿＿ I love to travel/study/experiment because I find I learn about myself and the world when I do.

23. ＿＿ I see no evil, hear no evil, speak no evil.

24. ＿＿ I feel most myself when I'm creating something new.

25. ＿＿ I want my life to make a difference, to make a mark on the world.

26. ＿＿ When I stay calm and centered, others seem quieted too.

27. ＿＿ If others could just see the light, they could have as wonderful a life as I do.

28. ＿＿ Since I've changed, my world has changed radically. Years ago, I would not have imagined things would turn out so well.

29. ＿＿ I think I'm justified in feeling superior to other people: I'm smarter, or better educated, or stronger, or more disciplined, or hardworking, or have better values, or because of my sex, my racial or ethnic heritage, my class, my accomplishments, my beliefs.

30. ＿＿ Tragedies (accidents, illnesses) often happen to me and those around me.

31. ＿＿ I work hard but do not expect to be rewarded or appreciated adequately for what I do.

32. ＿＿ If I could only win that jackpot, all my problems would be solved.

33. ＿＿ I feel good about myself and grateful for my life.

34. ＿＿ I would like to be more appreciated by others.

35. ____ I'll do whatever life requires of me. I want to make whatever contribution I can.

36. ____ I sometimes avoid or sabotage intimacy with others in order to maintain my freedom.

Innocent		Orphan		Wanderer		Warrior	
#5	_____	#1	_____	#3	_____	#4	_____
9	_____	8	_____	6	_____	10	_____
14	_____	13	_____	11	_____	15	_____
17	_____	20	_____	16	_____	18	_____
23	_____	30	_____	22	_____	25	_____
27	_____	32	_____	36	_____	29	_____
Total	_____	Total	_____	Total	_____	Total	_____

Martyr		Magician	
#7	_____	#2	_____
19	_____	12	_____
21	_____	24	_____
31	_____	26	_____
34	_____	28	_____
35	_____	33	_____
Total	_____	Total	_____

To see the relative importance of each archetype in your life, chart your scores on the grid below.

Appendix B:

Guildelines for Members of Hero Within Groups

1. Take full responsibility for your own journey. Others can guide and support you but only you can find your own grail, your own truth.
2. Whether or not the group has a leader, take your own share of responsibility for the effectiveness and health of the group. This means helping to keep the group focused on its task, and it also means paying attention to group process to be certain that the task does not get done at the cost of healthy relationships in the group.
3. Honor your own process and that of others. Let it be okay for members to be in different places and to see different truths. Remember, whatever truth there may be is certainly beyond any of our subjective truths. We are all like the proverbial blind men, each touching, respectively, a different part of the elephant and trying to describe the whole animal. We need all our perceptions.
4. Use "I" statements. ("When you say . . . , I feel . . . ." not "That is wrong/stupid," or worse, "You lousy . . . .")
5. Try to be mindful of others' likely feelings or reactions. This does not mean one should avoid conflict. It may mean, however, remembering to reassure others of one's respect, regard, or even affection when sharing a perspective that they might take as hostile to their own stance. Or it may simply mean remembering to be tactful. If you feel hurt or crazy or angry in response to what someone else says or does, tell them directly but also as empathically as possible. Never talk about group members behind their backs. If something bothers you, be forthright in raising it in the group.

6. Sometimes it is not appropriate to be tactful. Perhaps you are experimenting with a new way of acting—for instance, you want to break a family taboo against acting angry or bitchy. Then tell the group what you are doing, so people will not unnecessarily be thrown by your actions.

7. Talk with and to one another, not just to the leader (if you have one). Help one another when you feel someone needs comforting, reassurance, support, challenging, or encouragement to be more honest or confrontational.

8. Take responsibility for trying to get your needs met. Do not assume others (including any leader) can read your mind. Say what you want and need, but also be aware that you cannot always have everything you ask for (although asking certainly ups the odds of success).

9. Journeyers are equals. Even if your group has a designated leader, bring your full wisdom to the group. Do not disempower yourself by waiting for someone else to know what you know or see what you see. Often what we find missing in any group is what we alone could provide.

10. Take responsibility for group decisions. If the group decided to do something you did not want to do, take responsibility for not speaking up (if you didn't) or not being persuasive enough to change the decision (if you did). In short, take responsibility for being part of the decision-making process. If you would like things to go a different way, don't just complain. Bring it up to the group as persuasively and constructively as you can.

11. Take responsibility for your own participation or nonparticipation. Do what fits for you and not what does not. Use your creativity to tailor exercises or activities to your own style, priorities, and needs. Ask for assistance from others when you need it.

12. Stay in touch with your deeper, wiser self to know if you should be in this particular group or not. If you believe you should, then be as fully present as you can. If not, go where you heart leads you.

Appendix C:

The Twelve Steps of A.A.

1. We admitted we were powerless over alcohol—that our lives had become unmanageable.
2. Came to believe that a Power greater than ourselves could restore us to sanity.
3. Made a decision to turn our will and our lives over to the care of God *as we understood Him.*
4. Made a searching and fearless moral inventory of ourselves.
5. Admitted to God, to ourselves, and to another human being the exact nature of our wrongs.
6. Were entirely ready to have God remove all these defects of character.
7. Humbly asked Him to remove our shortcomings.
8. Made a list of all persons we had harmed, and became willing to make amends to them all.
9. Made direct amends to such people wherever possible, except when to do so would injure them or others.
10. Continued to take personal inventory and when we were wrong promptly admitted it.
11. Sought through prayer and meditation to improve our conscious contact with God *as we understood Him,* praying only for knowledge of His will for us and the power to carry that out.
12. Having had a spiritual awakening as the result of these steps, we tried to carry this message to alcoholics, and to practice these principles in all our affairs.

Taken from *Alcoholics Anonymous,* copyright © 1939 by Alcoholics Anonymous World Services, Inc. Reprinted by permission of AA World Services, Inc.

NOTES

Preface

1. Carol Pearson and Katherine Pope, eds., *Who Am I This Time? Female Portraits in American and British Literature* (New York: McGraw-Hill Book Co., 1976).
2. Pearson and Pope, *The Female Hero In American and British Literature* (New York: R.R. Bowker and Co., 1981).
3. Joseph Campbell, *The Hero with a Thousand Faces* (New York: World Publishing Co., 1970).
4. Carol Gilligan, *In a Different Voice: Psychological Theory and Women's Development* (Cambridge, Mass.: Harvard University Press, 1981).
5. Jessie Bernard, *The Female World* (New York: The Free Press, 1981).
6. Anne Wilson Schaef, *Women's Reality: An Emerging Female System in the White Male Society* (Minneapolis, Minn.: Winston Press, 1981).
7. Shirley Gehrke Luthman, *Collections* and *Energy and Personal Power* (San Rafael, Calif.: Mehetabel and Co., 1971 and 1982, respectively).
8. Starhawk, *The Spiral Dance: A Rebirth of the Ancient Religion of the Great Goddess* (San Francisco: Harper & Row, 1979) and *Dreaming the Dark: Magic, Sex & Politics* (Boston: Beacon Press, 1982).
9. Gerald G. Jampolsky, *Love Is Letting Go of Fear* (Millbrae, Calif.: Celestial Arts, 1979).
10. W. Brugh Joy, *Joy's Way: A Map for the Transformational Journey* (Los Angeles: J. P. Tarcher, Inc., 1979).
11. See James Hillman, *Re-Visioning Psychology* (New York: Harper Colophon Books, 1975) for a full discussion of the premises of archetypal psychology.
12. William Perry, *Forms of Intellectual and Ethical Development in the College Years: A Scheme* (New York; Holt, Rinehart and Winston, 1970).
13. Lawrence Kohlberg, *The Philosophy of Moral Development* (San Francisco: Harper & Row, 1981).

Introduction

1. For an introduction to Jungian psychology, see Edward C. Whitmont, *The Symbolic Quest: Basic Concepts of Analytical Psychology* (Princeton, N.J.: Princeton University Press, 1969).

Chapter 1

1. Joseph Campbell, *The Hero with a Thousand Faces* (New York: World Publishing Co., 1970), p. 136.

2. Carol S. Pearson and Katherine Pope, eds., *Who Am I This Time? Female Portraits in American and British Literature* (New York: McGraw-Hill Book Co., 1976) and Pearson and Pope, *The Female Hero in American and British Literature* (New York: R. R. Bowker and Co., 1981).
3. Carol Gilligan, *In a Different Voice: Psychological Theory and Women's Development* (Cambridge, Mass.: Harvard University Press, 1982), passim.
4. See Isabel Briggs Myers, *Gifts Differing* (Palo Alto, Calif.: Consulting Psychologists Press, 1980) for a full discussion of differences by type.
5. Box-Car Bertha, *Sister of the Road: The Autobiography of Box-Car Bertha*, as told to Dr. Ben L. Reitman (New York: Harper & Row, 1937), p. 280.
6. Annie Dillard, *Pilgrim at Tinker Creek* (New York: Bantam Books, 1975), p. 278.
7. Harriette Arnow, *The Dollmaker* (New York: Avon Books, 1972).
8. Shirley Gehrke Luthman, *Energy and Personal Power* (San Rafael, Calif.: Mehetabel and Co., 1982), pp. 56–69.
9. See Anne Wilson Schaef, *Women's Reality: An Emerging Female System in the White Male Society* (Minneapolis, Minn.: Winston Press, 1981), pp. 146–160, for a complete discussion of the concept of "levels of truth."
10. Philip Slater, *The Pursuit of Loneliness: American Culture and the Breaking Point* (New York: Beacon Press, 1976), pp. 105–123.

Chapter 2

1. Shel Silverstein, *The Giving Tree* (New York: Harper & Row, 1964), passim.
2. Dorothy Dinnerstein, *The Mermaid and the Minotaur: Sexual Arrangements and Human Malaise* (New York: Harper & Row, 1977), passim.
3. Ntozake Shange, *for colored girls who have considered suicide/when the rainbow is enuf* (New York: Macmillan Publishing Co. 1976), pp. 26–28.
4. See William Perry, *Forms of Intellectual and Ethical Development in the College Years* (New York: Holt, Rinehart and Winston, 1968) for a full discussion of the stages of cognitive development in young adults.
5. Elisabeth Kübler-Ross, *Death: The Final Stage of Growth* (Englewood Cliffs, N.J.: Prentice-Hall, 1975).
6. *A Course in Miracles* is available from the Foundation for Inner Peace, P.O. Box 365, Tiburon, Calif. 94920.
7. T. S. Eliot, "Four Quartets," *The Complete Poems and Plays, 1909–1950* (New York: Harcourt, Brace & World, Inc., 1962), p. 145.

Chapter 3

1. Carol Gilligan, *In a Different Voice: Psychological Theory and Women's Development* (Cambridge, Mass.: Harvard University Press, 1982), passim.
2. Daniel J. Levinson, *The Seasons of a Man's Life* (New York: Alfred A. Knopf, 1978), passim.
3. Erica Jong, *How to Save Your Own Life* (New York: Holt, Rinehart and Winston, 1977), p. 243.
4. See Jessie Weston, *From Ritual to Romance* (Garden City, N.Y.: Doubleday, 1957) for a fuller discussion of this pattern.

5. Jean M. Auel, *Clan of the Cave Bear* (New York: Bantam Books, 1980), passim.
6. Auel, *Valley of the Horses* (New York: Bantam Books, 1982), passim.

Chapter 4

1. David W. Johnson and Frank P. Johnson, *Joining Together: Group Theory and Group Skills* (Englewood Cliffs, N.J.: Prentice-Hall, 1975), pp. 1–33.
2. Thomas J. Peters and Robert H. Waterman, Jr., *In Search of Excellence: Lessons from America's Best Run Companies* (New York: Warner Books, 1982), pp. 235–278.
3. Betty Harragan, *Games Mother Never Taught You: Corporate Gamesmanship for Women* (New York: Warner Books, 1978), passim.
   Anne Wilson Schaef, *Women's Reality: An Emerging Female System in a White Male Society* (Minneapolis, Minn.: Winston Press, 1981), passim.
   Carol Gilligan, *In a Different Voice: Psychological Theory and Women's Development* (Cambridge, Mass.: Harvard University Press, 1982), passim.
4. Ursula K. Le Guin, *A Wizard of Earthsea* (New York: Bantam Books, 1968), passim.
5. Gilligan, pp. 24–63.
6. Schaef, pp. 134–135.
7. Susan Griffin, *Women and Nature: The Roaring Inside Her* (New York: Harper Colophon Books, 1978), pp. 193–194.
8. Tom Robbins, *Even Cowgirls Get the Blues* (Boston: Houghton Mifflin, 1976), p. 130.
9. John Irving, *Hotel New Hampshire* (New York: Pocket Books, 1981), p. 403.
10. Tom Brown, Jr., *The Search* (Englewood Cliffs, N.J.: Prentice-Hall, 1980), p.171.

Chapter 5

1. Carol Ochs, *Behind the Sex of God: Toward a New Consciousness—Transcending Matriarchy and Patriarchy* (Boston: Beacon Press, 1977), pp. 31–46.
2. Geoffrey Chaucer, *The Works of Geoffrey Chaucer*, ed. F. N. Robinson (Boston: Houghton Mifflin, 1957).
3. Joseph Heller, *Catch-22* (New York: Dell, 1955), p. 414.
4. Edward Albee, *Who's Afraid of Virginia Woolf?* (New York: Pocket Books, 1973), p. 191.

Chapter 6

1. See Carl G. Jung, *Man and His Symbols* (New York: Dell, 1968), pp. 1–94, for a discussion of Jungian psychology and the Shadow.
2. Ursula Le Guin, *A Wizard of Earthsea* (New York: Bantam Books, 1968), p. 180.
3. Le Guin, *The Farthest Shore* (New York: Bantam Books, 1972), p. 180.
4. Phillip Ressner, *Jerome the Frog* (New York: Parent's Magazine, 1967).
5. Madeleine L'Engle, *The Wind in the Door* (New York: Dell, 1978), p. 205.

6. Tom Robbins, *Even Cowgirls Get the Blues* (Boston: Houghton Mifflin, 1976), p. 43.
7. Robbins, p. 239.
8. May Sarton, *Joanna and Ulysses* (New York: Norton, 1968), passim.
9. William Willeford, *The Fool and His Sceptor: A Study of Clowns and Jesters and Their Audiences* (Chicago: Northwestern University Press, 1969), pp. 156–157.
10. Joseph Heller, *Catch-22* (New York: Dell, 1955), p. 342.
11. Claremont De Castilejo, *Knowing Woman: A Feminine Psychology* (New York: C. J. Jung Foundation, 1973), p. 178.
12. Marion Zimmer Bradley, *The Mists of Avalon* (New York: Alfred A. Knopf, 1983), pp. 875–876.
13. Shirley Gehrke Luthman, *Collections 1978* (San Rafael, Calif., Mehetabel and Co., 1979), p. 14.
14. Luthman, *Energy and Personal Power* (San Rafael, Calif., Mehetabel and Co., 1982), pp. 33–34.
15. Jung, *Synchronicity: An Acausal Connecting Principle* (Princeton, N.J.: Bollingen Paperback Edition, 1973), passim.
16. See Luthman's *Collections 1978* for a more complete discussion of how mirroring works.
17. Matthew Fox, *Whee! We, Wee All the Way Home: A Guide to a Sensual Prophetic Spirituality* (Santa Fe: Bear & Co., 1981).
18. Margaret Drabble, *The Realms of Gold* (New York: Alfred A. Knopf, 1976), p. 29.
19. See Marion Weinstein, *Positive Magic* (Custer, Wash.: Phoenix Pub., 1981), for a discussion of affirmations and for the text of the "perfect happiness" affirmation.
20. Madonna Kolbenschlag, *Kiss Sleeping Beauty Goodbye* (New York: Bantam Books, 1981), p. 218.
21. Margaret Atwood, *Lady Oracle* (New York: Simon & Schuster, 1976), passim.
22. See Anne Wilson Schaef's "Living in Process" book in progress for a full discussion of what it means to "live in process." Tapes available from the Learning Center for Healing Process, #8 Wild Tiger Lane, Sugar Loaf Star Rt., Boulder, Colo. 80303.
23. Alice Walker, *The Color Purple* (New York: Harcourt Brace Jovanovich, 1982), pp. 167–168.
24. Starhawk, in a "Creating Rituals Workshop," Institute in Culture and Creation Spirituality, Philadelphia, Penn., August 1984.
25. Mary Staton, *From the Legend of Biel* (New York: Ace Books, 1975), passim.
26. Le Guin, *The Dispossessed* (New York: Avon Books, 1975), p. 242.

Chapter 7

1. Jessie Weston, *From Ritual to Romance* (Garden City, N.Y.: Doubleday, 1957), passim.
2. Dorothy Norman, *The Hero: Myth/Image/Symbol* (New York: New American Library, 1969), p. 12.
3. Joseph Campbell, *The Hero with A Thousand Faces* (New York: World Publishing Co., 1970), p. 12.
4. James Hillman, *Re-Visioning Psychology* (New York: Harper Colophon Books, 1975), p. ix.